Collins

Public
Speaking

Collins

HarperCollins Publishers
Westerhill Road, Bishopbriggs, Glasgow G64 2QT

The Collins website is www.collins.co.uk

First published 2001 as Everything You Need to Know Public Speaking
First published as Collins Public Speaking 2004
Reissued with new cover 2005

© Essential Books 2001, 2004
Quotation compilation © HarperCollins 2004, 2005

Reprint 10 9 8 7 6 5 4 3 2 1

ISBN 13 978 0 00 720856 2
ISBN 10 0 00 720856 1

A catalogue record for this book is available from the British Library

Typeset by Davidson Pre-Press Graphics Ltd, Glasgow G3

Printed and bound in Great Britain by Clays Ltd, St Ives plc

CONTENTS

INTRODUCTION

Have you ever been to a job interview? Have you ever been asked to give a presentation to potential clients? To stand up and 'say a few words' about one of your colleagues as she's presented with her leaving present? To speak to a journalist? To speak to your peers at a trade conference?

I expect most people have had to face at least one of these questions and, although you might not have thought about it in this way, they're all forms of public speaking.

Oh – if you said you'd never been asked to do anything like that, watch out! I reckon you're probably next in line.

Your initial instinct might be to say, 'Not on your nelly!' But if your boss tells you your promotion rides on that presentation, or the person leaving this time is your best friend and no one else could do her justice, you might start to reconsider that stark 'no'.

Whatever the occasion – even if it's just having the courage to speak up in a meeting at work – the ability to speak clearly and confidently is a great skill to have.

And it is a skill you can learn. All you need are a few tricks of the trade and time to practise. Oh, and this book, of course.

In fact, I'm going to give you one of those tricks of the trade right now, before you've even got to the first chapter:

One of the first things journalists are taught is that every story must cover:

- Who?
- What?
- Why?

- When?
- Where?
- How?

The rule applies equally well to public speaking. We shall be covering these points in detail, but if you remember nothing else, remember to answer all these questions before giving any speech. The rest of the book will show you exactly how they apply.

WHAT THE ICONS MEAN

The Web Tip icon alerts you to where relevant website addresses appear in the text. If you are browsing through the book or specifically looking for website information, these icons will take you straight there.

Throughout the book, true stories have been used to illustrate the points being made in the main text. These are highlighted by the Real Life icon.

The Jargonbuster note is there to highlight and help explain any buzz words or phrases which may crop up.

> **JARGONBUSTER!**
> URL (Universal Resource Locator) is a web address.

1

GETTING STARTED

THE BASICS

- WHY AM I GIVING THIS SPEECH?

- WHO AM I TALKING TO?

- ALWAYS BE RELEVANT

- WHAT AM I TRYING TO ACHIEVE?

A speech is like an iceberg. The part below the surface that no one sees, the preparation of the speech, is 90 per cent of it – but the audience only sees the 10 per cent that is the presentation.

Having been asked to make the speech, you'll be gagging to get on with writing it and won't want to waste any time. STOP! If you've bought this book, you must be willing to do some preparation before committing your eminent wisdom to paper. And this chapter is the most important in the whole book.

Hold your horses until you've really thought through your answers to the next three questions – the holy trinity of public speaking.

WHY AM I GIVING THIS SPEECH?

No one asks you to speak in public without having a good reason.
It might be because you're an expert in your field. It might be because
you have experienced something that you can convey to an audience.
It might be because you're part of a campaign or charitable
organisation. Or it might be because the person asking you *thinks* you
are one of the above.

The very first thing you need to do is to stop and think about why
you've been asked. If you can't answer that question, you may not be
the right person to talk and you should bail out right now, before you
waste any more time.

Real
LIFE *I was once asked to give a presentation about the importance of
PR to independent production companies. I was asked because
I was then head of PR for a large production group. I didn't research my audience
well enough and when I arrived, I discovered they were all tiny companies –
one-man bands – and there was no way they could afford an in-house PR.
The fault was partly that of the organisers – but I should have done the research.
I had to rejig my presentation quickly so that I could say something that would
be relevant to the audience.*

WHO AM I TALKING TO?

Even if you *are* the right person, talking about the right subject, there is
still one potential stumbling block. Are you talking to the right people?

☞ Before you go any further, ask yourself: Why have I been
asked to speak? Has whoever asked me explained the
speech's purpose?

Actually, stop there and rewind. What we should be asking is whether you're pitching the speech at the right level for the audience you've got. If not, it's not the wrong audience, it's the wrong speech. In other words, it's your fault.

The most finely crafted speech, delivered in the clearest style, with the wittiest gags and the most stylish visual backup, will be as dull as ditchwater if you've pitched it wrongly.

CHECKLIST OF QUESTIONS

Make sure you know the answers to all the following questions:

Do I know who will be in the audience?
    If not, who can I ask? ❏

How much does the audience know about the subject? ❏

Are they volunteering/paying to listen to me –
    or are they being forced to attend? ❏

How many people will there be? ❏

Will they want facts and statistics or a general message? ❏

What preconceptions might they have about the topic? ❏

Will there be a wide age range? ❏

Will there be a wide range of experience/status? ❏

What will they want to do with the information? ❏

Are they used to listening to verbal presentations? ❏

A young advertising executive was asked to talk about effective communication. The event was a trade conference and delegates ranged hugely in age and status. The executive based his entire presentation on children's television of the 1970s. The programmes and advertisements had communicated so effectively with him that they had always stayed with him. Delegates of the same age were amused and gripped by his speech. The older delegates had some idea what he was talking about, although they were usually at work when these programmes were shown. The younger delegates had no idea what he was going on about. They didn't identify with him, they were bored and they got nothing out of the session. He was probably not the right person to speak about effective communication!

ALWAYS BE RELEVANT

If you were asked to talk to schoolchildren about road safety, you would probably keep the information to the bare essentials. You might take them into the playground and demonstrate how to cross the road or how to use a pelican crossing.

A talk to their parents about the same issue would be much more hard hitting. The audience would probably stay indoors, sitting down, and you might discuss specific accident blackspots in the area, while debating what improvements could be made.

Get these round the wrong way and the children would be bored and frightened, while the adults would feel silly and patronised.

A talk to local policemen, again about road safety, would be different altogether. You would probably be even more specific, more hard hitting and you would use more statistics and examples. You would also need to tell the policemen how to educate the children and parents of the area.

Coincidentally, the policemen may also be parents but, in this context, they are expecting a professional and businesslike approach.

Find out what the audience expects of you – always tailor your speech to the right context and never patronise your audience!

☞ **If you're speaking to the employees of a company, phone in advance and ask the human resources department for more information.**

WEB TIP *DO AN INTERNET SEARCH TOO. Most larger companies now have their own websites, including recent press releases, financial information, etc. By reading this, you'll be able to find out their current priorities.*

If you don't know their web address (otherwise known as a URL), try guessing! It's not as daft as it might sound. Try typing www.[nameofcompany].co.uk or www.[nameofcompany].com.

For example, if you wanted to find out about Tesco, you would type '**www.tesco.com**'. And you would be right! If that doesn't work, try to track it down through one of the search engines, such as **www.google.com** or **www.yahoo.co.uk** (see chapter 2 for more on using the internet for research).

URL (Universal Resource Locator) is a web address. Usually looks like this: www.nameofcompany.co.uk or www.nameofcompany.com.

http:// You sometimes see these symbols at the beginning of a web address. They simply tell the computer that the address is for a web page. The letters 'http' actually stand for Hypertext Transfer Protocol, which is the method the internet uses to send web pages.

JARGONBUSTER!
http:// These symbols simply tell the computer that the address is for a web page.

☞ Most browsers don't actually need you to type http:// at the beginning of the web address – they will add it automatically. But it won't hurt if you do type it. It's often included to help readers recognise it as a web address, especially if the address doesn't include the letters www.

www.bazza.com This bit is the address itself – the name of the computer that holds the web server that hosts the site.

/sj/humour If you see forward slashes and other words after the main site address, they are simply directing you to the actual pages you want to see. They are usually a good thing because they save you having to find your way around a site that may be unfamiliar.

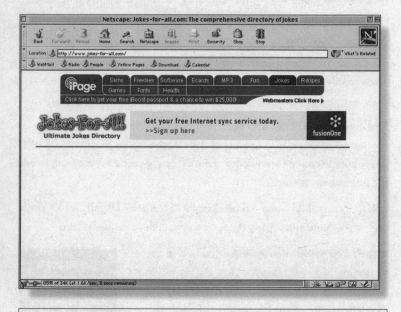

ILLUSTRATION 1   Screen grab of search page of jokesforall.com

htm Some web addresses end with the letters 'htm' or 'html'. This stands for Hypertext Markup Language and is the code in which web pages are written. If the web address doesn't end like this, the computer will usually use a default document.

WHAT AM I TRYING TO ACHIEVE?

You know why they've asked you and you know who you're talking to. Now we can really get to work. I'll be referring to this section right through this book, so you might as well concentrate while you're here.

What do you want to achieve from this speech? To help you answer, let's break it down into two elements:

1 What's my Objective?

2 What do I want the End Result to be?

At first, these might seem to be the same, but let's have a closer look:

OBJECTIVES

There are several possible objectives for a speech, but they usually fall into one of the following:

- to inform

- to prompt an action

- to provoke emotion

- to entertain

- to promote discussion

If you are asked to speak at a wedding, you will be expected to entertain. You will be speaking to friends and family, to whom you would normally speak informally, even though a wedding is a fairly formal occasion.

If you are so incensed about road safety in your area that you decide to set up an action group, you will need to inspire other parents to join you. Your presentation to them must make them share your anger and prompt them to do something about it.

A presentation to your board of directors about sales figures for the last quarter will mainly need to inform. The information itself should be enough. Forget jokes and emotional declarations.

But if those sales figures were poor, you'll have to inspire the sales team, when you get back to the office. You might need to scold or cajole the team – probably a bit of both. This will be much more informal and personal and with much more emotion.

END RESULTS

Once you've worked out your Objective, you can get more detailed and personal, and work out what your End Result should be.

CHECKLIST

It's easy to get carried away dreaming about what you want your End Result to be. Ask yourself, is my End Result. . .

Definable?   ☐

Reasonable?   ☐

Possible?   ☐

Imagine you've delivered your speech. Everything's gone really well and members of the opposite sex are falling at your feet with admiration for your immense speaking talents. What should happen next? (Apart from picking out the cutest of your new fans and taking them for a drink, I mean.)

Do you want the audience to do something? What? Do you want them to apply their new-found knowledge? How? Your Objective might be a bit airy-fairy, but your End Result should get down to specifics.

If you have the End Result clear in your mind, you will be more likely to achieve it.

Objective: To inspire fellow parents to join me in a fight for road safety improvements in the village.

End Result: The parents will sign my petition and write to the council. They will be inspired enough to come to another meeting next week.

If I had simply worked out my Objective, I'd have some idea where I was going. But I'd have no way of knowing exactly how to pitch it, nor could I measure how successful the speech was because I hadn't worked out the End Result.

Have another look at the End Result for the road safety campaign. You'll see that it was all three things required of any End Result. It was:

Definable = I can look at the petition and see how many people have signed. And how many turn up next time.

Reasonable = I'm not asking for the moon on a stick. People are busy and I can't expect everyone to devote hours and hours to this. But they can sign a petition, write a letter and turn up next week.

Possible = It's important to note that my End Result wasn't to improve road safety. That's because it's simply not possible for this meeting to achieve that. Only the council can authorise the money and the work.

☞ **Write down your Objective and End Result on a piece of paper. Stick it up somewhere obvious while you're writing your presentation.**

S U M M A R Y

You should now have answered the questions we set at the beginning of the chapter. Let's recap:

Why have I been asked to speak?

Think about the person who asked you – are you clear about their agenda?

Who am I talking to?

Think about who is in the audience and how you can find out more about them, including their needs, expertise and expectations.

What do I want to achieve?

Set your Objective and your End Result. These will be the solid foundations on which you build your presentation.

2

PLANNING AND
STRUCTURE

- MAKE YOURSELF A MIND MAP
- TURN IT INTO A ROUTE MAP
- FLESH IT OUT WITH RESEARCH

You're already on your way. You've established your Objective and worked out from that what you want your End Result to be. You know your audience and what they expect from you.

But even setting your Objective probably got you thinking about dozens and dozens of associated subheadings and topics. You know they're not all relevant to this audience – they might be too far reaching – and they're not all relevant to your End Result. But how on earth do you decide what to include and what to leave out?

There will probably be a million thoughts milling around in your head. First of all, don't panic. All you have to do is think through your presentation in a logical manner and there are a number of ways to help you do this.

Planning is the key to constructing a good speech.

MAKE YOURSELF A MIND MAP

In order to know where we're travelling, we all need a map. And as you're taking the audience on a journey through your topic, they, and you, need exactly that.

There are three main steps to drawing up your map, and you can run through these either by yourself or in a brainstorming session.

There are several ways of drawing up your plan, but my favourite is to create a Mind Map.

> ☞ When you're working out the structure of your talk, take the Objective, End Result and audience as your compass and you won't steer far off course.

If your subject is new to you, or requires a lot of thought, you might want to kick the creation of your Mind Map off with a brainstorming session. Some of the brainstorms I've been to were both fascinating and intellectually stimulating. Others were less of a brain*storm* and more a brain *damp breeze*. There's a trick to them.

> ☞ Listen to all the ideas at a brainstorming session but make sure someone is in charge to keep the meeting on course.

1 Only invite a maximum of eight people, unless they know each other very well (large groups can intimidate people and kill creativity).

2 Invite people who know the topic well and some who don't know it at all (they'll bring no baggage and preconceived ideas with them).

3 Provide water, tea, coffee, wine, beer, nibbles – anything that will make people more comfortable.

4 Run through the reason for calling the brainstorm.

5 Appoint a manager to channel suggestions and make sure everyone gets a say.

6 Appoint a writer to scribble down suggestions on a whiteboard, flip chart or Post-it notes, which are then stuck to a wall. You choose what method.

7 Open the floodgates.

8 Don't stop until you've exhausted all possibilities. Only when you've got a long list should you start to decide on which ideas are the best.

Brainstorms are supposed to be free-for-alls, but it might help to apply a few simple rules.

- Business or social hierarchy is left at the door. Everyone is equal.

- No one can rubbish anyone else's ideas.

- All ideas must be shared, even if they seem stupid.

- All ideas must be written down.

- Managers can't try to influence anyone's thinking.

Whether you decide to make your Mind Map yourself, or you want to enlist other people to help you, there are just three simple stages. Using a piece of paper, a flip chart, a whiteboard or Post-it notes, as suggested above:

IDENTIFY YOUR CENTRAL MESSAGE This will normally be your Objective, or a word or phrase closely associated with it. Write it in the middle of the page.

IDENTIFY SECONDARY POINTS These are the subheadings, which in turn suggest their own subheadings.

ALL AROUND THE CENTRAL MESSAGE, draw arrows to your secondary points. Where the secondary points suggest further points, continue the arrows out like a ladder. When you've exhausted the possibilities,

LEAVE THINGS OUT These are the bits you dream up as secondary points and then decide to cross out. Return to your Objective, End Result and audience profile and consider which of your points are vital and which beyond the scope of your speech. Cross out anything that doesn't fit in. Be ruthless!

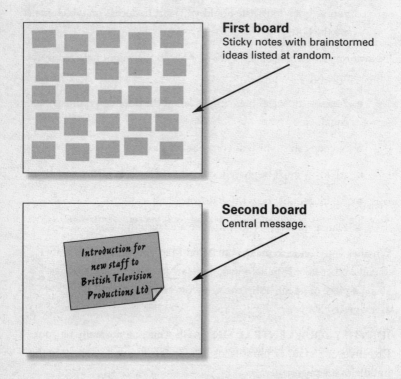

First board
Sticky notes with brainstormed ideas listed at random.

Second board
Central message.

Introduction for new staff to British Television Productions Ltd

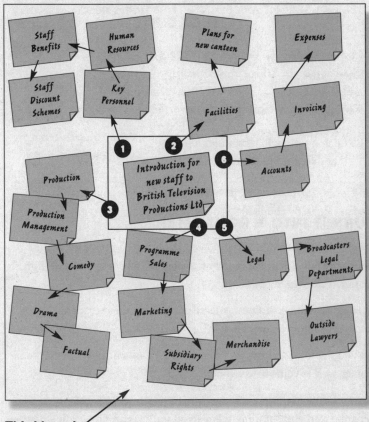

Third board
Secondary ideas sorted into Mind Map around the central message.

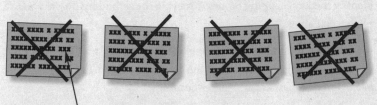

Secondary points not required for this presentation.

ILLUSTRATION 2   Stages in planning a Mind Map

CHECKLIST

When deciding what to include, ask yourself the following questions:

What will they expect me to cover first?   ❑

Which points will best pave the way
    to explain my later points?   ❑

TURN IT INTO A ROUTE MAP

You've done your Mind Map, so you know which points are in and which are out. But at the moment, the bones of your speech skeleton are scattered all over the page.

It's all down there, but now you've got to meld those scattered bones into a sensible structure. How?

As you think these through, it will probably become obvious that some points need to come before others.

If your Route Map isn't obvious, try jotting down each point onto a separate card and shuffling them about until you get the right structure.

When you have found the most logical route through your topic, identify the key Stepping Stones (probably the secondary points you established above).

It might help to think of this stage like a book, with your Objective, or central message, as the title of the book and your key points, or Stepping Stones, as the chapter headings.

FLESH IT OUT WITH RESEARCH

Now you have the skeleton of your speech, you need to put some flesh on those bones and fill in what you're going to say about each Stepping Stone. The first thing to do is to tackle any necessary research. The internet has revolutionised research: almost everything you need to know about anything is out there on the World Wide Web.

We touched on this subject in chapter 1 when we discussed researching the audience, but let's take a more detailed look at the vast resource that is the World Wide Web.

SEARCH ENGINES

Unless you know exactly what you're looking for and you know the URL of the site, start with one of the search engines or directories (see below).

JARGONBUSTER!
A search engine is a huge index of websites.

There are dozens of major search sites. They create their own indexes which are constantly updated by special programs called spiders. A search engine will ask you for a key word to search. When you've typed it in, a kind of electronic gopher rushes out and scours the Web for that word. It will display a list of sites containing the word or words you were asking for.

Different sites have programmed their gophers in different ways, so it's worth trying the same word in a few search engines – you'll probably get different results.

DIRECTORIES

As an alternative to the search engines, you might want to use a directory, such as Yahoo! These are lists of web pages, sorted into categories. You *can* search most directory sites using a key word, but the best way is to use the category links. Scroll down the page a bit until you can see them all. Then click through sub-categories until you find what you want.

SOME OF THE BEST SEARCH ENGINES

Yahoo! UK and Ireland	www.yahoo.co.uk
Excite	www.excite.com
Lycos UK	www.lycos.co.uk
UK Plus	www.ukplus.co.uk
AltaVista	www.altavista.digital.com
Infoseek	www.infoseek.co.uk
Ask	www.ask.co.uk

(this one works slightly differently: you key in a question, such as 'Where can I find out about labradors on the Web?')

SEARCH TIPS

The simplest way of searching is to click the cursor into the textbox, type in a single word and then click on the 'search' button. You will then be presented with a list of sites that match your keyword.

DO use capital letters if you want to find capital letters. So if you want to find out about London, type 'London', not 'LONDON' or 'london'. For ordinary words, such as 'poetry', simply use lower case.

DO put quote marks around the word to find a phrase. So 'love poems' will search for love poems and not just 'love' or 'poems'.

DO use + and – (a hyphen will do). If you are looking for, say, hotels in Chicago, try typing: 'hotels + Chicago'. But if you're trying to find out other things about Chicago and don't want to know about hotels, try typing: 'Chicago – hotels'.

Given the vast amount of information on the Web, refining your search makes sense in order to avoid ploughing through thousands of sites.

FAVOURITES OR BOOKMARKS

If a site looks interesting, add it to the Favourites or Bookmarks section of your web browser. That way you'll be able to find it again easily. If you're using Internet Explorer this facility is called 'Favourites'. Netscape, another popular browser, calls it 'Bookmarks'.

> **JARGONBUSTER!**
> Favourites/bookmarks: most web browsers allow you to save website addresses to a special file.

When you've done a search, you can also add the results page to your Favourites list and come back to it in the future.

When you've found a site you think you might want to come back to, go to the menu bar at the top of the screen, click on 'Favourites' or 'Bookmarks' and follow the straightforward steps.

Then, when you want to retrieve the site, go back in and click on the address. It'll whizz you straight to your chosen site.

When the search engine gives you a list of results, click on a title to go through to the site it has suggested. Don't worry, you won't get lost – you can always click 'Back' in the top left of your computer screen.

BUSINESS SEARCHES

If you're looking for a particular business or service, try the online versions of *Scoot* or *Yellow Pages* (Yell).

WEB TIP *Yell can be found at **www.yell.co.uk***
*Scoot is at **www.scoot.co.uk***

Both sites allow you to search by business name or type and by location. They will present you with a list of company names, addresses and telephone numbers. If the company has a website or email address, the site will usually include a link to these as well.

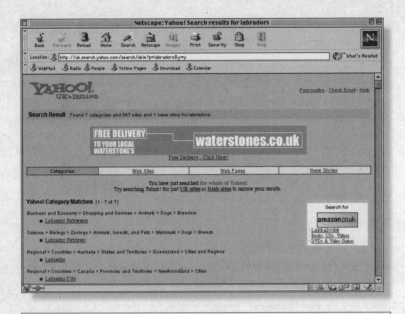

ILLUSTRATION 3   A typical search engine results page will look like this

OTHER USEFUL SOURCES ON THE INTERNET

The trick to getting the most out of the internet is
to think laterally.

If there is a trade body, charity or society associated
with your subject, take a look at their website.
Most carry useful background information about
their subject, either under obvious category
headings or under the heading FAQ.

> **JARGONBUSTER!**
> FAQ (Frequently Asked
> Questions): a document
> containing some of the
> most commonly asked
> questions, plus answers.
> A useful resource if
> you're new to a topic.

The Government has pledged to get as many services online as it can,
as quickly as it can. Government departments already have their own
sites. While they're almost universally ugly and utilitarian, they contain
useful statistics, press releases and reports.

Local councils also have websites, which can be useful for local
information.

WEB TIP *Most of these sites have URLs ending in the suffix '.gov.uk', for example, the website of the Ministry of Agriculture, Fisheries and Food is* www.maff.gov.uk.

You can get the URLs for all government departments and local councils at www.open.gov.uk – a really useful directory which covers all government bodies, including organisations such as the Association of Police Authorities and ACAS (the Advisory, Conciliation and Arbitration Service).

The national newspapers have been mystifyingly slow to catch on to the potential of the internet. However, most of them now have sites up and running, with useful archive sections, containing old news reports and features. By far the best is the one for the *Guardian* – www.guardianunlimited.co.uk. The *Financial Times* website, www.ft.com, is also an impressive resource.

BBC Online is also a brilliant resource. The news service is pretty good and the site has lots of other sections, covering subjects such as food, gardening, health etc. Find it at www.bbc.co.uk.

The trade paper for your subject might also have a site, e.g. www.businessweek.com; www.produxion.com (TV/radio trade site).

WEB TIP *For an absolutely mind-bogglingly vast directory of website addresses for newspapers around the world, visit the Internet Public Library at* www.ipl.org. *The UK section includes links to around a hundred national and local newspapers.*

Other sites you might find useful include:

- Dow Jones: **www.dowjones.com**
- Teletext: **www.teletext.co.uk**
- The History Channel.com: **www.historychannel.com**
- The World Wide Web Virtual Library: **www.vlib.org**
- Librarians' Index to the internet: **www.lii.org**

- Free internet Encyclopedia: **www.clever.net/cam/encyclopedia**

- The Living Encyberpedia: **www.encyberpedia.com**

- Ref Desk: **www.refdesk.com**

For more advice on research, together with links to dozens of features on the subject, try the US site
www.cs.cmu.edu/afs/cs.cmu.edu/mleone/web/how-to.

OTHER RESEARCH TOOLS

LIBRARIES. Books are valuable research tools but libraries nowadays also have video or audio tapes and CD-ROMs.

NEWSPAPERS AND MAGAZINES. Apart from the resources held on the internet, there are other ways of looking into the archives of a publication. Many produce their own CD-ROMs, such as the *Daily Mail's* excellent one. Some trade papers maintain their own archive, while others will be held by associated trade bodies. Some publications even issue annual indexes, which help you find your way round the year's issues. Call the publisher's office for information. The British Library Newspaper Division at Colindale in London holds copies of all main magazines and newspapers. These can be ordered ahead and may be viewable either in their original printed form, or, more likely, on microfiche or similar.

TRADE BODIES, CHARITIES AND COMMERCIAL ORGANISATIONS. Most of these now have their own websites, crammed with useful information. However, if you don't have internet access or your relevant organisation still lives in the Dark Ages, you may be able to access their information in other ways. Some may operate a library, or produce special publications, mailed to members or other interested parties.

S U M M A R Y

You have developed your thoughts and gathered them up into a coherent structure. Let's recap:

Your Mind Map ...

Help yourself to identify what should be included – and what you should leave out!

Your Route Map

Take the bones of your ideas and build them into a solid skeleton for your presentation.

Your research

Get to grips with research, including the internet – the library that comes direct to your desktop.

3

DECIDING ON
THE WORDS

- SCRIPTS VERSUS CUE CARDS
- HOW TO START
- HOW TO CARRY ON
- HOW TO FINISH BIG
- POLISHING THE SPEECH

Hooray! I'm delighted to tell you that, believe it or not, you've now done most of the hard work. Preparing a speech or presentation is a bit like decorating a room. The bit that you're itching to get to is choosing colours, slapping paint over the walls and putting all your belongings and new toys back into the room. But if you jump to that stage without first removing the old wallpaper, washing the walls and sanding down, the finish will be shoddy and the cracks will soon show. As it is in DIY, so it is in public speaking.

But you've now done all that boring preparation and you've got to the colour-chart stage – the stage where you pull the whole thing together and start writing your speech.

SCRIPTS VERSUS CUE CARDS

If you're not used to speaking in public, there's a huge temptation to write the whole speech out in full and simply read it out from your prepared script.

On the plus side, you'll never be stuck for a word, you'll never have to improvise and you'll know exactly where you are at any one time.

You could do it this way – many people do. But I would suggest that reading from a script is like riding your bike with stabilisers. You'll still move forward and you will, indeed, be safe from falling down, but you'll be restricted in what you can do. Remember the day you took the stabilisers off your bike? It was exhilarating, wasn't it? Suddenly you could whizz round corners and weave in and out of obstacles. You were free!

So I would urge you to remove the stabilisers of the script and move on to the freewheeling excitement (OK, maybe that's stretching the metaphor a touch too far!) of cue cards. Let's run through this approach and then you can make your choice.

Cue cards are

- easier to handle
- less likely to get damaged
- smaller and thicker – so it's less noticeable if you're shaking

You *can* jump straight from your Route Map to your cue cards. To create your Route Map, you identified your key points, the main stepping stones of your speech. These should now form the basis for your cue cards.

But if you're not a frequent speaker, I would suggest that instead of jumping from Route Map to cue card, you're probably better off getting there in three easy steps.

STEP 1: CREATE YOUR TEXT

Taking your Route Map and a clean pad of paper or new computer wordprocessing document, note down your Stepping Stones, or key points, one on each page. Under each key point, list the subsidiary points that you identified when you made your Mind Map.

Keep filling in, using your expertise and the research you've done, until you've roughed out the whole speech. Throughout this process, keep looking at the Objective and End Result that you wrote out and pinned up nearby.

STEP 2: TURN YOUR TEXT INTO A SCRIPT

In step 1, you pulled together all the information into a coherent whole. But you haven't yet got a speech.

There is a big difference between the written word and the spoken word. (Unless you're *Trainspotting* author Irvine Welsh, in which case there's no difference at all.) But generally, if you read out a passage directly from a book, exactly as it's written, you will find it sounds stilted and odd.

Read the tips in 'Polishing your speech', for more about the differences between written and spoken English.

At this stage, you should also start thinking about the visual aids you might want to use to support your presentation – you might note these cues in your script. (See opposite for the difference between a text page and a script.)

STEP 3: TURN YOUR SCRIPT INTO CUE CARDS

Using your main points as your framework, this is where you will distil your script down into key words or phrases.

If your speech is quite simple and short, you should be able to put one of your Stepping Stones, or key points, on each cue card. Write this in big letters and then add your key words and phrases.

But don't cram things onto the cards! If you've got a lot to say and only a few Stepping Stones, break things down a little further and devote a new card to each of your subheadings. The trick is to keep the information on each card to a minimum.

Number your cards, just in case you drop them on the floor! And move your thumb down the card as you move through the points. Then, when you look up to speak, you won't have lost your place.

You really should trust your memory – you will remember much more than you think.

If you're still not sure you can trust your memory, do two sets of key words – a minimum version and a more thorough one. Then you can practise with each. If you feel a bit nervous, use the more thorough version, but you may well find that you remember perfectly and that you speak more naturally with the minimum version.

☞ **Note the points at which you want to introduce any props or visual aids, but do this in a different colour. You'll be able to see it coming and this will prevent you from saying 'start slide show' out loud, by mistake!**

The reason I recommend the cue card approach is because I believe it gives *just enough* freedom. It frees you from the constraints of a written script, making your words sound fresher, more genuine and more conversational. But, unlike learning a speech by heart, it gives you a little support and, if you're getting off the point, it will take you straight back to your Objective.

TEXT PAGE

I would like to take this opportunity to welcome you all as new members of staff at British Television Productions Limited. For those of you who do not know me, my name is Joan Brown and I am the director of human resources.

The purpose of this meeting is to give you all a quick rundown of the different departments in the company and to explain how they relate to each other. You will be able to see how you fit into the bigger picture and, hopefully, it will help you to understand who your colleagues are and what their role entails. I am going to ask you to look at some slides, including photographs of the most senior staff. As you can see, BTP is run by an executive committee of eight people. This is the chief executive, Peter Hammond . . .

SCRIPT PAGE

(WELCOME)

For those of you who don't know me, I'm Joan Brown and I'm the director of human resources.

The purpose of this meeting is to give you a quick rundown of the different departments in the company and to explain how they relate to each other.

(DISTRIBUTE LEAFLETS SHOWING COMPANY STRUCTURE)

As you can see from the chart, BTP is run by an executive committee of eight people . . .

(TRIGGER FIRST SLIDE)

ILLUSTRATION 4   *Sample text page compared to sample script page*

CUE CARD 1

(Welcome)

Introduce self

Purpose: rundown of different departments

Explain slides

CUE CARD 2

(Distribute handouts showing company structure)

Explain executive committee

(Trigger first slide)

CUE CARD 3

Peter Hammond profile

(Trigger second slide)

Identify executive committee members

CUE CARD 4

(Trigger third slide)

Identify the human resources team

Move on to staff benefits

CUE CARD 5

(Trigger fourth slide)

Talk about new sports club

Explain staff discount schemes

CUE CARD 6

Explain facilities available to staff

(Trigger fifth slide)

Relate plans for new canteen

ILLUSTRATION 5   Part of your speech as it might appear on cue cards

HOW TO START

You've already decided on what your first point should be, and where you're going from there. Now you need to decide how to start saying it!

Beginnings are hugely important. This is the point at which you set the scene for the whole of the presentation. The audience will be at their most receptive and full of curiosity. It's at this point that they're going to decide whether they like you; whether you're going to be interesting; and whether they made the right decision in coming along at all.

Grab their attention now and they're more likely to stay with you throughout the speech. Lose them at the beginning and you'll never get them back.

BEGINNINGS SHOULD:

- have impact
- have authority: show the audience you know your subject
- show awareness of the audience's needs, expectations and interests
- be appropriate: don't tell a dodgy joke to an audience of professionals expecting a political speech, and don't let it jar with the rest of the speech

DON'T stare at an empty page, agonising about how to start. Write the main body of the speech first. So feel free to skip the beginning and come back to it later. You'll probably then find the beginning writes itself.

The key to a good intro is simply this: **give the audience a reason to listen**. There are several ways of doing this. Here are some examples:

1 Promise them something they want

I'm going to tell you about a product that will save you time and money AND improve your love life.

2 Tell them it's going to be short and simple

I know you've given up your free evening to be here tonight, so I'm only going to make three short points.

3 Tell them a story

We stand on a lonely, windswept point on the northern shore of France. The air is soft, but forty years ago at this moment, the air was filled with the crack of rifle fire and the roar of cannon. At dawn, on the morning of the 6th of June 1944, 225 Rangers jumped off the British landing-craft and ran to the bottom of these cliffs.

Ronald Reagan, 6 June 1984, taken from *The Penguin Book of Twentieth-Century Speeches.*

4 Create an image

Before I came here tonight, I went to visit little Johnny Smith in hospital. Johnny – a boy we've often seen trotting off to school – was lying in a hospital bed, fighting for his life, hooked up to all kinds of monitors and machines.

5 Shock them

I speak to you as a man who fifty years and nine days ago had no name, no hope, no future and was known only by his number, A, 70713.

Auschwitz survivor Elie Wiesel, 27 January 1995, taken from *The Penguin Book of Twentieth-Century Speeches.*

6 Make 'em laugh

The first time I took Tracey out on a date, I went to her house to pick her up. Her dad said she was just putting the finishing touches to her makeup. And then he said: 'Fancy a game of chess?'

7 Ask them questions

Do you find yourself constantly struggling because you haven't got enough time or money? Do you want to make your life easier?

All the above examples give the audience a reason for listening. You have made the speech directly relevant to them and so they want to know more.

HOW TO CARRY ON

You have your Route Map, so let the audience in on the secret; tell them where they're going. This isn't a magical mystery tour – the less the audience knows, the more time they're going to spend wondering, just when you want their attention.

Think about the times you have listened to speeches. If the speaker was boring you were drifting into a daydream, or trying to guess how long they were going to bang on because you were hungry/needed a wee/couldn't wait to get to the bar, etc.

Tell the audience where you are taking them.

So when preparing the speech, make sure you've answered all their possible questions.

And don't forget to present these in a positive light. Make the topic relevant, make yourself attractive to them, and tell them you're not going to speak for long. Today, we're so used to watching 60-second commercials. Airtime sales experts carefully place ads in programmes that the target market will be watching. So the ad is aimed at *you*, it's also visually gorgeous, may contain great music, *and* it gets its message across. Phew! How can you possibly compete?

Well, you *can* compete, because your speech is targeted directly at the dozen or couple of hundred people in the room. You've got something interesting to say and if you put it across properly, they'll listen.

Once you've answered their subconscious questions, move through the presentation by simply linking your different points.

Research has shown that most people have short attention spans. If you're speaking for 40 minutes, they'll start off listening intently and their interest will wane until it reaches its lowest ebb about 30 minutes into the speech. Then they'll sense the end is near and they'll perk up again.

But they'll listen more intently and more consistently to four ten-minute speeches. So why not try to break up your speech into shorter bursts, using visuals, a show of hands or some other stunt? You might even think back to those commercials and give your audience four five-minute breaks instead of one 15-minute break.

See 'Polishing your speech', for more tips on how to retain the audience's attention.

HOW TO FINISH BIG

In many ways, the ending is even more important than the opening. If you start well, keep them listening throughout the presentation and then limp to a sad little halt, that poor ending will undo all the good work you did at the beginning.

The ending is a chance to recap and should be the climax of your speech. When you are ending your speech:

DO pull people together.

DO reinforce the message.

DO call the audience to action.

There are a number of ways to ensure that your ending will prove a fitting climax. Here are some options:

LEARN IT BY HEART

Your finale should trip off the tongue and sound like you mean it. This is not a time for stumbling over your words. Make sure it's smooth and delivered with confidence.

GIVE ADDED VALUE

Today, we've looked at eight main points – People, Response, Organisation, Growth, Results, Excellence, Service and Sustainability. Put them all together, and we have PROGRESS.

Ending with a punchy and memorable little message should certainly help everyone to remember what it was you were talking about.

ADD DRAMA OR EMOTION

Above all, we give thanks for the life of a woman I am so proud to be able to call my sister: the unique, the complex, the extraordinary and irreplaceable Diana, whose beauty, both internal and external, will never be extinguished from our minds.

Earl Spencer, at the funeral of Diana, Princess of Wales, 6 September 1997, taken from *The Penguin Book of Twentieth-Century Speeches*.

Fortunately, not everyone will have to give such an address, but an emotional or highly dramatic sting in your speech's tail will certainly make it more memorable.

GIVE AN IMPORTANT FACT

As you know, our main competitor has just been taken over. I've found out that the new parent company has one million pounds to invest in researching new markets. If we're to remain market leader, we need to act now.

Something which is of great importance to your audience will have the same effect as a dramatic or emotionally charged ending.

PROVIDE A PAY-OFF YOU SET UP AT THE BEGINNING

So I'd like to say a special thank-you to Tracey for becoming my wife. I think you'll all agree that she makes a beautiful bride – and that she's really achieved something today: all her makeup done to perfection and only 10 minutes late at the church!

A pay-off line provides a neat, well-rounded ending.

CHECKLIST

Have I told the audience

my topic: what I'm talking about?   ❏

my reason for speaking?   ❏

the limits – what I can and can't tackle in this presentation? ❏

the time allowed for questions at the end   ❏

MARTIN LUTHER KING's 'I HAVE A DREAM' SPEECH, 28 AUGUST 1963

BEGINNING: I am happy to join with you today in what will go down in history as the greatest demonstration for freedom in the history of our nation.

Fivescore years ago, a great American, in whose symbolic shadow we stand today, signed the Emancipation Proclamation. This momentous decree came as a great beacon light of hope to millions of Negro slaves who had been seared in the flames of withering injustice. It came as a joyous daybreak to end the long night of their captivity.

But one hundred years later, the Negro still is not free. One hundred years later, the life of the Negro is still sadly cripped by the manacles of segregation and the chains of discrimination. One hundred years later, the Negro lives on a lonely island of poverty in the midst of a vast ocean of material prosperity. One hundred years later, the Negro is still languished in the corners of American society and finds himself an exile in his own land. And so we've come here today to dramatise a shameful condition …

ENDING: This is our hope. This is the faith that I go back to the South with. With this faith we will be able to hew out of the mountain of despair a stone of hope. With this faith we will be able to transform the jangling discords of our nation into a beautiful symphony of brotherhood. With this faith, we will be able to work together, to pray together, to struggle together, to go to jail together, to stand up for freedom together, knowing that we will be free one day. This will be the day, this will be the day when all of God's children will be able to sing with new meaning

'My country, tis of thee, sweet land of liberty, of thee I sing'

… And when this happens, when we allow freedom to ring, when we let it ring from every village and every hamlet, from every state and every city, we will be able to speed up that day when all of God's children, black men and white men, Jews and Gentiles, Protestants and Catholics, will be able to join hands and sing in the words of the old Negro spiritual: 'Free at last! Free at last! Thank God Almighty, we are free at last.'

WEB TIP *For the full text of Martin Luther King's speech, visit* **www.stanford.edu/group/King/**

JOHN F KENNEDY'S INAUGURAL ADDRESS, 20 JANUARY 1961

BEGINNING: Welcome ... we observe today not a victory of party, but a celebration of freedom symbolising an end, as well as a beginning, signifying renewal, as well as change. For I have sworn before you and Almighty God the same solemn oath our forebears prescribed nearly a century and three quarters ago.

The world is very different now. For man holds in his mortal hands the power to abolish all forms of human poverty and all forms of human life. And yet the same revolutionary beliefs for which our forebears fought are still at issue around the globe, the belief that the rights of man come not from the generosity of the state, but from the hand of God ...

ENDING: ... And so, my fellow Americans, ask not what your country can do for you; ask what you can do for your country.

My fellow citizens of the world: ask not what America will do for you, but what together we can do for the freedom of man.

Finally, whether you are citizens of America or citizens of the world, ask of us the same high standards of strength and sacrifice which we ask of you. With a good conscience our only sure reward, with history the final judge of our deeds, let us go forth to lead the land we love, asking His blessing and His help, but knowing that here on earth God's work must truly be our own.

WEB TIP *For John F Kennedy's complete speech,* visit **www.bartleby.com**

ILLUSTRATION 6   *Beginnings and endings of two famous speeches*

POLISHING YOUR SPEECH

Right, you've got the words down on paper and in your mind – and in the right order too! But don't rush off to deliver the presentation just yet. To make the difference between a good enough speech and a really good speech, you need to get out the literary Mr Sheen and polish up your English.

Here are a few suggestions that might help.

GET CHATTY

As we discussed above, spoken English is very different from written English. Listen to real conversations (a great excuse for nosy Parkers). Next time you're on the bus or waiting in a queue, listen to the words and sentence structure people use.

You will find that their speech patterns are full of abbreviations, such as 'you'll', 'didn't', 'wouldn't', etc., and they break off in the middle of sentences and use 'incorrect' grammar.

In your speech, you need to find a healthy balance between the boring correctness of written English and the muddled informality of having a chat.

DO read your draft speech out loud enough times to get comfortable with it. If you're using cue cards, this should be easy. If you've decided to ignore my good advice and read from a script, then you'll find it harder. Don't stick too closely to the written word – let your natural speech patterns come out. It will be much more interesting for your audience.

If you rush the audience, or blind them with long words, they'll be too busy worrying about the bits they missed to concentrate on the later pearls of wisdom.

Think about the three key differences between written and spoken words:

WRITTEN	SPOKEN
at reader's own pace	at speaker's pace
can be re-read	heard only once
can be read in any order	only heard in the order it's presented

Real
LIFE
Although he's hardly read these days, W W Jacobs is one of my family's favourite authors. His comic short stories were hugely popular at the beginning of the 20th century and he was admired by many better-known writers, including P G Wodehouse.

One of Jacobs's charms lies in his ability to convey normal speech patterns and dialect on the written page.

Take this extract from the opening chapter of his book Deep Waters:

'A sailorman – said the night-watchman musingly – a sailorman is like a fish, he is safest when 'e is at sea. When a fish comes ashore it is in for trouble, and so is a sailorman. One poor chap I knew 'ardly ever came ashore without getting married; and when he was found out there was no less than six wimmen in the court all taking away 'is character at once.'

Jacobs's writing was unusual for its time – he was a middle-class man himself, but a shrewd observer of the speech and language of all kinds of people. This 'chatty' style is easy to read and, in the above extract, we learn more about the night-watchman than could be conveyed in pages and pages of description.

DO avoid boring, passive words and phrases and go for exciting, active, thrilling language.

DO say, 'Our approach gets results fast! We could boost your productivity by a third in just six months.'

DON'T say, 'It has been found that our training course can improve productivity by an average of 33 per cent within six months.'

The same goes for phrases – make sure you keep them dynamic!

When you are thinking about your style, try reading the tabloid newspapers. If you're a snob about newspapers, you're in for a shock. It's the tabloids that are the true masters at conveying complicated stories in the simplest, most dynamic language. Sometimes they use terrible 'journalese', but ignore this and try to break down how they've put the story across. You might want to compare the same story in different types of newspapers.

DON'T SAY	DO SAY
you might want to	you should
I think you should	you should
can we think about	let's think about
shouldn't we try to	we must
may	can
could	can
might	will

USE THE RIGHT WORDS

Remember that words convey different emotions. Think about what buttons you want to press for your audience and use words that feel appropriate.

Real LIFE

As I wrote those words, I was casting around for a good example to illustrate what I meant. My partner works for one of the big food chains, so a copy of The Grocer magazine happened to be lying on the coffee table. I just opened it at a random page and found an ad for the launch of a new range of chicken ready-meals.

The ad said in big letters: 'Quality chicken. Altogether more tempting.'

It went on: 'With more thought for food, Birds Eye have once again made chicken altogether more tempting with the launch of two delicious and original dishes – Thai Chicken and Honey and Mustard Chicken.'

The copywriters and product developers have really thought about what the average household is looking for and they've pulled out all the right words to get that message across.

Health scares have rocked our confidence in the safety of meat, so 'quality' is there to reassure. But it's food, so it must be 'tempting' – a ready-meal is a bit of a treat, not something most families have every day. And so it goes on – the food is 'delicious' and 'original' – it's got to taste good, and how many home cooks are bored with preparing the same food, week in, week out?

Another example:

My newspaper property section carries an ad today that warns:

'Prepare to be converted. Nightingale Court features a range of large, elegant apartments of unreserved luxury set in two landmark Victorian listed buildings in extensively landscaped mature grounds. These magnificent apartments

combine traditional Victorian architecture with modern design and materials, blending the very best of old and new.'

Talk about pushing the right buttons! The developers know their customer – probably a well-off but busy commuter. He likes the character of older properties but hasn't the time or skills to do up an old wreck. He wants the best home, for the minimum fuss. He wants to put his deckchair outside on occasion, but he doesn't want to do the gardening. A different kind of buyer might be looking for a cosy family home – not our man! He wants to impress guests, so his home needs to be 'magnificent'.

Without realising he's being manipulated, our buyer will be very interested in this particular property.

Keep your Objective in mind all the time.

You can make your speech even more relevant to your audience by choosing the right words. Go back to your Objective. Is your speech about selling a product that can save the audience time? Use snappy words; appeal to their busy, stressed lives. Is it about asking them to join a campaign? Appeal to their emotions with warm, powerful words.

DO jot down what you want to say and then use a thesaurus to find a more exciting way of saying it. For example, if you jotted down 'Your profits will increase', the thesaurus offers you all kinds of interesting alternatives for 'increase': amplify, heighten, inflate, snowball, magnify, boost, multiply, escalate, enlarge, proliferate ... there is plenty of choice.

THINK ABOUT RHYTHM & FLOW

Giving your speech rhythm is a major key to keeping the audience's attention. Why is it that we remember song words but not dry facts? Why do we have little rhymes to help us remember dates ('In 14 hundred and 92, Columbus sailed the ocean blue'; or the fate of Henry

VIII's wives: 'Divorced, beheaded, died; Divorced, beheaded, survived')? Because rhythms appeal to our ears and make speech more attractive.

There's more later about how to change the rhythm with your voice, but here you should be thinking about the rhythm of the actual words themselves. When you're practising your speech out loud, you should be able to hear the beat – if a section feels too clumsy to say, change the rhythm.

There are many ways to introduce rhythm and energy into your speech:

Vary the length of your sentences

I understand. I know abandonment and people being mean to you, and saying you're nothing and nobody, and can never be anything. I understand.

Jesse Jackson, 19 July 1988, taken from *The Penguin Book of Twentieth-Century Speeches.*

Ask rhetorical questions (those you answer yourself)

What, then, are we doing to our capital city now? What have we done to it since the bombing during the war? What are we shortly going to do to one of its most famous areas – Trafalgar Square? Instead of designing an extension to the elegant façade of the National Gallery which complements it and continues the concept of columns and domes, it looks as if we may be presented with a kind of vast municipal fire station, complete with the sort of tower that contains the siren.

Prince Charles, taken from *The Penguin Book of Twentieth-Century Speeches.*

Speak in threes

Our daily deeds as ordinary South Africans must produce an actual South African reality that will reinforce humanity's belief in justice, strengthen its confidence in the nobility of the human soul and sustain all our hopes for a glorious life for all.

Nelson Mandela, 10 May 1994.

Try removing one of the three prongs of Mr Mandela's sentence. The balance goes all wrong, doesn't it? Threes just work.

Echo your phrases

> *We can never be satisfied as long as the Negro is the victim of the unspeakable horrors of police brutality. We can never be satisfied as long as our bodies, heavy with the fatigue of travel, cannot gain lodging in the motels of the highways and the hotels of the cities. We cannot be satisfied as long as the Negro's basic mobility is from a smaller ghetto to a larger one. We can never be satisfied as long as our children are stripped of their selfhood and robbed of their dignity by signs stating 'for whites only'. We cannot be satisfied as long as a Negro in Mississippi cannot vote and a Negro in New York believes he has nothing for which to vote. No, no, we are not satisfied and we will not be satisfied until 'justice rolls down like waters and righteousness like a mighty stream'.*

Martin Luther King.

Use alliteration

> *What do we want for our children – prison and poverty?*
> *Drugs and delinquency? Vandalism and vice? Or peace and positivity?*
> *Democracy and dialogue? Victory and valour?*

Repeat and reinforce

Repeating words and sounds can help drive your message home.

> *I know that I will be silenced for many years; I know that the regime will try to suppress the truth by all possible means; I know that there will be a conspiracy to bury me in oblivion.*

Fidel Castro, 16 October 1953.

Use imagery and metaphor for added impact

Comparing two things for dramatic effect can be useful. If you have a complicated topic, it can help people understand. Or it can help to paint a mental picture that will inspire the audience.

Beware of mixing metaphors (using more than one metaphor at a time).

In his first broadcast as Prime Minister, on 19 May 1940, Winston Churchill knew that Britain was losing the war. Germany was overwhelming every army in its path, but Churchill knew he had to fight on. And he had to get the nation behind him, however hard it might be. Not one for flowery language, he did, however, make use of metaphor in the climax of his speech:

Side by side, unaided except by their kith and kin in the great Dominions and by the wide empires which rest beneath their shield – side by side the British and French peoples have advanced to rescue not only Europe but mankind from the foulest and most soul-destroying tyranny which has ever darkened and stained the pages of history. Behind them – behind us – behind the Armies and Fleets of Britain and France – gather a group of shattered States and bludgeoned races: the Czechs, the Poles, the Norwegians, the Danes, the Dutch, the Belgians – upon all of whom the long night of barbarism will descend, unbroken even by a star of hope, unless we conquer, as conquer we must; as conquer we shall.

WEB TIP *For complete texts of Winston Churchill's speeches, visit* ***www.winstonchurchill.org***.

Imagery is closely linked to metaphor – and can be equally powerful. Look at these two examples:

Last Tuesday, 8-year-old Johnny Smith was knocked down and seriously injured while crossing the main road through the village.

Or: *Last Tuesday, Mary Smith waved her little son Johnny off to school – just like every mother in this audience. She was just loading the washing-machine when she got the knock at the door that every parent dreads. A policeman had come to tell her that Johnny had been knocked down and was fighting for his life in hospital.*

The first example is perfectly correct, but the second conjures up an emotional image that has an immediate impact on the audience. The first will make them think. But the second will make them feel.

The Reverend Jesse Jackson is a master of language. How many examples of polish can you find in this excerpt from one of his speeches?

> *I have a message for our youth. I challenge them to put hope in their brains and not dope in their veins.*

> *I told them that like Jesus, I, too, was born in the slum, and just because you're born in a slum does not mean the slum is born in you and you can rise above it if your mind is made up.*

> *I told them in every slum there are two sides. When I see a broken window that's the slummy side. Train some youth to become a glazier; that is the sunny side.*

> *When I see a missing brick, that is the slummy side. Let that child in a union and become a brick mason and build; that is the sunny side.*

> *When I see a missing door, that is the slummy side. Train some youth to become a carpenter, that is the sunny side.*

> *When I see the vulgar words and hieroglyphics of destitution on the walls, that is the slummy side. Train some youth to be a painter and artist, that is the sunny side.*

> *We leave this place looking for the sunny side because there's a brighter side somewhere. I am more convinced than ever that we can win. We will vault up the rough side of the mountain. We can win.*

GET EMOTIONAL

If your subject is particularly emotional, it's fine to use your feelings to help persuade the audience to your point of view, but let it come naturally. False emotion is all too easily spotted.

TELL 'EM A STORY

Anecdotes can be an extremely useful weapon in your vocal armoury. But irrelevant anecdotes, however amusing they may be, just leave the audience baffled, while they try to work out the link.

CHECKLIST

Make sure your anecdotes do at least one of the following:

Reinforce ❑

Highlight ❑

Explain ❑

Summarize ❑

Tony Blair made history by being the first British Prime Minister to address the Irish Parliament, on 26 November 1998. He made good use of anecdotal material to emphasise the links between himself and the people of Ireland. See how he makes the transition to very personal experiences, without straying from the bigger picture.

> *Ireland, as you may know, is in my blood. My mother was born in the flat above her grandmother's hardware shop on the main street of Ballyshannon in Donegal. She lived there as a child, started school there and only moved when her father died; her mother remarried and they crossed the water to Glasgow.*

> *We spent virtually every childhood summer holiday up to when the troubles really took hold in Ireland, usually at Rossnowlagh, the Sands House Hotel, I think it was. And we would travel in the beautiful countryside of Donegal. It was there in the seas off the Irish coast that I learned to swim, there that my father took me to*

my first pub, a remote little house in the country, for a Guinness,
a taste I've never forgotten and which is always a pleasure to
repeat.

WEB TIP *Taken from The History Place, Great Speeches*
Collection, www.historyplace.com.

MAKE 'EM LAUGH

A store detective once told me that the motto of her profession is: 'If in
doubt, leave it out.' It's a pretty good motto for many things – jokes in
a speech being one of them. Humour is the most difficult thing to get
right. And the easiest way of offending people. But everyone likes a
laugh and it's a good way to get the audience relaxed, engaged and on
your side. So you'll just need to tread carefully.

WEB TIP *Try the following sites for some topical gags that you*
can just throw into your speech:

www.bazza.com/sj/humour/

www.jokes-for-all.com

BANISH JARGON

Beware of jargon! You might know what it means, but does your
audience? Even if you're talking to a group who should understand the
terms, simplify them! Just a slight misunderstanding about a word's
meaning can make all the difference.

While we're on the subject of jargon, a quick mention of buzzwords,
or management-speak – you know, those phrases that someone always
trots out in a meeting. You may work for a company that loves
buzzwords, but recent reports have shown most people find them
a turn-off.

DON'T ever say:

- Let's run this up the flagpole and see who salutes it.

- Let's put that on the backburner.

- You need to think out of the box.

- Let's touch base.

And don't even think about dreaming up new ones. You'll just sound incomprehensible, like the person who said: 'In order to skin the cat, you need a better mousetrap', or 'I'd like to have a scuba in your think tank' or, perhaps worst of all, 'I want to stick a couple of ideas into your intellectual toaster and see what pops up'.

Think like a listener – not like a speaker.

IDENTIFY YOUR RELATIONSHIP WITH THE AUDIENCE

Put yourself in the audience's shoes and work out what you need to do to keep their attention and help them to remember what you're saying. Visuals, anecdotes and all the stylistic polishes we're talking about in this chapter should help.

DO talk about 'our business', 'our profits', 'the difference we can make', if you're talking to a group that you're part of. Make sure they know that you identify yourself with them.

DO make it clear, if you're not part of the group, that only they can make the difference – motivate them. Talk about 'your rivals', 'your opportunities', 'the best thing you can do'.

DON'T stand up there banging on about 'me' and 'I'.

S U M M A R Y

Should I write the speech out in full?

Text/script/cue cards. The cue cards will serve you far better.

How should I start?

You need impact, authority and awareness – and make sure it's
appropriate.

How do I end?

Pull people together, reinforce your message and demand
action. Make sure your ending gives them something to
think about.

Polishing your speech

Be chatty, be dynamic, think about rhythm and pace, use
imagery and emotion, banish jargon, make 'em laugh and
banish jargon.

4

WORDS ARE NOT
ENOUGH

- WHY VISUALS ARE IMPORTANT

- DIFFERENT TYPES OF VISUAL AIDS

- TYPES OF EQUIPMENT

- PREPARING YOUR VISUALS

- INSIDER TIPS ON WORKING WITH
  VISUAL AIDS

- USING HANDOUTS EFFECTIVELY

A picture paints a thousand words – and the audience is probably tired of looking at you by now, anyway.

If you've mapped your way through your speech, you'll probably already have had some ideas for visual material. Some points would obviously be better illustrated by a graph or chart of some kind – and you'll already have planned these in.

But you might think about using visuals to emphasise the most important points or to add interest or humour to the presentation. You may even want to think about using sound or video, to add interest or variety, or to explain a point better.

WHY VISUALS ARE IMPORTANT

Pictures are certainly more memorable than words – more even than
you might think. A designer who can create a memorable logo for a
company is highly prized – and highly paid. The best brands simply
seep into your mind, without you even realising. Just seeing that certain
shade of pale blue makes me think of Barclay's Bank. And a green
carrier bag says Marks & Spencer to me, even if I can't see the company
name. Nike's 'swoosh', Coca-Cola's 'dynamic ribbon' and McDonald's
'golden arches' are so instantly recognisable that the manufacturers can
use them to brand a product without using the company name at all.

You could simply say: 'Sales figures were rising at a rate of about
2 per cent a year until the introduction of the new system in 1998. Since
then, sales have gone up by 25 per cent a year.' But if you show them a
graph like this, the information is more likely to stick in their minds.

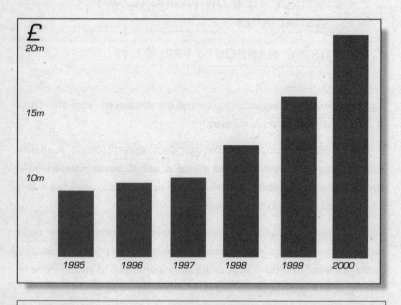

ILLUSTRATION 7   *A graph will help to make information stick in the minds
of your audience*

CHECKLIST

It's a great idea to include visual material in your presentation, but there's no point in including it if it's not there for a reason.

Go through this checklist and ask yourself: Would my choice of visual material do least one of the following:

show what something looks like? ❏

reinforce a point? ❏

illustrate something abstract or unseen? ❏

show information patterns? ❏

interpret figures? ❏

summarise key points? ❏

Just as logos make a lasting impression so too do visuals used during a speech. They can give a statement real impact and help to explain things like sales figures.

THE RIGHT EQUIPMENT FOR THE RIGHT INFORMATION

Different types of graphics and equipment all have their place, and they're all suitable for different purposes.

- To help the audience remember key points: **use key words**
- To emphasise easily illustrated specifics: **use photographs**
- To drive home key points and add humour: **use cartoons**
- To show something changing over time: **use a line graph**
- To compare data: **use a bar graph**

- To show how percentages relate to each other as part of the whole picture: **use a pie chart**

- To show how departments or events are related to each other: **use an organisational chart**

- To show a process or step-by-step approach: **use a flow chart**

- To show key points for large audiences: **use slides**

- To show key points for a small audience: **use an overhead projector (OHP) or a computer presentation**

- To show key points for very small audiences or when cash is tight: **use a flip chart**

- To show an imagined scenario, or to illustrate a narrative point better: **use video**

Before making a final decision about what visuals you want to use, contact the organisers, or the venue itself, and ask what facilities they have. Some are specially equipped for slides and computer presentations and can project your visual material onto a huge screen, with fantastic quality. It's not going to be a good day if the speaker who's wowing them before you takes advantage of this and then you turn up with your flip chart or handwritten OHP notes that no one beyond row three can even see.

Take some time out of the office – visit the venue to examine the facilities and see how the seating will be set up. Make an appointment to meet the technician there. He or she should be able to give you a demonstration and chat to you about the best approach.

If the venue isn't quite so high-tech, it might still have its own OHP, which would save you taking your own. (See chapter 5 for tips on checking visual equipment.)

If you're using a lot of visual material, you can really make it work for you. Use the visuals as your notes. They'll jog your memory and it'll look impressive if you're not constantly referring to cue cards.

Some experts will try to tell you how many visuals you should include per hour – and this is a useful crutch for people who like to be told what to do. But it is ridiculous to lay down rules about visuals because no two presentations are the same. A presentation about how to identify wild flowers might be based entirely on visuals – imagine how much time you would have to waste in describing those particular colours or petal shapes, without a picture to refer to.

But many of the greatest speeches in the world have conjured up impressive visual imagery, using nothing but the power of words.

However, once you have decided to use visuals it *is* a good idea to present the material fairly regularly throughout your presentation. Let's have a look in more detail at the kinds of visual material that might help back up your points.

DIFFERENT TYPES OF VISUAL AIDS

WORDS Editing your main points down to a few key words is an extremely effective way of driving them home. This form of visual aid is simple, quick and cheap to prepare and can be adapted to tie in with whatever equipment you've decided to use for other support – flip charts, OHPs, computer presentations or slides, for example. It can also look very professional, especially if you use computer-generated graphics.

DO edit ferociously. The key words method will only work if you have no more than about six words.

PHOTOGRAPHS If you work for a design company, for example, or your presentation is deeply rooted in visuals for some other reason, it makes sense to use photographs.

Original photographs can obviously be freely used, although they can take some time to prepare. You may need to gather together the things you want to photograph, or travel to the right place. You will then have to schedule some time to scan them into a computer or allow time for them to be processed as slides.

Or you could invest in a digital camera; they're fairly cheap now. Digital photos can then be downloaded directly into your PC. The advantage of computerised photographs is that you can crop or otherwise alter them with a simple-to-use program such as Photoshop. And when you need them again a year later, the edges won't be all bumped and curled up!

WEB TIP *To buy a digital camera, you could visit* **www.ukdigitalcameras.co.uk** *or* **www.internetcamerasdirect.co.uk** *or* **www.digital-cameras.com**. *If you're not sure what you're looking for, Yahoo! (**www.yahoo.co.uk**) has a particularly useful buyer's guide, as has Computer Shopper (**www.computershopper.com**). Photoshop software can be bought at **www.jungle.com** and other software sites. When I looked, it was priced at about £500.*

If you commission a professional photographer, this can be an expensive exercise. Most photographers charge at least £200 a day for their services, plus the cost of materials. If you have to hire a studio, you're really bumping up the price.

WEB TIP *Search for local photographers on Scoot or Yell (the Yellow Pages). You'll find Scoot at **www.scoot.co.uk** and Yell at **www.yell.com**. Both sites will allow you to search for services by name, type and location.*

If you use someone else's pictures, you'll probably have to buy them in, paying for the copyright. However, the main photographic agencies are

JARGONBUSTER!
Trannies: from 'transparency', i.e. slides.

extremely helpful and knowledgeable. You simply call up and describe what you want and they will send you sheets of slides (usually called 'trannies' in the business). There will be a basic search fee and then you pay for the images you use. If you need prints, rather than trannies, professional photographic studios can usually make prints in around 24 hours.

Many of the main picture agencies have websites, where you can search yourself. Leading photograph agencies include
Corbis – **www.corbisimages.com**;
Rex Features – 020 7278 87294 – **www.rexfeatures.com**;
London Features – 020 7723 4204

DO use photographs for slide and computer presentations as they reproduce well.

DON'T use them on OHPs as they don't work so well.

CARTOONS These don't have to be hilarious. No one's treating your presentation as a guest spot at the Comedy Store. Unless, of course, it is a guest spot at the Comedy Store. In which case, go ahead. Be hilarious.

But even in ordinary speeches or presentations, your audience will probably welcome any attempts at humour if it's appropriate to the subject matter.

DO keep it simple and representational if you decide to draw something yourself. Stick figures will work better than even the best-drawn figures. It's not an art class, it's just meant to get your message across.

If you're using cartoons you've already seen in a publication, remember that copyright laws may apply. Call the publication concerned. They'll usually be able to put you straight in touch with the cartoonist or advise you on the copyright situation.

If you want to commission cartoons, don't forget to include this cost in your budget. To find a cartoonist, you could look at newspapers and publications until you find someone who's doing the kind of work you're after. Trade magazines can be good sources as their resident cartoonist will already know something about your industry. The publication should be able to put you in touch.

WEB TIP *Many cartoonists have their own websites, which enable them to show the range of different styles. For a great directory of links to cartoonists' sites, visit The Cartoonists' Guild's site at **www.pipemedia.net/cartoons/index**.*

☞ **The receptionist at a publication probably won't have a listing for the cartoonist. If the cartoon you like is on the news pages, ask to be put through to the news editor. If it's on a features page, ask for the features editor.**

GRAPHS AND CHARTS These make all the difference if you're discussing statistics of any kind. Abstract figures can baffle even the most attentive egg-head, but most people can see that a line on a graph which is plunging downwards is news.

If you're generating your graphs on a computer, you can, of course, come up with all sorts of whiz-bang representations for your charts. These are particularly useful if you're pitching for business and want to impress a client, but simple representations are fine if all you want to do is get your message across. If you, or someone you work with, already know how to do the whiz-bangy things, all well and good. If not, it's easy to get sidetracked into learning how to show company profits as increasingly huge moneybags when you *should* be researching the content of your speech.

Anyway, you should be careful of anything too flashy – sometimes people get carried away with their own cleverness and forget that the purpose of the exercise is to make the statistics easier to read. Too many shadows and logos can get in the way of your message.

DO keep words to a minimum on charts. Make the letters large, clear and plain.

PIE CHARTS If you're using pie charts, make sure the slices tally with the percentages they represent. Use the sofware on your PC to construct the chart and produce a 3-D pie.

By now, you should have a good idea of the best kinds of visual aids to back up your points. But there are so many choices of equipment. Which is the most suitable?

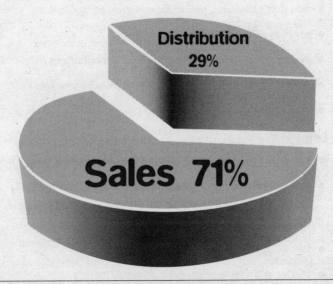

ILLUSTRATION 8   A pie chart can often illustrate your point better than a graph

TYPES OF EQUIPMENT

Before you decide which type of equipment to use for your presentation, a word of warning: never choose an important speech to use new equipment for the first time. Either use something with which you are familiar, or practise using new gadgets well in advance.

WEB TIP *If you need to hire equipment, try visiting* **www.scoot.co.uk** *or* **www.yell.co.uk**. *If the company has a website, there will usually be a link from Scoot or Yell, so you can simply click through.*

FLIP CHARTS AND WHITEBOARDS

This is the 'back to basics' approach.

DO use a flip chart if:

- you don't have any power for electrical equipment
- you haven't got much money
- you're going to write down audience contributions
- you need to explain things by illustration as you speak
- you've got a small audience

Don't use one if:

- you really don't want your visuals to look messy
- you're likely to change the running order or refer back (flip charts: it's a pain to flip through all that paper; whiteboards: you might have already rubbed it out)
- you've got illegible handwriting
- you've got a lot to show (size is limited)

With flip charts you can either write the material as you go along, or you can prepare it in advance; using different coloured pens helps to make things stand out and adds variety.

You could even get really whizzy and have two flip charts! One, at the left side of the room, could list your main points, while you use the other to go into detail. While you're talking, the audience will be able to remind themselves where they are and what you're talking about.

If you're using a whiteboard, you can also use magnets to secure sheets of paper to the board, which is useful if you want to show other visuals.

For whiteboards, 'dry erase' pens are easy to remove, so are better if you want to change things quickly. 'Wet erase' pens are less smudgy and a bit more permanent. But you can still get the marks off with a proper eraser.

CHECKLIST

Things you'll need for flip charts and whiteboards:

Flip chart

plenty of marker pens in the right colours (if you
    get a dud one, throw it away at once so you
    don't pick it up again) ❏

enough paper in the pad ❏

ruler (if you need one) ❏

something to point with (optional) ❏

Whiteboard

plenty of special whiteboard pens (ordinary marker
    pens are permanent – beware!) ❏

whiteboard rubber ❏

ruler (if you need one) ❏

something to point with (optional) ❏

magnets (if you're using other visuals on paper) ❏

☞ If you are planning to write on the sheets as you go along, you can prepare by lightly pencilling notes in the corners. The audience won't be able to see them and it will look as if you have the memory of an elephant.

DO leave a blank sheet between charts. Sometimes the paper is thin and almost see-through.

DO make a sample chart or sheet and then stand at the back of the room and check that you can see the information clearly. If not, start again. You should check this even if you're planning to write on the sheets as you go along, instead of pre-writing them. It will give you an idea of how big the figures need to be.

DO practise writing quickly and legibly while standing at the side of the board or chart.

DO number the pages if you are pre-preparing a flip chart presentation, so that you don't skip a page and can find your way back if necessary.

DON'T try to write and talk at the same time: you have to turn away from the audience to write and then you won't be able to project your voice properly. Important points may go unheard.

DON'T worry about the silence; the audience will be perfectly happy watching what you're writing. When you've finished writing, turn round and start talking again.

If you're really going back to basics, you could use a blackboard. But that's taking low-tech to almost ridiculous lengths.

PORTFOLIO

A smart folder, possibly with clear pockets on the inside, can be useful. They are used for carrying artwork or other presentation material. Some have a built-in mechanism that allows the portfolio to be propped up, while you flip the sheets over.

Do use if:

- you're presenting to only a few people
- you're making the same presentation lots of times
- you need the presentation to be very portable
- you can't guarantee you'll have an electrical source
- you need to change the running order, or flip back a lot
- you want to look professional

Don't use if:

- you're presenting to a large audience
- you've got more to show than you can fit in the portfolio

DO buy a strong, good-quality portfolio that's the right size for your presentation material.

DO check that everything is in the portfolio before you go off for a presentation.

DO make sure the light's not glaring off the plastic pockets.

DON'T use cards or a script for your speech – it will look weird. Use the visuals as your prompt.

OVERHEAD PROJECTORS

An OHP is a lightbox which projects words or images from acetate sheets onto a wall or screen. You can also get a gadget that connects the OHP to your computer, projecting your computer screen onto the wall screen. OHPs have been refined a great deal since the old days. They're now smaller, brighter and project a more even image.

Do use if:

- you're not very good at technology
- you're worried about equipment breaking down, as they are pretty reliable

- you haven't got much money: they are cheap to buy or hire

- you need to give your presentation in different locations: new models are fairly portable

- you're likely to go back and discuss points you made earlier

- you want to add notes to your visuals as you go along

- you can't darken the room much, as new models are still bright enough to see clearly

Don't use if:

- it's important that you have a cutting-edge look

- you've got an old model and you're not sure the room will be dark enough and that the machine might be too noisy

- you're worried about damaging or losing the acetates

- you don't have power, a screen or a blank wall

- colours or photographic detail are important to your presentation

Although OHPs don't work well for big audiences, they have the advantage of being flexible. If a question, for example, refers back to one of the visuals, it should be easy to find it and display it once more. With slides, you would have to run through the whole lot. If you can, you should print your OHP sheets on acetate rather than handwriting them. It looks a lot more professional and you can plan out the whole page before you start printing. You can also print an exact copy on paper, for you to refer to, instead of craning your neck round or staring at a brightly lit OHP. You can also hand out the copies after the presentation.

If the presentation includes some pages where you start at the top and work slowly down, remember to exploit the medium. Cover the acetate on the OHP with a piece of paper, which you may then slide down to reveal the points as you speak. This will stop the audience from sneaking a look at what's coming up and thinking about that, instead of what you're talking about now.

Remember to take care of your acetates: put a piece of plain white paper between them as you make them. This will stop them from sticking together. And don't leave them on a hot OHP for too long.

CHECKLIST

Things you'll need for overhead projectors:

Power supply and extension lead, if necessary ❑

Tape to secure the lead to the floor, if it's plugged in anywhere that people might walk. (The best is 'gaffer' tape, or Elephant Tape, available from DIY stores, but any parcel tape will do, as long as it will come unstuck again afterwards) ❑

Screen or wall space ❑

Table with enough room for acetates and your PC (if using it) ❑

Spare OHP bulb ❑

Handkerchief (in case you need to change a hot bulb) ❑

Something to point with (optional) ❑

Acetate marker pens (if you're writing as you go along) ❑

Soft cloth to polish lens and mirror ❑

Once you have placed each sheet on the OHP, stand next to the screen, so the audience doesn't have to gaze at only one or the other. Do this unless you're making notes on the acetate as you go along. If you do make notes, make sure you're not blocking anyone's view. You will find it easier if you place the OHP in the middle of the table. Put the unseen sheets on one side and, as you remove them from the machine, place them on the other side. And finally, try to plan your speech so you don't have to keep switching the OHP on and off – it could blow the bulb.

DO set up before anyone arrives, making sure the image is large enough and not distorted.

DO practise changing the sheets, so that you don't fumble.

DO have a 'title-page' up as the audience comes in. It will look professional and the audience is less likely to notice the noise of the machine than if you switch it on after they've settled down.

DO check the conditions at the same time you're planning to do the presentation. A new model means the room doesn't have to be very dark. It might be dark enough at 5 pm, but if your presentation is from 9 am to 10 am, the bright morning light could make your visuals invisible.

DO number the sheets, in case you drop the lot on the floor. You might want to mount the acetates in a cardboard frame. They will be easier to handle but bulkier.

DO make sure the actual machine isn't blocking anyone's view.

Use an overhead projector with two bulbs, in case one blows.

SLIDE PROJECTOR

A slide projector is a familiar piece of kit that is now usually powered by remote control and can be linked up with a specially recorded soundtrack, which triggers the slides at the right point in the commentary. They're also a bit brighter and clearer now.

Do use if:

- you can project the image large enough for the room size

- photographic images are important to your presentation

- you need to take your own presentation equipment to the
  venue (projectors are pretty portable and slides are light and
  robust)

- you often present using a range of images (slides are easy to
  get and easy to store)

Don't use if

- it's important not to put a subconscious barrier between
  yourself and your audience (turning out the light can do this)

- you don't have power and you can't darken the room at all
  (although new models are much brighter)

- you might need to change the running order

- you're on a tight budget and you're only going to use the slides
  once

- you're on a tight deadline and can't wait for the trannies to be
  produced

CHECKLIST

Things you'll need for a slide projector:

Power supply and extension lead   ❏

Tape to make sure no one trips over the lead (see OHPs) ❏

Table for the projector   ❏

Laser pointer or special torch for pointing (optional)   ❏

When you are preparing your slides, make a mark in the top right-hand corner of the slides, so you don't put them in upside down. Allow time to do a run-through with the projector at the venue before anyone gets there, to make sure the slides are all there and all in the right order.

Remember, if you need to talk about something else between slides, insert a black slide, and if you are using an OHP remove the sheet so that the audience concentrates on what you're saying.

DO number your slides, in case you drop the lot on the floor.

DO use a remote changer and stand by the screen.

DO take a directional lamp or do your speech without referring to notes if you're working in a darkened room.

VIDEOTAPE AND AUDIO TAPE

A change of voice is usually welcomed by the audience and calls them back if their minds were wandering. Copyright considerations might apply, but if you're recording your own footage this will, of course, be fine.

Do use if:

- you want to record delegates acting out scenarios and play them back for analysis
- you need a narrative technique to illustrate your point
- you have a power supply
- you have a big enough TV and/or speakers that are loud enough without distorting
- the venue has a number of TVs linked up to a single video player

Don't use if:

- (for video) everyone can't see the screen, because of the lighting or the size of the room

DO test the equipment in the room in which you're going to use it.

DO have the tape cued up and ready to go.

DO plan what you're going to do while it's playing. For audio you can stay where you are, for video you should probably sit with the audience and watch it. Try to look interested, no matter how many times you've seen it before.

CHECKLIST

Things you'll need for videotape and audio tape:

Power point and extension lead   ❑

Tape for wayward leads (see OHPs)   ❑

Video or audio tape   ❑

COMPUTER-GENERATED PRESENTATIONS

There are several software packages aimed specifically at presentation, but the best known is Microsoft PowerPoint. No matter which one you choose, they all have the advantage of providing a series of templates. You just fill in the details and – hey presto! – professional graphics. They also give you the option of printing out the pages, so you can easily produce handouts for the audience.

It is also easy for you to store the presentation and alter it later for subsequent presentations. This is useful if you're presenting similar material to different audiences, because you'll be able to tweak the material and personalise it. You can incorporate photographs or video clips into the presentation, which will save you from having to switch equipment part-way through. And you can download images from the internet, or have people mail images direct to your computer.

If you've just learned how to use the software, avoid getting carried away with your new skills. Too many animations and flashing logos can just be distracting.

These are the main options for a computer generated presentation:

1 LCD (Liquid Crystal Display) projection panels – link to an OHP, to project what would normally be seen on a computer screen. The computer can deliver sound at the same time.

2 LCD and DLP (Digital Light Processing) projectors – project the computer screen images onto a wall or screen and deliver stereo sound. Brighter than LCD panels. Many conference centres have systems installed.

3 Large screen computers – suitable for small groups. Speakers provide sound.

Do use if:

- you've got a fast computer with a big memory (when you buy presentation equipment, check with the supplier that your computer will be compatible and fast enough)

- it's important that you appear to be using 'cutting edge' technology

- you make presentations on a regular basis

- you've got some cash to invest in the right equipment

- you're pitching for business and you're in competition with another firm

- your presentations might change at short notice

- the venue has compatible projection equipment, then you'll only need to take a laptop

- the room can't be darkened: most screens work in normal light

Don't use if:

- you have no idea how to fix it if it goes wrong

- you can't give any kind of presentation if it goes wrong (they can be a bit unreliable)

- you're not sure your PC will be compatible with the projection equipment

- you don't have access to a projector and you're presenting to a large group of people – they'll never all be able to crowd round the screen

- you're hard up

- photographic detail is really important – they're still not quite as good as slide projectors

If you decide to go down this route you should probably go on a course and then practise a lot. Know the hardware and software inside out: it can be very embarrassing if the whole thing goes down at the beginning of the presentation.

DO practise setting up.

DO back up your presentation onto disk and if visual aids are vital, put an OHP or slide projector (plus accessories) in the car, just in case. Or take an expert with you.

DO link to the internet in advance if you need to, and then store the information on file, just in case the link doesn't work.

INTERNET, CD AND DVD PRESENTATIONS

If you regularly repeat the same presentation, it might be a waste of time for you to traipse up and down the country yourself. Instead, you might want to put all the information onto the internet or a CD or DVD (Digital Video/Versatile Disk). Your target can watch it whenever they want, can choose which bits they want to look at

> **JARGONBUSTER!**
> DVD: Digital Video Disk or Digital Versatile Disk. A new generation of information storage. Holds more information than CDs. Extremely high picture and sound quality.

first (by clicking on the right sections) and can watch it over and over again. They can also pass it on to colleagues or friends.

To get the best out of a CD, internet or DVD presentation, you may want to hire a specialist company.

WEB TIP *If you're not sure where to find an internet presentation specialist, try typing 'internet presentations' into one of the search engines. In October 2000 there were 1,660 listings, so you shouldn't be short of people to try.*

If you're planning to use any kind of visual aid which involves darkening the room, don't schedule it for straight after lunch – everyone will be nodding off. Try to use anything like this in the morning, when everyone is (theoretically) alert. Another disadvantage of darkening the room is that it breaks your eye contact with the audience, so you can't 'read' their feelings about how the presentation is going and rectify any problems.

Once you've thought about what you'd *like* to use, and you've examined what you *can* use, it's time to start preparing your visuals.

PREPARING YOUR VISUALS

It is much better to prepare your visuals on a computer. We'll look later at the sophisticated software specially designed for presentations but, that aside, ordinary word-processing packages alone will make all the difference to your visuals. They allow you so much flexibility – you can go back and alter anything at any time.

☞ Putting the name and the date of the presentation at the bottom of each page will make the audience think you've done all that work especially for them. Even if you just changed the name and the date from the presentation you did last week.

They also look more professional.

They will allow you to establish a coherent style and design.

WHAT'S YOUR STYLE?

The overall style is the first thing to consider when preparing visual material. Firstly, choose a font by clicking on the Format button on your computer tool bar. Play around with the fonts on your computer, but don't get carried away!

Apart from the style of the lettering, you should also decide on the size, colour, where you put the words on the page and whether you're going to use boxes, borders, symbols or bullet points, etc. Think about the overall design and the presentation will hang together as a coherent whole.

If you're not sure of your way around your word-processing program, it's worth buying a book. Don't be scared of going to a computer store to buy a guide; they're not all full of geeks who'll laugh if you don't know what you're talking about. If you're not convinced, go to **www.amazon.co.uk** and use the search tools to find the book you want.

Make sure you choose a 'point size' that can be seen at the back of the room. It can be changed in the Format menu on the toolbar at the top of the screen or by going to View on the same toolbar, scrolling down to Toolbars and selecting Formatting. Then you'll be able to change the point size as you go along, without going into Format all the time. Simply click on the arrow and scroll down to the number you want.

JARGONBUSTER!
Point size refers to the size of letters on a computer.

Be consistent about where you use italics, underlining, bold or centred text, etc.

Think about what colours to use. Dark colours show up better than light ones. Even red can fade away in the wrong light. But try to use different colours for variety, and use them consistently. You might want to assign a certain colour to a certain issue, name or subject.

some fonts are fiddly and difficult to read

OR JUST TOO SQUASHED UP

or simply trying too hard

But some are friendly and clear

Some can look like notes.

This might be useful

Some can look old-fashioned.

Don't use them if you're talking about a
product that's supposed to be state of the art.

ILLUSTRATION 9   Different fonts can determine the style of your presentation

And don't forget that we associate different colours with different emotions or subjects. Here are a few examples:

Red = stop, danger or hot

Green = go, safe, natural, calm, neutral

Blue = water, cool, efficient, corporate

Purple = wealth, luxury, wackiness

Yellow = sunlight, warmth

Try writing '**GO**!' in red or '**HOT**!' in green. Some people don't find this particularly freaky, while others find it very weird, so bear it in mind when deciding on colours. Also remember that however warm and sunny it might be, yellow barely shows up at all against white.

Avoid sloppy spelling, poor punctuation and grammatical gremlins.

Your words are going to be on display to everyone – possibly on a massive screen above the stage. Now is not the time for sloppy and inconsistent spelling and shaky grammar.

MAKE SOME RULES FOR YOURSELF!

Make yourself a style-guide: a list of words and punctuation to look out for, including correct spelling and whether a word has a capital letter at the beginning – and stick to it.

CAPITAL LETTERS Many people fall into the trap of scattering capital letters around like they're going out of fashion, especially if they're giving a presentation. Maybe they think it makes the words look more important. Capital letters are for the beginnings of sentences and for proper nouns, such as London Road, Jacey Lamerton and Essential Books.

I've broken my own rules a couple of times in this book – for example by giving capital letters to Objective and End Result. This is because I'm turning them into proper nouns for the purposes of the book and I want them to stand out. You might want to start your bullet points with capital letters. It's up to you. But make it consistent.

DATES AND TIMES Decide how you're going to write these and stick to your rule.

Most English newspapers write 'day, date, month, year' – Thursday 23 March 2000 (note that the date number stands alone, so it's 1 April, 20 May – not 1st April, 20th May).

You may also write times as 5 pm or 17.00 hrs – you decide. No system is *right*; just choose the one you feel comfortable with and stick to it.

QUOTATIONS If you're using quotations, decide how you're going to identify them. Here are a few suggestions, pick one (or make up your own):

'The future doesn't belong to the fainthearted.'
Ronald Reagan, 28 January 1986

'The future doesn't belong to the fainthearted.'
Ronald Reagan, *28 January 1986*

'The future doesn't belong to the fainthearted.'
RONALD REAGAN, 28 January 1986

'THE FUTURE DOESN'T BELONG TO THE FAINTHEARTED.'
Ronald Reagan, *28 January 1986*

ACRONYMS It's clearer and more modern NOT to put full stops in acronyms, e.g. UNESCO. This also applies to people's names, e.g. James T Kirk.

SINGULARS In the written word, companies are singular. Yes, it sounds weird when you say it out loud but it's correct. So you should say: 'Granada Television makes programmes.' The singular rule also applies to:

> **Team** (unless you're writing for the sports pages, in which case it's plural – don't ask me why there's one rule for the front of the paper and another for the back, it's just one of those journalistic anomalies)

Staff

Government

Department

Group

Committee

APOSTROPHES Probably the grammar point most likely to trip people up.

These are the most common problem words:

It's = It is

Its = The thing belonging to it – *The car was new but its tyres seemed worn*

You're = You are

Your = When something belongs to you – *Your dog has fleas*

There's = There is

Theirs = Something belonging to them – *That car? Oh, it's theirs.*

The dog's bowl = The bowl belonging to the dog. One dog.

The dogs' bowl = The bowl belonging to the dogs. One bowl. More than one dog.

The cat's whiskers = The whiskers belonging to the cat. One cat. Lots of whiskers.

If ONE person owns the book, the apostrophe goes BEFORE the 's'.

If MORE THAN ONE person owns the book, the apostrophe goes AFTER the 's'. It doesn't matter how many books there are. That's irrelevant.

CHECKLIST

Are my visuals:

legible? ❏

full of the right amount of information? ❏

the right size so even those at the back can see? ❏

in the right font? ❏

in a consistent style? ❏

checked for spelling? ❏

checked for grammar? ❏

double-checked for figures? ❏

If your word processor has a grammar check it will underline problem words or phrases in green. Take note: 99.9 per cent of times, you'll be right and the computer will be wrong. But just check those bits over again.

☞ Grammar not too hot? Ask at your local library for one of the modern grammar guides.

If your grammar is not too hot, mug up with one of the latest guides – they're not as dull as they used to be! Good ones to try include *Mind the Stop* by G V Carey, published by Penguin, or the *Oxford Dictionary for Writers and Editors*. Or you could try Strunk & White: *The Elements of Style* at **www.columbia.edu/acis/bartleby/strunk**.

INSIDER TIPS ON WORKING WITH VISUAL AIDS

The more fancy-schmancy the equipment, the more chance there is that it could go wrong. So think carefully about what you are going to use and make sure you have a backup in reserve if possible.

DO remove any visuals left behind by the previous speaker – you don't want the audience's minds lingering on what someone else has told them.

DO look at the audience, not your visual aids.

DO check, check and double-check the figures you use for any charts or graphs.

DO stand on the left of the screen, from the audience's point of view. They will read from left to right and it will make more sense to them if you're on the left.

DO make sure you know where everything is if you need to dim the lights.

DO allow yourself plenty of time to get familiar with the equipment.

DO structure your speech so that the visual aids support your most important points.

DON'T use visuals that people can't see – if you see what I mean.

USING HANDOUTS EFFECTIVELY

Of course it wouldn't happen to you, would it? You do all this work; you plan your speech meticulously; you write it lovingly, packing it full of all the best and most dynamic words you can summon up; you illustrate it thoughtfully; you deliver it clearly and rousingly; and you answer questions knowledgeably and graciously. And then the audience walks out of the room and forgets every damn thing you've just said. No. It would never happen to you.

But just in case pigs start to fly or Hell freezes over – or maybe just in case human beings act like human beings and have flawed memories, you'd better think about handouts.

WHAT SHALL I GIVE THEM?

Handouts for every presentation will vary but, depending what you're speaking about, you might want to provide:

1 a timetable, especially for a conference, or presentation lasting several hours or days

2 a list of your key points

3 copies of your visual aids

4 information about you

5 a list of sources or further reading suggestions

6 a proposal

And remember to continue the style and grammar structure you worked out for your visual aids.

Even if you're told how many people will be in the audience, check numbers the day before the presentation. You don't want to waste resources by printing off dozens of copies when only six people are going to attend. Having said that, when you've confirmed numbers, chuck in a couple of spare copies, just in case.

PITCHES

If your speech is a professional pitch for business, you'll probably have a proposal anyway. The client will obviously receive a copy of that.

SHOULD I JUST GIVE THEM SOME BITS OF PAPER?

Handouts printed on to A4 and stapled together are perfectly acceptable. However, if you really want to make a good impression, and you've got a bit of a budget, you might want to invest in some kind of wallet or folder.

The simplest ones may just be acetate folders, or you might have access to a binder or laminator. Always print a title-page and use a colour printer, if you have access to one.

Always include your own contact information. If you do a good job, audience members might hire you in the future, or pass on your name to friends and colleagues.

Even if you make presentations regularly, it's highly unlikely that you will be making *exactly* the same presentation over and over again. So it's probably not worth having your handouts printed into a booklet.

Because corporate brochures are so quickly out of date, invest in professionally designed folders, which include pockets for loose-leaf sheets. These can then be printed in large numbers (saving money on print costs) and used by all the different departments – they simply insert their own sheets into the folder.

You might also want to include a specially cut slot in your folder to hold a business card.

ANYTHING ELSE?

You may want to offer them a transcript of your presentation. If your speech is fairly rigid and prepared, you might want to take a few copies along with you. If lots of people want a copy and you don't have enough, offer to forward it to them. If you're speaking more spontaneously, you could record the speech and then prepare a transcript, which can be posted to anyone who requests it.

WHEN SHOULD I HAND THINGS OUT?

If your presentation has a clear timetable, it's best to hand this out before the speech. If the audience know where they are, it will stop them wondering how long they've got to wait until a tea-break.

Knowing there's going to be a change of any kind can also act as a subconscious wake-up call. You can leave this material on their seats, ask someone to hand it out as the audience enters or, if you're addressing a small group, it's more friendly to hand it out personally.

Biographical material about you is also better handed out before. It could be posted out in advance, although some people will inevitably not read it. If you hand it out immediately before the session starts, it might distract people. The best time might be as people arrive, particularly if you're serving tea or coffee first.

Reading the information will give people something to do while they wait for the speech to start. If the members of the audience don't know each other, it might also help to break the ice.

The printouts of your visual aids, however, are a different question. My advice would be to hand them out in advance only if really necessary. Any material given out in advance can be a distraction. Don't do anything that might drag them away from your words of wisdom!

When presenting your first visual aid, let people know you will be handing out copies of all visual material at the end of the session. That way, they won't be anxiously trying to copy your graphs and charts and they can sit back and concentrate on what you're saying.

BUT THEY'RE STAYING FOR COFFEE AFTER THE SESSION – WON'T THEY LOSE THE NOTES?

Now you're getting cynical! You're probably right, though. The best time to hand out your support material is when your audience is about to leave the venue – whether that's immediately after your speech or a while later.

You might want to give people the option of posting the notes to their offices. Or, if you know the names of all the delegates in advance, you might want to produce personalised notes.

Not only will they feel more obliged to take care of them, you'll be able to forward them if they *do* get left behind.

COPYRIGHT

Copyright can be a tricky area, which you're most likely to encounter when preparing visual aids. It can refer to text, letters, art, audio, advertisements, maps, charts and tables – even to information published on the internet, so beware! This doesn't mean you can't use copyright material – but you

> **JARGONBUSTER!**
> Copyright: the sole legal right to print, publish or perform, film, or record a literary, artistic or musical work.

need to check what credit you should give and if you need to pay a fee.

Photographs are also copyright – and the photographer owns the copyright, unless it was taken during the photographer's employment, in which case it belongs to the employer. If you commission photographs, it doesn't mean you hold the copyright, unless this was arranged in a written agreement.

The same rule applies to all material – if it's created in employment, or signed over, it belongs to the employer or commissioner. If not, it belongs to the originator.

Photocopying can, surprisingly, infringe two sets of copyright: that of the creator of the work, *plus* that of the publisher, who has typeset the page.

If you're presenting copyright material for the purposes of reviewing it, you don't normally need to get formal permission – as long as credit is given. This means written acknowledgement of the author and publication alongside the material you have used. If you're not sure who to credit, get in touch with the publisher (see below).

If you're presenting to the public or any event for which people have paid, you'll need to get proper permission to show copyright material, and you might have to pay a fee. Again, you should contact the publisher.

You can use extracts from magazines or books in your presentations, but beware, because the law is very hazy on this point. Reproducing a 'substantial amount' needs permission, but no one really knows what this means!

To try to help, some bodies have set down clearer guidelines, known as 'fair dealing', about how many words you can reproduce without permission. BUT these guidelines only apply to material used for criticism or review and you will need to include the author's name and the title of the book (it's also courtesy to include the publisher's details).

But bear in mind that these guidelines are not included in law and they don't cover music, lyrics, work to be used in anthologies, work which has been changed in any way, or complete articles, however short.

It's always best to check with the copyright holder before going ahead. When you write to the publisher, or other copyright holder, you need to:

- ask for non-exclusive permission to reproduce the item
- include details of where you'll be reproducing it from
- include an explanation of what you want to use it for
- ask exactly what credit you need to publish
- ask if your planned acknowledgements are OK

The fair dealing guidelines say you can reproduce:

400 words as a single extract, from a single book

800 words as various extracts from a single book, provided no individual extract is more than 300 words

less than a quarter of an article from a newspaper or magazine

less than a quarter of a poem, or a number of extracts that add up to less than a quarter of a poem

WEB TIP *For more about copyright issues, try the Copyright Licensing Agency's website, **www.cla.co.uk**. The site includes details about general copyright issues, up-to-date information about rights concerning the internet, plus links to other bodies dealing with copyright.*

SUMMARY

You now have a good idea of your options with visual aids – you're aware of what to use and when. Let's recap:

Visuals aren't just eye candy

Make sure visual aids are there for a reason.

The right gear for the right fact

Decide which equipment is best at conveying your point.

Preparing your visuals

Establish style and avoid mistakes.

Insider tips

Remember the advice on page 71

Handouts

Give them something they can use – at the right time.

Beware of copyright issues.

5

COPING WITH
THE VENUE

- ● CHECKING THE FACILITIES
- ● ADAPTING THE VENUE
- ● SPOTTING POTENTIAL PROBLEMS

When people are asked to speak at an event, the speech takes over every waking thought. But many of the opportunities and potential pitfalls come from the venue itself, and from other presentation techniques, such as the equipment you use to back up your speech. Don't skip this section – I know you're worried about drying up and forgetting your words but this is really where most things go wrong!

If you've booked the venue yourself, you'll need to be even more careful. Don't worry about upsetting the caretaker – make sure they know EXACTLY what you need and make sure you have all their contact details in case there's a problem. Get the details of the booking in writing.

Make sure the audience have the correct information, too.

Of course, you already know what the venue looks like, don't you? Because you're Mr/Ms Organised, aren't you? You checked it out and discussed the facilities before you even set pen to paper, didn't you? You'll already have requested a mike and PA system, plus spares for the audience to use during question and answer sessions.

> ☞ It might sound obvious but double-check the time, date and venue of the presentation and call the day before to check everything's still on course.

You'll have told them you need a flip chart and an OHP and you'll have discussed where that should be. Then you called the day before, to double-check they knew what your requirements were.

CHECKING THE FACILITIES

Now you've arrived at the venue in plenty of time and you're going to check that everything's in order.

If, because of distance or some other reason, you can't visit the venue beforehand, get the name of the facilities manager or caretaker and have a detailed chat about the venue.

Remember – it's a pain, but getting there in plenty of time could mean hours before you're actually 'on'. You might not be speaking at the conference until 12 noon, but if the first speaker starts at 9 am, you'll need to get there around 8 am to check that everything's working. If it's not, that will give the facilities people time to do something about it. Don't worry – you can while away the intervening time by criticising other people's speaking techniques!

If you're not speaking at a venue that's accustomed to hosting presentations, you'll have to do a bit more work yourself.

Arm yourself with a mental straggly beard and long greasy hair, because we're heading into Roadie territory.

Certain elementary checks may seem too basic to bother with but the simplest of things can go wrong and scupper your presentation.

POWER POINTS AND EXTENSION LEADS

In a conference venue, these should be plentiful and well placed. If you're speaking in the church hall, though, you might find the points are all at the 'wrong' end of the room.

Even if you do see a point in the right place, don't assume that it's working: check it!

Work out how many power points you need and where they need to be. If there aren't enough in the right place, make sure you take a four-plug extension lead to the presentation.

ELECTRICAL EQUIPMENT

We looked at electrical equipment in the last section, so you should be fairly clear about the choices, advantages and possible pitfalls. But don't forget:

DO test the equipment beforehand – at the venue.

DO take a simple repair kit of spare bulbs, electrical screwdriver, masking tape, scissors and fuses; or,

DO take a flip chart or other low-tech alternative in case the whole thing goes wrong. If a piece of equipment is vital to your presentation, get the number of an engineer who offers an express service.

SOUND EQUIPMENT

Get someone to help you do a sound check. The best way to test the mike is by speaking into it. It's easy to get overenthusiastic when you're tapping it and you'll either deafen the audience or break the equipment.

☞ A top showbiz tip is to position the mike about half an inch below your chin: you'll be less likely to get feedback from being too close to it and the audience will be able to see your face. Bonus!

HEALTH AND SAFETY

While you're still planning which electrical equipment you'd like to use, it's worth bearing a few health and safety rules in mind. If you've got a crowd of people tramping in and out, one of them is bound to trip over that trailing lead that you thought would be OK. And if that person is you, that's even more embarrassing.

If you *must* have cables trailing across the floor, make sure they're taped down securely. The best tape to use for this is the 'gaffer' tape or 'elephant' tape used by television crews. It's usually black or grey and about two inches wide. You can buy it from DIY stores but most venues will have a supply. Ask in advance!

TOILETS AND FIRE EXITS

If the audience is unfamiliar with the venue, they will need to be told where the toilets and fire exits can be found. You might want to make these kind of 'housekeeping' announcements, including when they can expect a cup of tea, before you start your presentation proper.

If there is an emergency, don't forget that they'll think of you as being in charge. If an alarm goes off, don't dither about, thinking it might be a drill. Tell people calmly and clearly to make their way to the fire escape (remind them where it is) and to assemble at the fire assembly point (remind them where that is, too). If it turns out to be a false alarm, shepherd them back in again and make sure everyone's settled before you re-start.

And don't be put off your stride – emergencies tend to break down barriers and the audience will probably be far more jovial than they were before.

REFRESHMENT ARRANGEMENTS

Make sure you know what time you're due to break for coffee/lunch/ the end of the day, so that you can pace yourself.

If refreshments are to be served in the same room, try to arrange for the caterers to wait outside until you tell them you're ready. Otherwise you might have got to the very climax of your speech, only to have the wind taken out of your sails by a doughty tea-lady, clattering her steel teapot against the plate of custard creams.

If you're in charge, make sure there's somewhere to make and serve the refreshments you have in mind. You'll need a kitchen with the right equipment, crockery, cutlery, a serving table, napkins, and possibly staff to make it, serve it, clear up and wash up.

If you want to offer a glass of wine, say, after the presentation, check first with the management. Many church halls don't allow alcohol to be consumed on the premises. The same goes for smoking. Make sure you tell people if they have to go outside to smoke – and ask them to be considerate about what they do with ash and cigarette ends.

While tea-breaks revive, lunch can send people to sleep. Try to wriggle out of doing your presentation immediately after lunch.

☞ **Don't present vital information to a dozy lunchtime audience.**

If you're talking all day, or if you *have* to have the post-lunch slot, bear that in mind when you're planning your presentation. Don't give them the most vital bits of info while they're nodding off under the weight of the steamed pudding they never normally eat but to which they've just treated themselves. Not to mention the delights of the bar to which a few always sneak off.

ADAPTING THE VENUE

SEATING

You might not be able to change this but, if you can, it's worth thinking about the best seating configuration for your needs.

Think about what you want to achieve.

A lively discussion, with lots of input from the audience?

Seat them in a U-shape. If it's a small meeting, seat them around a central table. If there are more people, arrange the tables and chairs in the U-shape. If you want it to be very lively and informal, don't give them tables at all.

Hold their attention – they can talk about it later.

Seat them in rows, facing you. They might still whisper to their neighbour, but they'll be less likely to make eyes at the person opposite – or flick elastic bands at them.

OTHER FURNITURE

DO make sure there's a table for an overhead projector or handouts for people to take as they leave the room.

DO make sure there's somewhere to set cups if people are going to have tea and coffee during the presentation.

DO give them something to lean on if you're going to ask them to take lots of notes.

SIZE

If you're in a huge barn of a room, with half a dozen people, it can make the presentation feel cold and flat, while the audience feels uncomfortable. If you can, move the furniture to make the room cosier. Ask if there are any room-dividers, display boards, large plants or anything that can be used to make the space more intimate.

If it's going to be too small, there's not much you can do except move to a completely different, larger venue, or just put up with it.

LIGHT AND SHADE

Make sure the lighting's appropriate and that you're not either blinded or standing in a dark corner, where the audience can barely see you. Equally, if you have visuals, you might need the lights down for a slide presentation. Make sure your visuals aren't ruined by glaring sunlight through a window that has no blinds.

DO tape up some black card at the windows if there are no blinds or curtains. It's not ideal, but if your visuals are very important to the presentation, the audience will have to see them.

DO rehearse closing and opening blinds or curtains that are there. You'll feel a fool if you're bumbling about with your back to the audience.

ATMOSPHERE

This is a tricky one to put your finger on, but can make or break your presentation. If the room is shabby but there's nothing you can do about it, you might want to take some display boards and pin up information about your company or campaign. If the place is a bit 'dead' and flat, a tablecloth, vase of flowers or plants might make all the difference. If you're at a hotel, ask the manager if they can supply these. Or pack your own.

If you're doing a business presentation, shabby and mismatched furniture could present the wrong impression. Consider hiring furniture for the occasion – it's not as expensive as you might think.

WEB TIP *Find a local furniture hire company through Scoot or Yell (**www.scoot.co.uk** and **www.yell.com**). Or you might want to get to know a company that offers a nationwide service. Try **www.roomservicegroup.com** or **www.denbe.com**.*

HEATING AND VENTILATION

Ideally, you should be able to change this within the room itself. If not, find out who can put the heating on if things get too chilly. Check if you can open a window if it gets too hot, but think about fans if the window opens on to a busy road, a school playground, or if you're in an airport flightpath. (See below for advice on how to deal with noise, and other distractions.)

You need your audience to be comfortable – too hot and they'll nod off through even the most thrilling presentation; too cold and they'll find it equally hard to concentrate and they'll be uncomfortable if they're muffled up in gloves and coats, dreaming about the hot cuppa they might get at 11 am.

SPOTTING POTENTIAL PROBLEMS

While you're still in Roadie mode, apply your new-found venue expertise to spotting possible distractions. Some of these you won't be able to do anything about, such as fire alarms going off or emergency vehicles screaming past, in which case you need to know how to handle them.

Others, you can do something about; but only if you recognise them as potential distractions. Here are some scenarios and possible solutions:

1 The venue is near a busy road which creates a great deal of background noise when the windows are open, but it's hot and we need air.

   DO get there early and open all the windows as wide as possible, to get some air circulating.

   DO close the window when you're ready to start; the sudden reduction in noise should actually help get the audience to quieten down too.

DO open the windows during any breaks. Request fans if it's really very hot.

DON'T open the windows if it is very noisy. Request or hire some fans, and specify that you need ones that operate quietly.

2 There is actually air conditioning but it's too noisy and people at the back of the room can hear nothing but the whirring of the machine's fan.

Treat this as you would the busy road (above). Switch off the system while you're talking, cranking it right up during any breaks if possible.

3 There's a loud ticking clock and it will hypnotise the audience to the extent that they'll fall asleep.

When you assess the venue in advance, ask if the clock can be stopped. If not, you'll have to work harder to counter its sleep-inducing effects.

DO move about, ask questions, use visuals etc.

DON'T talk with a clock right behind you. Cover it up or move it. Instead of listening to you, the audience will be grimly fascinated by how slowly its hands are moving.

4 It's a beautiful day and the sun is streaming in. People will be getting too warm and again might start to feel sleepy.

Use the methods above to keep the temperature down. It might be a bit miserable to shut out the sun, but you'll need to do it if it's very bright.

DO allow people to move their seats out of the direct sunlight if there are no blinds or curtains.

DO schedule some extra breaks and, on their return, ask if anyone needs to move.

DO try to be considerate about the environment; some people find that sunlight easily triggers migraine or sickness, not ideal conditions under which to absorb your presentation.

5   The room has a big window with an interesting view, but the view might just be too distracting.

Again, you'll have to be a miseryguts and close the curtains. If this isn't possible, try to change the layout of the room so that the window is behind, or to the side of the audience.

6   There's some sudden, but passing noise such as an emergency vehicle, a low-flying aircraft, a refuse lorry, etc.

DON'T pretend it's not there and simply get louder and louder. Your speech might be important but the rest of the world hasn't stood still.

DO stop and resume once the noise has gone. If you can, say 'I'll just pause while that plane goes over', then make a joke or light-hearted remark if you can, remind the audience what you were discussing and continue.

7   There's a lot of noise from the office outside the room.

If you think this is likely, stick a notice on the door, asking for quiet.

S U M M A R Y

You now know how important the venue can be. This section is a bit nerdy: there's lots to remember and there's lots to forget. I've put together a detailed checklist – tick it off before you go any further!

ASK YOURSELF:

Have I:

Checked the time, date and venue?   ❑

Got the details of the booking in writing?   ❑

Booked it on a day the audience can make?   ❑

Have I remembered:

My notes!   ❑

Any handouts?   ❑

Extension leads?   ❑

Gaffer tape?   ❑

Any presentation equipment not being provided
by the venue?   ❑

Spare bulbs for OHP or slide projector?   ❑

Spare fuses?   ❑

Pens etc. for visual aids?   ❑

Electrical screwdriver? ❑

Any catering equipment not being provided? ❑

Black card (if there is bright sunlight and no blinds)? ❑

Display boards or room-dividers (if necessary)? ❑

Information about my company or campaign
(if appropriate)? ❑

A tablecloth, vase of flowers or plants (if needed)? ❑

A notice asking for quiet (if needed)? ❑

Have I remembered to check:

Fire exits? ❑

Fire assembly point? ❑

Toilets? ❑

Refreshment arrangements? ❑

Power points? ❑

Sound equipment? ❑

Visual aid equipment? ❑

That trailing leads have been taped down? ❑

Refreshment arrangements? ❑

That I can offer wine (if wanted)? ❑

Smoking regulations? ❏

That the seating is organised as I want it? ❏

That any other necessary furniture is all there? ❏

That any hired furniture is definitely arriving? ❏

That I can close the blinds or curtains? ❏

That any additional 'dressing' for the room is there? ❏

Who can put the heating on/how to work it? ❏

Who can put the air-conditioning on/how to work it? ❏

Whether I can open a window? ❏

That clocks are stopped or unobtrusive? ❏

6

PERSONAL
PRESENTATION

- NERVES

- YOUR VOICE

- WHAT SHOULD I DO WITH MY BODY?

- ESTABLISHING CONTACT WITH
  THE AUDIENCE

Having spent so much time and energy preparing for your presentation, you may well be worried that you will let yourself down by becoming some kind of nervous wreck or suddenly developing an inability to control your arms and legs.

Don't worry. This chapter will, hopefully, give you some pointers on how to settle your nerves before, or even during, a presentation. You should also be able to use the advice in here to avoid moving or gesturing like a cartoon character.

Without a doubt, if you are able to put into practice even some of the advice laid out here, it should help you to develop enough confidence to tackle any situation, or to maintain your own confidence at a level that allows you to take almost anything in your stride.

NERVES

We've all heard famous and accomplished actors, politicians and television presenters banging on about how it's *good* to feel nervous – that we need a certain amount of extra adrenalin pumping round to make us perform at our best. That's all very well for them. The difference is that they know how to handle it and we ordinary bods simply don't.

So there it is, the nerves will come. The question is, how to stop your mouth going dry, your tongue gumming up, your hands shaking like a jelly and your voice sounding like that of a 90-year-old with a sore throat.

By now, you'll have done all your preparation and the speech has been honed to a veritable work of art. Keep reminding yourself that you've done all the groundwork and that should help a bit.

Real LIFE

Emma used to swim competitively as a child. She was so nervous before her first gala that she was sick six times before she even got to the leisure centre. She recalls that standing at the end of the pool, waiting for the starter's gun, was a form of torture. Even now, she says she can't watch swimming races on the television without feeling a shadow of that former terror. But she also remembered: 'As soon as the whistle blew and I was in the water, my nerves disappeared. I was just concentrating on my stroke, my breathing and my strength. I didn't give those nerves another thought.'

The chances are, the same will happen to you, as soon as you get the first words out of your mouth.

Remember that you're speaking to an audience of ordinary people who have the same fears and hopes as you have.

I'll bet you can talk to your partner or speak up in front of three, five or ten of your closest friends. It doesn't matter if you're speaking to three people or three hundred people. They're all individual people who know that speaking in public can be a bit daunting. You're not making a presentation to three hundred evil geniuses. Unless you're Ming the Merciless, in which case, if they heckle, you can just have them killed.

Other than that, you need to ask yourself a couple of questions.

- What am I afraid of?
- Is the worst likely to happen?
- Is there anything I can do about it if it does?

Now, let's look at a few of the most common fears.

- I might dry up.
- They might listen to me when I'm chatting in the pub but I'll never keep their interest for 30 minutes.
- I'm worried about my accent.
- I'm worried I won't use the right words.
- Someone in the audience might be an expert on this subject.
- Someone might ask a question I can't answer.
- Someone might heckle me.

Thinking about some of the questions above, let's see if those fears are founded, and what you can do about them.

I MIGHT DRY UP!

Yes, you might. Even the most seasoned professional will sometimes grind to an inelegant halt.

So plan what you're going to do if you dry up.

DON'T waffle on, expecting the words to come back to you miraculously – you'll spend all your energy cringing at the rubbish you're talking.

DON'T worry if you can't exactly remember the clever way you were going to convey the point. Just get the message across and the audience will never know they missed out on your best bons mots.

DON'T over-apologise.

DO look at your notes – that's what they're there for.

DO give yourself pause for thought to find the right words – it might seem like an eternal silence to you, but the audience will be grateful to you for marshalling your thoughts. It's the adrenalin that's making it feel like ages.

Have a quick look back at chapter 3 where we discussed how much to put in your notes and how much to keep in your head. Make sure you jot down figures and quotes because they are the only things that need to be accurate and the most likely to go clean out of your head!

I'M NO RACONTEUR – WON'T EVERYONE GET BORED?

If you've researched, mapped, written and polished your speech properly (see chapter 3), there's no reason why they should be bored. You've already thought about rhythm, balance, contrast and visuals. You're not a stand-up comedian and you're not auditioning to be the audience's best friend. You're not Churchill, rallying the nation. You're an ordinary person, speaking in the 21st century. You're there to put across your message in the most effective way.

DO keep your tone fairly conversational and you'll avoid the stilted 'lecture' that does bore people.

I'M WORRIED ABOUT MY ACCENT

Hang-ups about accents are much less common these days, with 'BBC English' risibly historic and our screens and cities populated by a wide cultural and economic mix. Everyone thinks they sound horrible the first time they hear their own voice – it's a cruel twist of nature. Famous speakers don't worry about their voice – they worry about getting their message across.

DON'T try to be something you're not – the accent will slip and you'll really look stupid.

DO think about making yourself understood. As I said before, you're there to put across a message, that's all.

DO think yourself lucky that you'll sound different from the last speaker. The audience will relish the change.

I'M WORRIED I WON'T USE THE RIGHT WORDS

Highly unlikely, if you're familiar with conversational English. Because if you're worrying about long words or jargon, you're better off without them. You may not have the vocabulary of Dr Johnson on the tip of your tongue – but neither will your audience.

DO try to be clear and concise.

DON'T try to impress the two or three audience members who know what your long words actually mean.

WHAT IF THERE'S AN EXPERT IN THE AUDIENCE?

If you've done all the research – YOU'RE an expert now! And if they're such an expert, what are they doing in the audience? Well, I do concede you might encounter a specialist, but don't be so defensive! See the sections on heckling and difficult questions in chapter 7.

DO use them as a resource – someone to add to your ideas.

DON'T forget that you're in charge – you've got the mike, the clock, the platform, the snazzy whiteboard or overhead projector. It doesn't matter how much they know – it's YOU that's been invited to speak and you're doing just that.

SOMEONE MIGHT ASK A QUESTION I CAN'T ANSWER

See chapter 7 for more help with answering difficult questions.

It is true that there is about a 50/50 chance of this happening to you, depending on the topic. However, if you've done all your research, you should have covered all the obvious bases.

DO turn the question back – 'I don't know, I've never thought about that. Why do you ask?'

DO consider whether the question is relevant to your presentation – if not, suggest you discuss it after the speech.

DO promise to find out later and get back to the questioner if you decide it's a valid point.

DON'T worry if you don't know everything – be confident. No one's come to see the all-seeing, all-knowing being.

DON'T waffle or lie. These sins will find you out – you'll be as transparent as a pane of glass!

SOMEONE MIGHT HECKLE ME

Well, they might – especially if you're planning to be controversial.

See the separate section on this; learn a few classy put-downs and don't forget you've got the mike. Just be yourself – only a bit louder, more confident, and slower.

You can get through life without practising what to say. You don't clam up when you ask for your bus ticket. And there's no single 'right' way of asking for the bus ticket. You just start speaking and you get your message across. Once you know what you want, public speaking is no different.

I STILL FEEL NERVOUS!

The way to handle nerves and regain control over your voice is to get control of your breathing. Most of the time we don't think about breathing, it's a reflex action. That's why we don't always have much control over it. Practise this breathing exercise:

BREATHING EXERCISE

1 Sit or stand quietly

2 Breathe in through your nose, count slowly to four and then stop

3 Hold your breath for a count of four

4 Release the breath through your mouth, to a count of four.

For the next breath, try to extend the 'breathing-in' count, until you can count up to maybe 16. But take it slowly, over a matter of weeks. Stop if you get dizzy. Practise a few times a day and then do it just before you start your speech. By then you should have much more control over your breathing and your body will have learned that it's time to relax.

Another surefire way to relax is to tense up. That sounds mad, but it's a yoga trick that really works. If you're feeling nervous just before your speech, nip off to the toilet, or somewhere else that's private, and run through the exercises here in boxes.

RELAXATION EXERCISE 1

1 Breathe in and tense the muscles in your shoulders and neck as tight, tight, tight as you can. Pull your shoulders right up to your ears, tense as hard as you can.

2 Relax. Breathe out and as you do so, push your shoulders back and down and then relax totally.

3 Repeat as many times as you want.

RELAXATION EXERCISE 2

1 Screw your face right up into a horrible grimace (this is
   why it's important to do this exercise somewhere private).
   Concentrate on screwing up your mouth, your eyes,
   your nose, your forehead, your whole face.

2 Stretch out your face as much as you can. Pull your
   mouth right open, open your eyes as wide as they'll go,
   even flare your nostrils out.

3 Relax.

DEALING WITH A DRY MOUTH, SHAKING HANDS AND OTHER PHYSICAL TICS CAUSED BY NERVES

GABBLING Sit quietly a few minutes before you're due to start.
Take long, controlled breaths in through your nose, hold them a second,
then breathe out through your mouth. Don't forget that adrenalin
speeds you up, so make an effort to slow down.

DRY MOUTH Have a glass of water nearby and don't forget that you
can take the time to drink from it.

SNIFFING Blow your nose before you get up and keep a clean
handkerchief at hand. If you need to use it, take the time. You're in
charge!

LOCKJAW If you're so nervous you feel you can't prise your mouth
open, nip into the toilets and do a few muscle relaxing exercises.

1 Roll your shoulders forward, up to your ears, back and down.
   Repeat ten times.

2 Screw up your face tight and then relax. Make sure no one's
   watching.

3 Drop your jaw as far as it will go, then open your mouth as wide as it will go. Then relax. Do this a few times to remind your mouth that it can move.

SHAKY HANDS We talked in chapter 3 about the advantages that cards have over paper, one of them being that the shaking looks much worse with paper. If you're a shaker, don't hold your notes. Put them down on the desk.

What you do with your hands depends on what resources you have. You may be able to lean on the desk, or hold on to the lectern. As the speech progresses, you might want to nonchalantly put them in your pockets for a while. Just remember, you feel more awkward than you look.

CALLS OF NATURE Don't let nerves make you drink more coffee, tea or cola than you're used to. Nerves will make you want to wee as it is; they'll just make it worse *and* you'll be shaking like a drug-crazed maniac, thanks to all the extra caffeine. If you're at a conference, avoid the temptation to be the life and soul of the hotel bar the night before.

And whatever you do:

DON'T fidget.

DON'T fiddle (if you're a fiddler, take your change and keys etc. out of your pockets beforehand).

DON'T scratch.

DON'T click your biro.

DON'T grip the lectern so tightly that your knuckles go white.

DO smile (not an idiot grin, but at least try to look as if you want to be there and that you're not going to put the audience through an hour of hell).

ALL OF THE ABOVE – AND WORSE!

If you've got it really bad, you could try two real Californian techniques: visualisation and affirmation. If you're *that* nervous, you've got nothing to lose! This honestly works – people have even beaten cancer with it sometimes. So believe in it and it will help. You weren't born with the hang-ups you've got – you learned them. So you can unlearn them. Try doing this before you go to sleep and you'll have the best chance of reprogramming your subconscious. If you start panicking before you are due to speak, replay your visualisation, use those affirmations to stop the negative thoughts. Just don't allow yourself to dwell on the negative.

Visualise yourself happy and confident on the podium, nodding modestly at the audience's rapturous applause. Or striding manfully across the stage, speaking articulately, your words creating powerful images for the audience, who are simultaneously inspired and charmed by you and your speech.

Then affirm this visualisation by replaying it over and over again – telling yourself it *can* be done, and it *will* become true.

Don't think for a moment that drink will help. If you're nervous to begin with, dulling your faculties will give you an extra reason to be afraid. Go in there as sharp as a pin – and head for the bar straight afterwards if you want!

WEB TIP *For more ideas on how to control your nerves, visit:* **www.stresscure.com/jobstress/speak college.hmco.com/ communication/speech/overcome** *For some relaxation exercises, try:* **www.easytaichi.co.uk/relaxation_techniques**

ILLUSTRATION 10   Tai chi is recognised as an excellent way of relaxing your body

YOUR VOICE

We've talked at length about the different types of equipment you might want to use as part of your speech, but the most important piece of kit is, of course, your voice. If your voice serves you perfectly well most of the time, it will serve you well in front of an audience, or on radio or television. Voice coaches might tell you an interesting piece of research.

When a voice-trained person delivers information, the audience retains 83 per cent of the content.

When an untrained person delivers the same information, the audience retains only 45 per cent of the content.

Well, I'm not sure about the scientific basis for such research, but I can believe it – up to a point.

Pitch, tone, speed, accent and clarity all help to retain one's interest – and you're more likely to remember something if you've actually listened to it in the first place.

But voice coaches will insist that you need professional training to achieve such results. I don't doubt a professional voice coach *would* improve almost everyone's delivery. But if you're not a regular public speaker, it's probably not worth the time and money.

So let's take the DIY approach for now, and start off by examining the surprising range of factors that have influenced the voice you have. These include:

- the influence of your family, friends and colleagues

- the vocal habits you developed as you grew up

- the physical make-up of your mouth, nasal passages and all the other bits and pieces used in speaking

- your general health

- your personality and outlook

So if any one of those variables changes, it can have an impact on your voice. And you might have to work on one or all of them if you want to change your voice.

I bet that if you've ever heard your voice on tape you'll think it sounds awful. Everyone's voice sounds awful when they're not used to hearing it on tape. The lovely echo chamber that is my head (no jokes please) makes my own voice sound rather resonant and low-pitched to my ears. Vocal glitches and a slight accent sound interesting and possibly even cute.

Real
LIFE

My friend Daisy has to do lots of presentations, as part of her job. When I asked her for her public speaking tips, she let me into a secret and revealed she worries about her accent. She said: 'I'm a bit of a sponge for other people's accents, so I like to think I've developed a "go anywhere" kind of voice – not posh, not common, but universally acceptable.'

But one of her presentations was video recorded and she was horrified by what she heard when the tape was played back. She wailed: 'I sound like some kind of mutant with Sandra Dickinson's high pitch wedded to an accent that veers between the glottal stops and strangled vowels honed by spending my formative years listening to the estuary English of Margate, before escaping to London, working with posh people and living with a Yorkshireman. I've given up listening to tape recordings of my voice. It was giving me anorexia of the larynx.'

Yes, your voice sounds horrible. But only to you. So try not to worry about it.

But if you really do want to change your voice for any reason, be reassured that you *can*. People change their voices all the time. Actors regularly see voice coaches to get the right accent and intonation for a part. People who have had accidents sometimes have to rebuild their voices from scratch.

And, perhaps surprisingly, one of the biggest areas of voice therapy is for transsexuals. The hormones administered during the sex-change procedures do some of the work but the patient usually needs to refine his or her new voice with a course of speech therapy.

So, you *can* change your voice – and if you don't want to change it, you can also make the very best of the voice you have, making it more powerful and resonant.

It takes practice and it takes some time. Get into the habit of practising while you're doing something else – don't sing in the bath, speak! Talk to yourself whenever there's no one around. You'd better tell your partner what you're up to though, or you could find yourself practising in a padded cell. And the acoustics in those places are terrible.

BECOME A LISTENER

Before you can train your voice, you need to train your ear. Become sensitive to sounds and voices.

Every sound has four characteristics:

- Pitch = the highness or lowness of a sound

- Volume = the loudness of a sound

- Quality (or timbre) = the character of a sound; what makes one voice different from another

- Duration = the length of time a sound lasts

Cultivate your sensitivity to these four characteristics. Try these exercises:

Listen to a news programme. See how the presenter varies his or her voice to fit the different material; solemn news, sad news, news of international importance, light-hearted news, travel news, the weather, interviews.

Collect accents. Listen out for as many different ways of saying the same word as you can.

Listen to someone whose voice you like. Then listen to someone whose voice you find ugly. Try to identify what it is about each of the voices that you like or dislike.

LISTEN TO YOURSELF

When you've got used to listening to other people, start listening to yourself. Tape record yourself talking and reading out loud. Include your name and some bits of your speech – the whole thing if you like. Then listen really hard with your newly trained ear.

First, listen straight through, without stopping the tape or taking notes. What is your overall impression? Then listen again, this time in a more detailed way. Concentrate on:

- 'ums', 'ahs' and 'likes', etc.

- how you pace your speech

- how you pitch your speech

- where you place your emphasis

- how clearly you say the words

- how fluent you sound

Analyse what you hear and compare the elements with those of the person whose voice you admiringly listened to in the previous exercise. Ask a number of other people what they think of your voice and see if there is any common ground in their answers.

Listen to your voice as you speak and when you make those verbal tics you identified in the first exercise. Is it when you're tired? Or nervous? Or speaking to specific people?

WORK ON YOUR VOICE

So many of our verbal characteristics are learned – how we speak defines us in society. If you went to public school, you've probably got a posh accent and people will judge you according to their own preconceptions of posh people. And vice versa, if you grew up on a council estate in the East End of London. If by some quirk of fate you'd moved to the other end of the country when you were three years old, you would have a different speaking voice today.

You need to free your voice – to explore what your voice is capable of. So have fun with the following (in the privacy of your own home!):

VOICE EXERCISE

1   Make animal noises.

2   Imitate musical sounds – really try to make your voice
    sound like an instrument. Say 'ding' like a bell, letting
    the 'ng' die out very slowly.

3   Try saying these words in as many different ways as you
    can: Good morning, Hello, Yes, No.

4   Count out loud. As you say each number, make it sound
    different from the one before – louder, softer, more high-
    pitched, deeper. Try injecting emotion into the numbers –
    sound excited for one, solemn for the next, and so on.

HOW CAN I MAKE MY WORDS SOUND MORE INTERESTING?

We all know that monotonous speakers are dull, boring and hard to
listen to – even if the listener is really *trying* to pay attention.

**Most of us have interesting voices, complete with light and shade,
varied pitch and modulation and changes in speed. We just don't
realise we're doing it, because we're not thinking about speaking,
we're just talking.**

So when we stand up to speak in public, we suddenly realise
everyone's listening to us; we get all self-conscious and the interesting
voice disappears, to be replaced by a nervous, shaky monotone.

You've worked on your voice. Now for a few tips on making your
words sound more interesting at all times.

BE CHATTY If you prepare for your big speech by watching tapes of
Winston Churchill, Hitler or Mussolini addressing vast crowds of
people, you might end up sounding like a pompous fool when you

finally take to the stage. Unless, of course, you *are* speaking to vast crowds of people and the purpose of your speech is to inspire them to revolution or something. In which case, I'm highly flattered that you're reading this book, and can I have a seat in your new government? Or an important honour, at the very least?

Assuming you're not the next Fidel Castro, or leading your people to freedom from an evil dictator, I'd advise you to develop the chatty kind of style adopted almost universally by modern speakers.

If we're talking world leaders, the conversational style of speaking was good enough for Franklin D Roosevelt, who made it his personal trademark and used it in his famous 'fireside chats', intended to make radio audiences feel he was in their living-rooms with them. (Quite a scary thought, actually!)

So if it was good enough for Roosevelt, it's good enough for us. Practise reading your speech until you're really familiar with it. Avoid trying to speak written English (see chapter 3) and speak as you normally would – only a bit more clearly.

Apparently, the optimum speed to deliver speeches is around 150 to 200 words per minute. Which is little help really. Well, if you can be bothered to count out 200 words and time yourself until they fit into a minute, that's up to you. If you really have a tendency to gabble, it might be a worthwhile exercise. For me, life's too short and I think I'd forget it all when the nerves took over anyway. Personally, I think it's more useful to tackle the nerves that make you gabble in the first place.

CHANGE THE PACE If you paid attention in chapter 3, you should have written a few changes of pace into your speech already. We looked at how changes in rhythm keep the attention of the audience.

You can maximise this effect by thinking about your subject-matter, and varying your pace accordingly. Speed up when you're talking about exciting things and slow down when you get to more serious points.

If you find the adrenalin is making you gabble, despite your relaxation exercises, remember to take a deep breath before a new sentence and to pause for a second before a new paragraph. It will stop the gabble and will reinvigorate your lungs, making your voice sound more powerful.

Change the pitch Equally, we all have the capacity to make our voice louder and softer. So in those speedy, exciting bits, you can also raise your voice. You could even practise dropping your voice to a 'stage' whisper – it will make people lean forward to hear you and increase the atmosphere in the room.

If you're feeling particularly mischievous, you might carry on lowering and lowering your voice until the room is very quiet indeed. And then shock them by suddenly bellowing really loudly. It will raise a laugh and wake up anyone who was getting a bit sleepy. But don't do it if you're making the annual address at the Heart Transplant Patients' Society. It won't be funny.

SHUT UP ALTOGETHER You can also use pauses to help add rhythm and emphasis to your presentation. You're probably standing there, bombarding them with new information. If you don't give them a few moments of silence, they won't be able to assimilate what you're saying.

Real LIFE

I commute to my office and use the time on the train to catch up on my reading. Often, I find myself staring out of the window. It's not because the book is boring – quite the opposite. I like to savour a particularly interesting point and turn it over in my mind. That's the reading equivalent of silence during a speech.

If you want to emphasise a point, try pausing for a second or two.

To move onto a new point altogether, pause for longer – about four seconds, or whatever feels comfortable. It will signal the fact that one point is ending and it will help the audience make the mental leap to the new topic.

BE CRYSTAL CLEAR It doesn't matter if you have an accent; what does matter is making your words clear. If you're out of breath before you've get to the end of long words, you're gabbling and you need to slow down.

GENERAL TIPS FOR SPEAKING DURING THE PRESENTATION

DO remember the easiest and most important thing: speak up and never mumble.

DO smile, if it's appropriate. It makes your voice sound more animated. If you're talking about something serious, then don't sit there like a grinning popinjay. (You've probably already worked that out for yourself.)

DO concentrate on meaning. Open a book at a random page, read a passage and concentrate on what it's trying to say. Then read it aloud.

Here are a few trade secrets that can help everyone make a difference to their voice:

1 Speak clearly and avoid filling pauses with 'uh', 'um' and 'you know', etc.

2 Vary your pitch and speaking speed – it will keep the audience interested.

3 If there's no microphone and you have a fairly large room, make sure you project your voice clearly. Speak from the chest, not the throat.

4 Pause slightly before important points, so that the audience can mentally prepare for them.

5 If you stumble over a word, take that as a sign that you need to slow down.

WHAT SHOULD I DO WITH MY BODY?

HOW SHOULD I STAND?

Start off by standing in a relaxed and balanced way. Spread your weight over both feet, with your toes and heels on the ground. Keep your knees slightly relaxed. Take a deep breath – lower and loosen your shoulders. Beware of unconscious rocking or swaying.

MOVING AROUND

Feel free to move around the stage if it suits you. But avoid moving in a set pattern or it will look like you're doing the tango.

Moving from side to side is more effective at ringing the changes than moving backwards and forwards because, if the room is large, it can affect the perspective. You may have noticed this when watching television. The moving camera that the runners are effectively running towards makes it look as if the athlete in second place is right on the winner's heels. But the camera at the side of the track shows there's a much bigger gap between them.

ILLUSTRATION 11   Moving from side to side is fine but avoid swaying

When you finish, thank the audience, gather together your papers and exit with aplomb!

GESTURES

The question of what to do with your hands is one that exercises fledgling public speakers out of all proportion to its importance.

You think back to other times when you've got up to say a few words and suddenly you've morphed into that Kenny Everett character who had enormous whirling hands.

You become aware that all eyes in the room are on you and every fear you've ever had of being clumsy and uncool comes rushing back to you, and every move you make seems meaningless, over the top and totally uncontrollable.

The problem is, delivering a speech isn't a dance routine. You can't choreograph gestures; if you try, they will look unnatural and unconvincing. But I'm not going to leave it at that and send you up to the lectern trembling because you feel like you're wearing somebody else's arms. Although you can't plan your gestures, there *are* some hints and tips to help you control your body and feel less self-conscious.

DO start with your hands together. That gets over the problem at the very beginning. As you begin to speak, you may forget your awkwardness and your hands will naturally move around and then come back together.

DO hold on to the lectern if there is one – but loosely! Don't grip so tightly that you can't loosen your grip and the audience can see your knuckles turn white. To avoid the temptation to grip, it's better to rest your hands lightly on the lectern.

DO use a desk if it's there. You can try placing your hands on top of it – but only if it's the right height. Don't feel you have to hunch over, just so that you can touch the table.

DO hold your notes if you're standing in the middle of the room with nothing in front of you – that will give you something to do with your hands. It will look slightly more professional to have your note cards on a table nearby – although this leaves you again with the problem of what to do with your hands.

DO create opportunities to gesture by using phrases such as 'on the one hand ... on the other'. You can also count on your fingers if you've numbered your points.

Different venues call for different gestures. Cinema actors pare down their gestures almost to nothing, because the camera does much of the work for them. By zooming in close, a face – or even part of a face – can fill an entire cinema screen, making a raised eyebrow speak louder than any words. When such actors transfer to the stage (as seems to be the trend for Hollywood stars at the moment), they often have problems making their gestures 'big' enough for the audience to notice. All that 'internal' acting is no good if the person sitting at the back of the Upper Circle doesn't realise that the actor is having a seminal moment.

The same principle can be applied to public speaking. If you're in a small meeting-room at the office, keep your gestures fairly small. Motion with your hands and forearms, bending your arms at the elbows. But if you're in a huge conference hall, you can afford to be more theatrical. Gesture with your whole arm – go on, don't be afraid!

Gestures made above elbow level carry more authority than those made below elbows. To an audience, the latter will look like the physical equivalent of muttering. Making a fist and pointing a finger looks aggressive on television but in a presentation it can add passion and emphasis.

Ask your friends what gestures you make when you're nervous. If they say you always fiddle with your hair or jingle your pocket change, make sure you avoid these movements during the presentation. If possible, take the temptation away – tie your hair back and empty your pockets.

Once you think you've got it sorted, videotape yourself and watch it back with the sound turned off. Watch carefully – most of your nervousness won't even show! But if there are any awkward gestures, make a mental note to avoid doing them. Keep the thought throughout the next few days, while in the office and at home. If you find yourself making the action, stop yourself. When you've stopped worrying that you look ugly or fat, once you've watched yourself on tape, you'll probably feel better.

ESTABLISHING CONTACT WITH THE AUDIENCE

If you're only speaking to a few people, don't sit at the table shuffling your notes and pretending you can't see them as they arrive. Get up and shake hands as they enter, sit them down, make sure they're comfortable. You'll be at an advantage before you even start.

If you're speaking to a larger audience, approach the stage (if there is one) with confidence. Smile as you introduce yourself or your speech.

Establish eye contact with the audience, including those lurking at the back.

If maintaining direct eye contact makes you feel uncomfortable, look at noses. They won't notice the difference. Get someone to try it on you, if you're sceptical.

During the presentation itself, when you've finished with a card, don't put it down on the table, put it to the back of the stack in your hand. That way the audience won't be distracted by trying to work out how long there is to go, whether you've got more cards in your hand or on the table!

That's it – everything's now in place. Breathe, relax. And deliver the killer presentation!

SUMMARY

I hope you're now feeling a little better about the personal element of the presentation. Let's recap:

Nerves – schmerves!

Kill the fear but deal with any nerves that persist.

Make yourself clear

Become a listener and remember that your aim is simply to be understood.

Control those bodyparts

Practise what you're going to do with all those arms and legs.

You and the audience

Meet, greet and act human.

7

TIME FOR

QUESTIONS

- THE PROS & CONS OF TAKING QUESTIONS
- PREPARING FOR QUESTIONS
- STAYING IN CONTROL
- DEALING WITH DIFFICULT PEOPLE

You've sorted out the speech, worked out the visuals, ironed out your verbal and physical tics, checked out the venue and you know the workings of your equipment so well that you're considering setting up as an engineer. Home and dry then, yes?

Well, no. There's still Question Time to contend with. If you don't have the ferocity, confidence and mental agility of Jeremy Paxman, you're probably a bit nervous about taking questions. It's understandable.

So skip it altogether then, yes? Scrap the Question Time. Ramble on until it's time for the coffee break and avoid the issue. Well, it's an option, but let's examine the situation first.

James Scott is a successful marketing manager – so successful, in fact, that he's often asked to speak at conferences and seminars.

James enjoys researching and delivering his presentations, but he dreads the moment when he has to throw the subject open for questions.

He says: 'I prepare like a loony for the presentation itself but once I allow someone else to speak, anything can happen. This is when I might really dry up. Someone might use it as an opportunity to take a pop at me. They might ask something really difficult that I just can't answer. They might go on and on and I won't be able to stop them.'

THE PROS & CONS OF TAKING QUESTIONS

Is it a short speech just to welcome, or close a meeting? Is it an informal speech – reminding your family why they're here to celebrate Granny's 90th birthday? If so, questions obviously aren't appropriate.

You might also think about scrapping the idea if you're speaking to a really huge audience. There's nothing worse than opening up for questions only to be met with a stony silence because everyone's too afraid to speak up. (Although there is a way round this – but we'll get on to it later.)

But if your presentation is controversial, complicated or (as it should be) a matter close to the audience's heart, they're bound to want to ask questions. If you're speaking at a conference, people may have paid hundreds of pounds to be there – and they want to get their money's worth. If they wanted to be talked at, they could have bought a video.

Question Time should be an opportunity to get in touch with the audience's opinions or feelings. If they have questions, or reservations, Question Time should root them out and give you the chance to convince them to buy your product/join your campaign/agree with your argument.

We discussed earlier that audiences have a limited attention span. If you've been banging on for a while, announcing Question Time will perk them up no end – even if it's because they're going to hear someone else's voice, or because they know they'll be able to go to the loo in ten minutes.

There are all kinds of good reasons for taking questions – let's summarise them:

1 You can communicate directly with your audience.

2 It offers a change of pace, boosting attention.

3 Handle it well and they'll admire you more.

4 You can clarify anything that you didn't communicate clearly enough.

5 You can find out exactly what's on their minds.

PREPARING FOR QUESTIONS

You can't prepare for questions, can you? You have no idea what people might ask! Wrong. You can't predict every possible one, but if you do a bit of work you can guess at several likely questions.

Depending on the subject-matter, people are most likely to ask:

- What's the first thing we should do?

- What will we get out of it?

- What if we don't do this?

- What should we do about this?

- How long will this take?

- What about the financial side of it?

Apply these questions to your own topic and think about how you might answer them.

If you're not confident about speaking off the cuff, jot down some notes. The audience won't mind – they'll just think you're really well prepared.

BRAINSTORM QUESTIONS!

Persuade, bully or bribe someone suitable to listen to you rehearse your speech. Don't ask them when they're in a rush – block out some time in their diary, even if it's your partner. Tell them you really need their help and appreciate their input. Then run through the presentation and spend an hour or so brainstorming questions. Don't let them interrupt – give them a pen and paper, so they can jot things down as they occur to them. If you can persuade family members to pay attention, they're often the best test audiences – because they can be brutally critical!

If there's any chance of getting two or three people to listen and brainstorm, so much the better. They'll bounce ideas off each other and the session will be more effective.

PLANTING QUESTIONS

Of course, one way of making sure you're fully prepared for questions is to plant some! You might be shocked at this; it seems a bit like cheating, doesn't it?

But most speakers routinely plant questions, asking someone they trust from the audience to open Question Time with a particular query. It can mean avoiding an embarrassing silence.

Not only will it make you look good when you answer the question confidently, but you'll make the audience feel better too. They might be burning with questions, but many will be too shy to be the first to put their hand up. Planting questions helps to break the ice.

GETTING BACK-UP

You might be really nervous about answering detailed questions. If so, it's fine to invite someone else along to provide backup. Don't hide the fact! Finish the main body of your speech and say:

'Right, now let me have a quick slurp of water and give you the chance to have your say. Feel free to ask any questions you like. I've asked John from marketing and Brenda from sales to come along and help out if we stray into their areas of expertise.'

Then if such a question does pop up, simply say:

'Well, I've got my own views about that, but John can really tell us what marketing makes of it. John?'

If you do draft in some 'experts' and there's not a separate chairperson for the meeting, remember that you're still in charge and will be expected to control the session (of which, more next).

Throughout Question Time, remember your Objective. Don't stray too far from your Mind Map.

STAYING IN CONTROL

When you kick off your speech, tell the audience that you will be allowing five minutes for questions at the end of the presentation.

If you anticipate lots of questions, allow more time – the audience will feel frustrated if you talk for hours but their questions have to be cut short.

SIGNAL A CHANGE As we found above, the audience will perk up when you announce it's time for questions. Make the most of this by changing the feel of the presentation. You might want to sit down, or wander about more. At the least, pour a glass of water and take a deep breath. Use that change of pace to relax and reinvigorate the presentation.

DO make sure you listen to what your questioner is asking. Sometimes it's a good idea to repeat the question.

DO make sure you've understood it.

DO make sure the rest of the audience has heard it.

DO diffuse aggressive questions. If you're asked, 'Why should I waste time and money asking the council for traffic calming, when we all know it won't do any good,' paraphrase this by saying, 'So, you want to know if the council will really pay any attention to our campaign.'

DO give yourself a few moments to think how you'd like to respond.

But **DON'T** repeat the question at smaller or more informal meetings. It can become an annoying habit!

PAUSE BEFORE ANSWERING Give yourself a few moments to think. The audience won't mind: it will seem like a much longer pause to you than to them, and they'll think you're taking the question very seriously. From your point of view, it will give you time to think of an answer that's relevant, concise and considered.

INVOLVE THEM You might want to welcome questions, saying 'That's a good point' or 'What an interesting angle'. When answering, start off by making eye contact with the questioner and addressing your remarks to them, but then move out and try to involve every-body. 'We can see why Jane has raised that particular point ...'

IS THE QUESTIONER HAPPY? Finish each answer by going back to the questioner and asking 'Does that answer your question?' or similar. Make sure they're happy. If they're not, the following section might help you more.

KEEP AN EYE ON THE TIME If you've said you're going to allow ten minutes for questions, allow ten minutes. If you're meant to finish at 12.30, stop your speech at 12.20 and open the question session. Then keep a close eye on the time. You may want to take off your watch and put it on the desk in front of you.

ILLUSTRATION 12   *Make sure you have a watch or clock in easy sight*

DO make sure the audience knows you're still in charge.

DO say, a couple of minutes before the end, something like: 'We've just got time for one final question before we break for lunch.' The audience will know they need to keep it brief – especially if they can hear stomachs rumbling!

BE FLEXIBLE! If the questions are coming thick and fast, the audience is obviously keen to continue for a while. You could say: 'Well, I have time for a couple more questions, if you'd like to extend this for a minute or two.'

FINISH ON A HIGH NOTE If you've just delivered a brilliant answer but there's still a minute on the clock, quit while you're ahead and jump straight to your closing comments. If, on the other hand, you've limped through a pathetic explanation, simply keep them there for another minute or so, while you take another question. Try to finish strongly!

DEALING WITH DIFFICULT PEOPLE

Ah, the thing that speakers fear the most: the Difficult Questioner.

Sometimes people don't mean to be difficult – they just stray off the point, or stumble into a sensitive issue. They might even be right on the money, but they've come up with an issue you hadn't even considered and have no idea how to answer. If this is the case, you have a number of options:

If you brought along back-up, now's the time to toss the question over. Or if you know there's someone else in the room who's likely to have the answer, draw them in. It's fine to say: 'Thanks George, I hadn't considered that before. I can see our head of human resources, Angela Owens, at the back of the room. Perhaps Angela can shed some light on the question?' Or you might even throw the question open to the floor: 'I'm sorry, I don't know the answer to that. Is there anyone here who does?'

You can also admit you don't know but whatever you do, don't waffle. The audience will see through it straight away and you'll lose any respect you built up during your speech.

DO say: 'Well, George, you've got me there. I've never looked into that aspect of it before. But it's a valuable point and I'll do my best to find out and get back to you this afternoon.'

DO get back to him, if you say you will.

DO shoot the question back: 'I don't know, I've never thought about that. Why do you ask?'

DO consider whether the question is relevant to your presentation. If not, suggest you discuss it after the speech.

DON'T worry if you don't know everything – be confident. No one can be expected to know everything.

But you do get the odd audience member who simply wants to cause trouble. These usually fall into the following beasts:

1 The Show-off

2 The Wanderer

3 The Time-waster

4 The Antagonist

5 The Doubter

There's no need to panic. It's easy to stay in control, even in the face of the most Difficult Questioner. You just need to find out the nature of the beast and have a plan.

Who are the people most used to public speaking, those we see regularly on our TV screens? Do you want to phone a friend? Yes, it's politicians!

And what are politicians famous for? No chance to go 50/50 here. Yes, you've won a million – *they don't answer the questions.*

Remember – if you don't want to answer a question, you don't have to. Tell the Difficult Questioner it's not within the boundaries of what you're trying to do in this session. Tell them you don't have time to answer that right now. Tell them you'll discuss it with them later – I bet you find they're not so keen to discuss it when there's no one to hear their points and when everyone has already gone to the bar.

Let's look at the beasts we identified above.

1 **THE SHOW OFF** Distinguishing characteristics: Tends to waffle on for hours without actually having a question to ask. Can be a fighter who tries to score points by making himself look cleverer than you.

   How to snare him: Stop him in his tracks. You're the one who's been asked to speak, not him. Tell him: 'Yes, Ivan, you're right. The system does have its foibles.' Don't let him drag you into a battle where you both try to prove who knows the most. Tell him he's very clever, then move on to something more interesting.

2 **THE WANDERER** Distinguishing characteristics: Seems intent on wandering off your Map and into the wilderness. May be well-meaning but she's taking the focus out of your presentation.

How to snare her: Steer her back on course. Tell her: 'As I said before, we only have scope to cover A, B and C in this session. If you want to talk about D, I'd be happy to discuss it with you after the session – or maybe we can set up a follow-up meeting to cover these issues.'

3 **THE TIME-WASTER** Distinguishing characteristics: Similar in appearance to the Wanderer, but more dangerous, because he's definitely doing it on purpose.

How to snare him: As for the Wanderer, but you might need to be firmer. If he's taking the focus away from your Objective, stop him! Say: 'Sorry, but we're a little short of time – can we have your question please?'

Say you're going to move on and take another question. If he still won't shut up, tell him: 'I'm clearly not going to sort this out in this session. I'd be happy to set aside some time later to discuss this. But now I must move on.'

4 **THE ANTAGONIST** Distinguishing characteristics: A particularly dangerous beast, she seems determined to disagree with you.

How to snare her: Try to play down your differences and concentrate on what you have in common. Suggest she may have misunderstood. If she gets personal, you might have to warn her to concentrate on the issues, not on any personalities. If all else fails, agree to disagree and/or discuss it later and move swiftly on.

5 **THE DOUBTER** Distinguishing characteristics: The Doubter tries to cast doubt on your expertise or your argument.

How to snare him: Don't pretend. Be confident enough to admit your limits. If you can, say you'll find out and tell him later. And do it. Remember, you're in charge, you've done your research and it doesn't matter if you don't know everything.

INSULTS & PUT-DOWNS

If things get really bad and the person just won't shut up, you might venture an insult or a put-down, although I'm not sure I'd recommend it!

Take a scan through some of these famous insults anyway – if nothing else, you can turn away and mutter them so no one can hear. It might just make you feel better!

> *When a true genius appears in this world, you may know him by this sign, that the dunces are all in confederacy against him.*
>
> Jonathan Swift

> Once at a social gathering, Gladstone said to Disraeli, *I predict, Sir, that you will die either by hanging or of some vile disease.* Disraeli replied, *That all depends, Sir, upon whether I embrace your principles or your mistress.*

> *Has it ever occurred to you that there might be a difference between having an open mind and having holes in one's head?*
>
> Richard Schultz

> *A cynic is a person who knows the price of everything and the value of nothing.*   Oscar Wilde

> *Don't be humble, you're not that great.*   Golda Meir

> *Every great thinker is someone else's moron.*   Umberto Eco

> *Let us be thankful for the fools. But for them the rest of us could not succeed.*   Mark Twain

> *Hating something is too much work to do. What you want to do is ignore something. It is more effective.*   Sridhar Ramaswamy

> *Never mistake motion for action.*   Ernest Hemingway

> *Only two things are infinite; the universe and human stupidity, and I'm not sure about the former.*   Albert Einstein

*I do not want people to be agreeable, as it saves me
the trouble of liking them.*   Jane Austen

During his 1956 presidential campaign, a woman called out
to Adlai E Stevenson: *'Senator, you have the vote of every
thinking person.'*
Stevenson called back: *'That's not enough madam, we need a
majority.'*

*Wisdom eventually comes to all of us. Someday it might even be
your turn.*   David and Leigh Eddings

*If men's minds were like dominoes, surely his would be the double
blank.*   P G Wodehouse

I've had a perfectly wonderful evening. But this wasn't it.
                    Groucho Marx

*Gentlemen, Chicolini here may talk like an idiot and look like an
idiot, but don't let that fool you; he really is an idiot.*
                    Groucho Marx

Don't say yes until I finish talking.   Darryl F Zanuck

*The trouble with her is that she lacks the power of conversation,
but not the power of speech.*   George Bernard Shaw

*I would like to take you seriously, but to do so would be an affront
to your intelligence.*   George Bernard Shaw

*If this is tea, please bring me some coffee ... but if this is coffee,
please bring me some tea*   Abraham Lincoln

Never interrupt your enemy when he is making a mistake.
                    Napoleon Bonaparte

*It's always easier to quote something that someone else has said,
than to have the courage to say something original.*
                    Virginia Frans

BUT above all, try not to worry. All that sounds very scary, but most people are perfectly straightforward and they will raise their hands, ask interesting questions and let you answer and move on.

CLOSING THE QUESTION SESSION

When preparing your presentation, you'll have worked out your killer ending: the climax to the speech. But if you're going to have questions, you'll need to work out a few more closing remarks, to say *after* Question Time.

These can give you another good opportunity to reinforce your main points. If you're stuck, you can use a cut-down version of your Big Finish. Try to give yourself enough flexibility to include points raised during question time, if you can.

You might want to look at your watch and say:

'Well, we're pretty much out of time now. Thank you so much for listening – and for your thought-provoking questions. Don't forget – if we all work together and take these few simple steps, it could make all the difference to the future of our village.'

Make your ending strong, relevant and appropriate. Don't let your speech limp to a close.

SUMMARY

You've discovered that there's actually a lot you can do to get ready for the question session. Let's recap:

Prepare for questions

Get ready for the most frequently asked questions and guess the rest.

You're in control

Learn the expert tips on dealing with Question Time – the final furlong.

Different people and hecklers

Master the art of keeping the upper hand.

8

SPECIAL

SPEECHES

- BUSINESS PRESENTATIONS
- HIGHLY FORMAL SPEECHES
- SPEAKING OFF THE CUFF

Some forms of public speaking have a special structure and, while these can vary quite a bit, this section should help to prepare you for tackling what can be rather imposing situations.

Like all speeches or presentations, you must always have a clear idea of what your Objective is from the outset. The structure of the meeting or presentation will then dictate how you tailor your speech to suit.

The key is to stay in control, if not of the entire event, then at least of your contribution to the proceedings. Be clear about what you want to say and put your message across in a logical manner and you won't go far wrong.

BUSINESS PRESENTATIONS

The tips for public speaking in general can usually be applied to
business presentations – indeed business presentations are often easier
to deliver, because your Objective is usually clear from the start and
you already have some familiarity with the subject-matter.

Broadly, business presentations have one of three main aims:

1 **TO PERSUADE** The majority of business presentations are
   aimed at persuading the audience. Sales presentations and
   pitches fall into this category, but it also includes product
   launches and talks when you need to challenge a point of view.

2 **TO INFORM** This kind of presentation is fairly
   straightforward. It's the presentation of factual material.
   You might be inducting new recruits to your company, or
   presenting company results.

3 **TO INSTRUCT** This takes the second step an stage further.
   It is intended to give the audience new information or skills
   plus the ability to use it. Training sessions fall into this
   category.

When establishing your Objective – to sell your product, inform staff
about health and safety procedures or to teach the new accounting
system to the department – you should also bear in mind which
category your presentation falls into.

THE BRIEF

If you've been asked to give the presentation, you will have been given
some kind of brief. This might have come from your boss, a different
department, or from the client herself.

You might not even realise you've had a brief – it's not necessarily a
detailed document; it could be an email, a phone call or a chat in the
corridor.

Rewrite the brief in your own words and send it to the person who's asked you to present. This will ensure, at an early stage, that you understand exactly what's required, and it will show your commitment to giving the presentation you really want. It can be done in the form of a letter, an email, an agenda, a memo – whatever you feel is most appropriate.

This is the time to include any questions about the brief.

Your confirmation might look like this:

MEMO

From: Greg Dempsey, development

To: Janet Smith, press office

Re: Demonstration of new meal range

Janet,

Just a note to confirm that I have booked the first-floor meeting-room for 12.30 on Wednesday 6 September for the meeting to show you the new meal range, so that you are well-prepared for the planned launch on 15 January.

I know you haven't been told much about this yet, so I anticipate the presentation will take about an hour – we intend to talk you through the story behind the new recipes (we have a five-minute slide-show to help with this), before we start sampling the dishes. Of course, we should be able to answer any other questions as we go along.

I will head the demonstration, with Dean Ambrose and Gemma Bonham explaining the development of the projects.

I understand that you, Joy and Simone will be attending from your department – do you think we should invite Carol Jones from Marketing?

Give me a call on extension 6831 if you have any further questions.

Greg

ILLUSTRATION 13   *Maintaining communication is essential to make sure everything runs smoothly*

You should also write a memo for yourself, so you don't forget that you promised to email everyone to tell them where the meeting is being held. This memo should then be copied to everyone involved – including your boss – to keep them informed.

CHECKLIST

Checklist for confirming a brief

Ask yourself, have I confirmed:

the Objective? ❏

the End Result? ❏

what the audience expects to see and hear? ❏

the level of audience knowledge about the subject? ❏

the estimated size of audience? ❏

the timing and structure of the presentation? ❏

the venue? ❏

the date? ❏

the time (arrival time and start time, if different)? ❏

the name of the presenter/names of the presentation team? ❏

breakdown of everyone's responsibilities (including those of the client)? ❏

a note of the visual aids you intend, or would like, to use? ❏

PREDICT ANY PROBLEMS

Even if you're utterly clear about your brief, there might still be a few tricky issues lurking around – that's business!

Ask yourself the following questions:

- Is this presentation a test for me? Does my promotion/assessment depend on it?

- Is this presentation particularly important for my boss? Will her job be affected by how well I do?

- What will the business get out of this? In the long term? In the short term?

- Is there anyone in the audience who might be difficult? Why? Can I do anything about it?

- Does the presentation include bad or controversial news? Why am I presenting it? How can I present it without associating the bad news with my own performance?

TALKING MONEY

Business presentations are more likely than other speeches to have a budget attached to them. Set this budget at an early stage; if there isn't a budget, costs can easily spiral out of control.

Consider the following costs when making a budget.

At the same time, think about the value of the whole presentation to your business. If you're not going to make much money out of it, keep the budget low. And there's no point in your colleagues spending hours preparing for a minor presentation – their time has a cost attached to it too.

Room hire	❑
Hire of equipment	❑
Training	❑
Preparation of visuals (including photography, commissioning illustrations and printing handouts)	❑
Research costs (external researchers, photographic agencies, etc., will charge for research)	❑
Travel	❑
Accommodation	❑
Entertaining/catering	❑

KNOW YOUR AUDIENCE

- How much do they know?
- Are they likely to be hostile?
- Are they likely to be receptive and open to persuasion?
- Are they likely to be supportive and keen to contribute?
- Are they likely to be suspicious?
- Are they likely to be bored?
- Are they likely to pick you up on every detail?

As for all kinds of public speaking, think about the audience.

Try to tailor your presentation to the reception you think you might get.

Here are a few tips:

HOSTILE AUDIENCE Play up the positives. Team presentation can help.

RECEPTIVE AUDIENCE Confirm their thoughts that this is a good proposal. Be persuasive but keep things fairly straightforward

SUPPORTIVE AUDIENCE They might want to jump in with extra points, or topics for discussion. Structure the meeting in advance and hand out a timetable. Stay friendly but keep a close eye on the time.

SUSPICIOUS AUDIENCE Make it positive and persuasive. Create an atmosphere of trust. Play up your successful business record.

BORED AUDIENCE Don't let them think they'd be better off elsewhere. Keep it short, include surprise, audience participation and simple visuals.

PICKY AUDIENCE Include lots of statistics. Get together with colleagues and brainstorm possible questions. The answers don't all have to be in the presentation, but have them at your fingertips.

WORK TO YOUR DEADLINE

Once you have the date of the presentation and the brief has been approved, break down the job into separate tasks that need to be done.

If you have a team of presenters:

DO assign jobs to different people.

DO work out a deadline for each of the jobs to be completed – then bring them forward by a few days, to allow for unforeseen circumstances.

DON'T just give your team a list of jobs and the date of the presentation – if you do, there will always be one who'll leave it all until the last minute and realise that the last minute is too late to complete a vital part of the presentation.

DO have regular meetings to see if you're still on schedule.
Emergencies do come up, though – if one member of the team is
particularly busy, be flexible enough to swap round the
responsibilities.

DO circulate your schedule to everyone on the team – they need to
know what their colleagues are up to.

If you don't have a team:

DO take the time to work out a schedule for yourself. When you're
full of enthusiasm for a project, it's easy to imagine you'll get
everything done. But when other things crop up, it's easy to forget
how much work is involved.

**DO write out your schedule and file it at the beginning of a new
folder.** Then put the dates into your diary. If you use Microsoft
Outlook, or another computer-based diary, this approach can be
particularly useful because as soon as you get into work and log in,
your computer will remind you what you're supposed to be doing.
If you don't do it, it will carry the task over to the next day – coloured
in red for danger!

**DO tick off steps in your diary and on the printed schedule in your
folder as you complete them.**

CREATE YOUR CONTENT

The main sections of this book will help you with research and
planning but, for business presentations, don't forget to keep all the
relevant people informed. Your boss might appreciate a regular update
– let her know what content you're planning to include.

CHOOSE YOUR VENUE

See chapter 5 for detailed checklists on what to look out for in your
venue. For a business presentation, you might want to pay special
attention to travel arrangements (arriving late could blow the whole
pitch before you've even started) and catering. If you're after someone's

money, make sure they're fed and watered. Keep it simple but buy
the best.

TROUBLESHOOTING

For important presentations, plan ahead for any possible emergencies.
Think about potential problems early on in the project. In fact, write
some time into your schedule to give this proper consideration. Here
are some possible problems and suggested solutions.

1 **A VITAL MEMBER OF MY PRESENTATION TEAM HAS
   FALLEN ILL** This demonstrates the importance of working as
   a team, and keeping the team fully informed. Make sure notes
   are kept in neat, clear files, so that another member of the team
   can step in, if necessary. When you allocate jobs to the
   members of the team, also assign them as understudies to other
   jobs. Let the client know if someone is a stand-in, as a matter of
   courtesy.

2 **MY EQUIPMENT HAS BROKEN DOWN** Handouts can
   come into their own in this situation. Instead of giving them
   out at the end, hand them out during the presentation and
   work from them.

   If you're presenting to a small audience, take back-ups of your
   visual material in a portfolio. If there are any problems, you
   can present from that.

   If words are important to your presentation, arrange to have a
   flip chart or whiteboard there, so that you can hand-write your
   points.

3 **THE VENUE HAS BEEN CHANGED AT THE LAST
   MINUTE** Rather than panicking, find out how the change of
   venue impacts on your plans.

   The main problem is likely to be with audiovisual equipment –
   either it's not provided at the new venue, or the new venue
   isn't suitable for what you had planned.

If it's too late to borrow or hire new equipment, fall back on the methods described above in 'My equipment has broken down'. If you've got a low-tech fall-back plan, you shouldn't go too wrong. If you had planned catering and there are no facilities at the new venue, contact a local café and ask them to deliver teas, coffees and suitable snacks. Most will be happy to do so. If you can't find anyone to do this, Marks & Spencer and Prêt à Manger both offer a sandwich delivery service.

If the change was very last-minute, the client or audience will be sympathetic to the lack of bells and whistles in your presentation.

4 **I'M STUCK IN A TRAFFIC JAM/THE TRAINS HAVE BEEN CANCELLED** Equip yourself with a mobile and all the relevant numbers before you leave. Try to allow for the vagaries of transport; if you're really early, you can always go and have a nice cup of tea first.

If you do hit problems, ring ahead, explain that there's been a crash or whatever, and give your client a realistic estimate of your arrival time. Let them know if you can shorten your presentation, and say you're extremely keen to go ahead.

5 **I HAVEN'T GOT THE RIGHT TYPE OF FURNITURE**
You may have asked for tables and chairs, but that still leaves plenty of room for misunderstanding. If it's vital that you have a certain type of table (for your audiovisual equipment, for example), pop a fold-down table in the car, just in case.

6 **THERE ARE MORE PEOPLE HERE THAN I EXPECTED**
Plan for this by taking extra copies of any handouts. If there are so many people that they can't see your visual aids, you can always give them a handout to use instead.

If you don't have enough handouts to go round at the end of the meeting, ask people to write their names and addresses on a sheet of paper and post on any follow-up material.

HIGHLY FORMAL SPEECHES

If you are asked to speak at a debating society, or other formal meeting, you'll need to know a bit about the complicated and old-fashioned rules that still govern this kind of thing. First of all, here is the jargon:

RULES OF ORDER

Applicable to Parliament and some formal business meetings, these are just the rules by which the meeting is governed.

THE CHAIR

Another term for the chairman of the meeting (who may or may not be a woman).

What does the chairman do? And what shouldn't he do?

- He keeps order and applies the rules of the meeting impartially.

- He avoids speaking for or against any issue. If he feels he must speak, he should vacate the chair.

- He shouldn't vote unless there's a secret ballot or he has to make the casting vote if there's a tie.

- In very formal meetings, he shouldn't say 'I', 'you' or 'we', etc., but should say things like 'Would the speakers please remember to address all comments through the Chair'. Equally, speakers should call him 'Mr Chairman' or 'the Chair'.

RISING TO BE RECOGNISED

In formal meetings, no one can get up to speak unless they are 'recognised' by the Chair. In a large meeting, this usually means you should stand up. In a smaller meeting, it's OK just to raise your hand.

Etiquette says you shouldn't interrupt another speaker to do this.

The Chairman should normally recognise speakers in the order they stood up, i.e. first come, first served.

HAVING THE FLOOR

Once you've been recognised, you 'have the floor'. That means you can speak and, under normal circumstances, no one else should interrupt.

There might be a time limit on how long you should speak. Apart from that, you can carry on as long as you are 'in order' (i.e., proper and relevant). The term 'proper' can be a bit difficult to define. But generally, remember you're in a formal situation, so you should be careful not to offend anyone.

The exception is if you're discussing an impeachment or something similar, when character judgements are necessary. But make sure anything you say would also stand up in court.

MAKING AND SECONDING MOTIONS

If the meeting has finished with everything on the agenda, and there's time for any other business, you can introduce a new topic in the form of a motion.

This is how you should do it:

> **YOU (MRS A):** (rising to be recognised) *Mr Chairman.*
>
> **CHAIRMAN:** *The Chair recognises Mrs A.*
>
> **MRS A:** (Briefly explain what you want to do) *So I move that such and such be done.*
>
> **CHAIRMAN:** (If he agrees this is in order) *It has been moved that such and such be done. Is there a seconder?*
>
> **MRS B:** *I second the motion.*
>
> **CHAIRMAN:** *It has been moved and seconded that such and such be done. Is there any discussion?*

Seconding isn't always necessary, but the reason for it is to check there's more than one person interested in a topic, before it's taken on for discussion.

ORDER OF BUSINESS/AGENDA

These are more or less the same thing but an agenda is more detailed. It sets out what the meeting is going to cover. When the meeting is underway, you must cover the topic that is currently being discussed. If you try to discuss another, it is literally 'out of order'.

Formal meetings usually go something like this:

CALL TO ORDER The chairman may rap his gavel (a wooden hammer, like that used by auctioneers) and say: *The meeting will please come to order*. This starts the meeting.

THE MINUTES The secretary records the proceedings of the meeting in a permanent record called the minutes.

Meetings usually start with the reading of the minutes of the last meeting. The secretary reads them out and the Chairman asks if the members agree with the changes.

When everyone is happy, the minutes are said to have been approved.

REPORTS Meetings may include reports by officers and committees. They are usually heard in the following order:

> *Officers:* President, vice-president, secretary, treasurer.

> *Committees:* Standing committees, special committees.

GENERAL ORDERS After all the reports have been read, the meeting moves on to general orders of business – motions that have been put down for discussion. For example:

> **CHAIRMAN:** *As the first general order of business tonight we have to consider the recommendation of the Environment Committee at the last meeting that we run all Society vehicles on unleaded petrol. Is there any discussion?*

UNFINISHED BUSINESS Sometimes meetings have to close without coming to any real conclusion about a motion. This then becomes unfinished business and is taken up at the next meeting, after general orders.

NEW BUSINESS This is your chance to bring up something new. It's a good idea to jot down what you want to propose as a motion, so you don't stumble over your words. You should also discuss it beforehand with someone else, to make sure it will be seconded. A more experienced member will also be able to give you advice on how to word your proposal. If possible, speak to the Chairman before the meeting and let him know what you're planning.

Some organisations say that anyone wanting to propose a motion under new business should supply it in writing to the secretary some time before the meeting.

But if it is all right to make the proposal in the meeting, wait for the Chairman to call for new business, rise to be recognised and propose your motion, as described above.

ADJOURNMENT The meeting goes on until it is in recess or adjournment. Recess is a short break. Adjournment is the formal end of the meeting. People might still sit around and chat, but the formal bit is all over.

WEB TIP *For more information on debating and formal speaking procedures, try **www.actein.edu.au/ACTDU/owndebate**.*

SPEAKING OFF THE CUFF

You may have been called upon to 'say a few words' at a colleague's leaving party, a family birthday party or the like. The shock of being called upon, totally unprepared, may have fazed you, and you might feel you stumbled through, sounding like an empty-headed fool.

It's trying to speak 'off the cuff' that has caused much of the general terror at the thought of speaking in public.

Even if this hasn't happened to you, we have all sat through such occasions, trying not to meet anyone's eye in case it *does* happen and one is forced to one's feet.

When you speak off the cuff, you literally make up your speech as you go along. So no chance of mind-mapping, setting an Objective or End Result, luxuriating in the pros and cons of script versus cue cards, and all the other preparation devices we've already covered.

This is true. But many of the other tips and hints included in the book will improve your performance, whether you're speaking from a prepared speech or off the cuff. If you know that your voice, stance and gestures have been considered, all you need to worry about is what you're going to say.

Speaking extemporaneously, as the dictionary would have it, is difficult for most people who are unaccustomed to public speaking. But some people can do it, so what's the trick?

The trick is that most of the time, they're not speaking off the cuff. Television and radio presenters may be hugely experienced wordmasters, but even when they appear to be speaking spontaneously, they might still be reading from an autocue, or performing a well-rehearsed piece. So don't punish yourself thinking that everyone else can do it.

Even if they haven't learned their speech, or don't have carefully hidden 'idiot boards' around the room, they might be using a few tricks of the trade.

The thing to remember is that there's 'off the cuff' and there's 'off the cuff'. Most of the time, you will actually have a chance to plan what you're going to say.

If a member of your staff is leaving, or you are likely to win a prize, you'll know about it in advance and you'll have a good idea that you might be asked to say a few words. Instead of burying your head in the sand and hoping it doesn't happen, take some time out to think what you *would* say, if you were asked.

Even if you have the shortest of short notices, decide your Objective in double-quick time. You might want to speak about the importance of family; the changes in the business over the years; or simply that your secretary was the best you've ever had. Keep that at the forefront of your mind, just as you would for any public speech.

If you have more time, think about your Mind Map – identify a few key points that you want to cover. Everyone knows you're speaking off the cuff, so they won't be expecting miracles.

Consider the following structure:

- State your Objective – your key message.

- Expand on it.

- Tell a story or give examples to illustrate your Objective.

- Return to your Objective, saying it in a different way – possibly with added strength.

- Shut up.

DON'T waffle on.

DO what you're asked: say a few words.

One high-profile example of an unrehearsed speech is Robert F Kennedy's eulogy to Martin Luther King Jr. King was assassinated in Memphis on 5 April 1968, just as Kennedy – then a candidate in the Indiana presidential primary – was on a plane to Indianapolis. He was due to speak on the tarmac to a group of people, who were already there, awaiting his arrival. The audience had no idea that King had been killed, but Kennedy heard the news mid-flight. He junked his prepared words and, on arrival, delivered the speech of his life.

Real
LIFE

Another famed – but underrated – off the cuff speaker is the former Labour Party leader, Neil Kinnock. His Welsh articulateness and passion failed to shine through when he was forced to deliver the carefully worded speeches written by advisors who, having been in

Opposition for some time, were more afraid of upsetting voters than anything else. But when Kinnock was given a free reign, he produced his best speeches. One such was delivered to the Welsh Labour Party at Llandudno on 15 May 1987. The following passage became the best known of the speech – see what dynamic language he chooses and how his words are based on normal, natural speech patterns:

Why am I the first Kinnock in a thousand generations to be able to get to university? Why is Glenys the first woman in her family in a thousand generations to be able to get to university?

Was it because all our predecessors were 'thick'? Did they lack talent – those people who could sing, and play, and recite and write poetry; those people who could make wonderful, beautiful things with their hands; those people who could dream dreams, see visions; those people who had such a sense of perception as to know in times so brutal, so oppressive, that they could win their way out of that by coming together?

Were those people not university material? Couldn't they have knocked off all their A-levels in an afternoon?

But why didn't they get it?

Was it because they were weak? – those people who could work eight hours underground and then come up and play football?

Weak? Those women who could survive eleven childbearings, were they weak? Those people who could stand with their backs and their legs straight and face the people who had control over their lives, the ones who owned their workplaces and tried to own them, and tell them, 'No, I won't take your orders.' Were they weak?

Does anybody really think that they didn't get what we had because they didn't have the talent, or the strength, or the endurance, or the commitment?

Of course not.

Taken from The Penguin Book of Twentieth-Century Speeches.

WEDDINGS

Many people are called upon to speak at a wedding at one time or another – even if it's just their own. Because of this, and because of the maze of special rules that govern weddings, I've devoted an entire chapter, the following one, to the subject.

SPEAKING TO THE MEDIA

There are dozens of reasons why you might be called upon to talk to the media. Again, there are special rules and special skills involved. I have given a whole chapter to the subject, chapter 10.

SUMMARY

Special speeches require special skills, so make sure you've run through all the sections. Let's recap:

Business presentations

Confirm the brief

Predict any problems

Set your budget

Know your audience

Work to your deadline

Create the content

Choose the venue

Troubleshooting

Formal public speaking

Familiarise yourself with all the terms and you'll be fine

Speaking off the cuff

State your Objective

Expand

Tell a story

Return to your Objective

Shut up

9

SPEAKING AT
WEDDINGS

- WHO SAYS WHAT? AND WHEN?
- BREAKING FROM TRADITION
- TRICKY MATTERS
- RESEARCHING YOUR SPEECH
- SUGGESTED INTRODUCTIONS
- TOASTS
- READINGS

Although weddings are becoming more informal, family traditions vary and some people are keen to follow the conventional or 'proper' way of doing things. In order to subvert something, you first have to understand it, so we'll run through the traditional way of doing things, and then look at some alternatives.

When you think of wedding speeches, you probably think of the slightly risqué best man's speech that upsets some maiden aunt. Or of the father of the bride's speech which embarrasses the bride!

In fact, one of the main purposes of wedding speeches is to thank the various members of the wedding party. And one advantage of doing things the traditional way is that everyone who should be thanked, gets thanked.

The speeches also congratulate the newlyweds and include the toasts – and no one minds the latter!

Different cultures and faiths have different traditions – even within Britain. Irish and Scottish weddings might follow a different speech order to English weddings – and the Irish are famous for their way with words, so they tend to go on a bit longer!

It's outside the scope of this book to deal with lots of different types of wedding – a specialist publication will do that much better. So forgive me for dealing with the English wedding – the Scots, Irish and Welsh aren't usually *too* different. And if your family follows its own traditions, I'm sure the mothers of the bride and groom will be happy to volunteer any changes to the suggestions I include here!

WHO SAYS WHAT? AND WHEN?

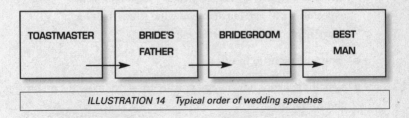

ILLUSTRATION 14   Typical order of wedding speeches

TOASTMASTER

There may be a toastmaster; if there is, he'll introduce the speeches. If not, this job falls to the best man. Whoever is doing the job simply asks for silence and introduces the first speaker.

BRIDE'S FATHER

As the first speaker, you will effectively set the scene for the rest of the speeches. Traditionally, this is because the bride's father pays for – and therefore hosts – the wedding.

Officially, you speak on behalf of your wife and yourself. A great part of your speech will be about your daughter and, although fathers and daughters are supposed to have a special relationship, try to steer clear of clichés and talk about your own relationship. Real life anecdotes say more about that relationship than any amount of generalisation about fathers and daughters. Don't be afraid to talk about the times you didn't see eye to eye – probably during her teenage years – as long as you counter this with something about how she's grown into a wonderful woman, or how you always loved each other underneath it all. Traditionally, your speech should include:

- a welcome to the groom's parents, both families and other guests – particularly if they've travelled a long way

- mention of how proud you and your wife are of your daughter

- something about the events leading up to the wedding

- some anecdotes about the bride's childhood and earlier adulthood – how she has surpassed or changed your expectations of her, how you view the strength in her relationship with her new husband

- congratulations to the groom

- something about how happy you are to get to know the groom and his family

- something expressing confidence in the couple's future together

- advice to the couple for the future

- an invition to the other guests to wish the newly-weds well

- a toast to 'the health and happiness of the bride and groom'

You might also want to add a few words about your own relationship with the groom – how you met him, what you thought at the time, something that surprised you about him or something you have learned from him.

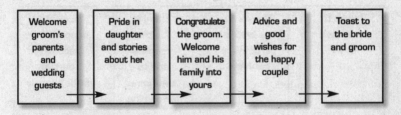

ILLUSTRATION 15 Main points of the father of the bride's speech

If the father of the bride is not there for any reason, this role is normally taken by the person who gives her away.

BRIDEGROOM

If you're the bridegroom, you speak on behalf of your wife and yourself. This gives you the opportunity to open with the words 'My wife and I', which you can use to raise a chuckle or a bit of heckling. Don't forget that, if the bride is not speaking herself, you are speaking for the two of you. You should include:

- thanks to the bride's father for the toast

- thanks to the bride's father for his daughter's hand

- thanks for the wedding and reception

- thanks for being welcomed in to the family

- how happy you are and how lovely your bride is

- praise for the bride's parents on their daughter

- happiness at becoming part of their family

- thanks to your own parents for your upbringing

- response to the advice given by the bride's father

- any anecdotes about meeting your wife and your relationship (if the stories cast you in a slightly embarrassing light, the audience will love them even more)

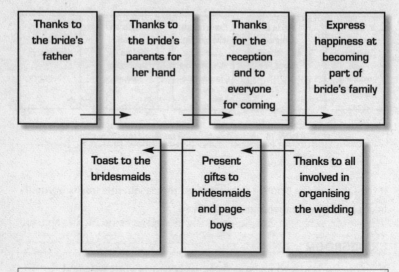

ILLUSTRATION 16   Main points of the bridegroom's speech.

- comments addressed directly to the bride about how happy you are and how much you're looking forward to the future

- thanks to guests for attending, for their good wishes and gifts

- thanks to the best man, ushers and anyone else who has helped – present them with their gifts, if you have bought gifts

- thanks to the bridesmaids and praise for their good looks

- presentation of gifts to the bridesmaids and page-boys

- a toast to 'the bridesmaids'

You might also want to include:

- further comments to the bride's father – if he has said something nice about you, you might want to return the compliment by saying how hard you'll try to fulfil his expectations, or that you are proud to be his son-in-law

- remarks about how the wedding is going – especially if anything funny has happened

- thanks to anyone else who has played a particularly important role – providing flowers, cake, food, outfits, etc.

- a few words pretending you're dreading the best man's speech but saying something nice about him (this will also act as an introduction to anyone who doesn't know him, if he hasn't already spoken)

BEST MAN

The best man has specific things to say as well as being the life and soul of the party.

If you're the best man, you're obviously meant to be hilariously funny and possessed of the public speaking skills of a major broadcaster, politician or comedian. Of that, more later. Cut down to the bone, you're supposed to respond on behalf of the bridesmaids.

You may include:

- the bridesmaids' thanks for their gifts

- your own compliments to the bridesmaids, page-boys or ushers

- admiration of the bride and something about the groom's luck in having such a lovely bride

- congratulations to the happy couple

- something about being delighted to be best man

- a toast to 'The bride and groom's future happiness'

- thanks to the host and hostess on behalf of yourself and the guests

- a toast to 'The host and hostess'

- any telegrams or similar messages from guests who can't make it to the wedding

- a toast to 'Absent friends'

- stories and anecdotes about the groom – but see the special section on this!

- what's happening for the rest of the evening

A word of caution! Don't forget that this is the day on which the bride and groom have pledged their lives to each other. Also, consider the other guests. I'm not saying you have to dilute your speech so much that it wouldn't offend a Victorian spinster, but do bear in mind that there are likely to be guests of different generations, cultures and outlooks. Your risqué story might be funny down the pub, but don't risk ruining the day for anyone – especially the bride.

Mix your humour with kindness and your embarrassing tales with sincerity. Mention how you first met the groom, how you came to be such close friends, what you like and admire about him, how you viewed his relationship with the bride – mention how you first realised it was serious, or how he told you he was going to propose. You should also wish them the best for the future. You might also like to include:

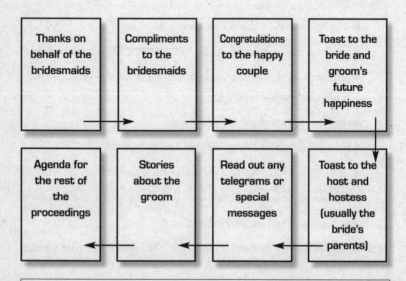

ILLUSTRATION 17   Main points of the best man's speech

- anecdotes about the wedding preparations, especially near-disasters or anything funny

- some more about the bride – try to talk to and about her as well as the groom (sometimes I think the best man would have been better off making his speech at the stag night, for all the thought he spares for the bride)

- props – I've seen a slide show (with embarrassing photos from the groom's past), a specially written song, performed by the best man and ushers, and enlarged photos, copied several times so they could be passed round the room

As I mentioned above, it can be a bit daunting to be asked to be best man at a wedding. You'll probably be speaking to a large group of people, some of whom you know and some of whom you will never have laid eyes on before. And they'll all be expecting you to be funny, warm – and audible. Quite a task.

Don't panic, you've got a number of advantages on your side:

ADVANTAGE ONE Although the best man feels the most pressure to be funny, his is usually the speech people look forward to most of all. And that goodwill can count for a lot. It's a weird phenomenon but when people know they're supposed to laugh, they usually do. How else do you explain the gales of audience laughter achieved by even the worst sitcoms on TV?

ADVANTAGE TWO If there's no toastmaster, you will have been taking control of the proceedings, giving you the advantage of already being familiar to the audience.

ADVANTAGE THREE You're on last. In the star slot. Several toasts will already have been drunk – not to mention the wine guests drank during the meal and the sips they've been taking throughout the speeches. The potential hurdles have all been overcome and everyone is now relaxing, looking forward to an evening of dancing and chatting to their friends and relatives.

So all in all, they're highly likely to greet even your lamest of gags with a roar of laughter.

BREAKING FROM TRADITION

So much for the traditional wedding. There are dozens of reasons why people choose not to stick to this format.

It might just be a matter of personal preference – the bride doesn't speak, traditionally, but many modern women are appalled by the idea of sitting quietly while the men speak on her behalf on her big day. Women who routinely chair business meetings, or pitch to high-level clients, or field questions from the media, day in, day out, might balk at the idea of the traditional, mute bride.

And the same might go for her mother. I know plenty of families where the mother is the one who sits on committees, who is a member of an amateur dramatic group, or who is simply an accomplished chatterer. Why should she sit and smile while her husband does all the talking?

THE BRIDE

The very fact that brides traditionally don't make a speech is going to free you to make the speech you want to make.

Unlike the best man and your father, you don't have years of expectation colouring what you want to say. You don't have to be uproariously funny like the best man; nor do you have to be the doting dad. But when anything goes, it's hard to know where to start.

Even though the bride's speech is a relatively recent idea, some 'new' traditions have taken root. This might be a good place to examine your thoughts about what you want to say.

The first question to tackle is *where* does your speech fit in, in the traditional order?

The father of the bride's speech is traditionally about the daughter, so if your dad is not there for any reason – or if it's been decided that he shouldn't speak – you might want to take that slot.

Or you might want to do a kind of double act with your new husband. We saw above that the groom's speech is traditionally made on behalf of himself and his new wife, so if you do want to speak, this would seem to be a logical time to do so.

However, you may prefer to let him have his say alone and keep your own words as a surprise. If this is the case, you could speak just before or just after the brand-new 'old man'.

OR (yes, there is yet another alternative), you might want to go last – although personally I think the slot after the best man is the most difficult of the evening. Give yourself a break!

Anyway, whenever you decide to do it, what do you say? Again, anything goes, really, but you might want to think about the following:

- thanks to the guests for coming, especially if they've travelled from afar

- thanks to everyone who's helped with the preparations (As traditional roles break down, more and more people get involved with the planning of a wedding and this might be a good time to thank your long-suffering best friends. After all, they've probably helped you to choose all kinds of accessories – not to mention drying your tears when you were having second thoughts about the entire thing! But best not to mention that specifically; not at the wedding!)

- a special thank-you to your mum, for helping with the wedding (if she has done so) and also for bringing you up and for your continuing relationship

- a thank-you to dad – if he's just related lots of embarrassing but heart-warming tales about you, the least you can do is to return the compliment

- a thank-you to anyone else who helped significantly with the wedding preparations

- a few words about your husband. This is your chance to put your side of the story of how you met and about any anecdotes he might be planning to tell about you. It's also the time to say something very, very nice about him

- a thank-you for any presents

- normally the groom thanks the bridesmaids but as they are your helpers on the day, it might make more sense for you to do this job

- as most wedding speeches end with a toast, the Americans have introduced a tradition that the bride proposes a toast to the guests

THE BRIDE'S MOTHER

If the bride's father is not at the wedding for some reason, his traditional role might well fall to the bride's mother. More of that below.

But what if the bride's mother *chooses* to speak – what should she say? Generally, I would advise that she sticks to a similar structure to that of the father of the bride (see above). The mother of the bride might wish to relate some tales of her own about the bride's childhood, which would give a nice, different perspective.

THE GROOM'S FATHER

The groom's family traditionally have virtually no role to play in the wedding. But many couples find this out of date – particularly if they have contributed financially to the wedding.

So you might want to consider asking the groom's father to say a very few words. He needn't say much – I would recommend that he echo the sentiments of the bride's father, thanking the latter for his welcome and saying a few words of greeting to his own family, while saying how pleased he is to meet so many members of the bride's family.

THE BEST WOMAN

Just as the best man speaks for the groom, some couples have asked the bride's best friend to perform a similar role for the bride. If you go down this route, simply review the guidelines for the best man and adapt them, as necessary.

WARNING! Having said all this, I would be wary about making speech time an opportunity for everyone to get up and have their tuppen'orth. You could go on for ever, inviting your mother's best friend's cousin to get to her feet. Don't. It's fine to dispense with tradition, but have a care for your guests. They're itching to get to the bar/chat to their favourite nephew/go to the loo/get away from their husband/chat up the bridesmaids, and they don't want to sit around the dinner-table all night.

So that's all the happy families stuff. More difficult are the situations when families don't fit in to the traditional pattern outlined above and speakers are changed not out of choice, but out of necessity. Divorce, death, adoption and stepfamilies aren't modern phenomena. But today's society is happier to acknowledge them, not to gloss over them. Which brings us on to:

TRICKY MATTERS

Of course there are still highly traditional white weddings, in which the parents are still married to each other; there are no family feuds and the bride and groom are each other's first serious partners and only just about to set up home together for the first time. Well, I suppose there are. There must be. It's just that I've never been to one. And neither has anyone I've asked.

Let's have a look at what the internet calls the FAQ (Frequently Asked Questions list):

1   What if the bride or groom has been married before?

2 Who speaks if one of the key cast is ill or dead – or has recently died?

3 What if the bride or groom has a child by a previous relationship?

4 What if parents of the bride or groom are divorced?

Weddings can be extremely difficult times. But they should be happy times. Let's have a look at those problems again and try to come up with some solutions that work in the real world – not just in the etiquette sections of the big newspapers. (See suggested intros below for speech suggestions.)

WHAT IF THE BRIDE OR GROOM HAS BEEN MARRIED BEFORE?

Whatever the circumstances, this is a difficult situation. Either partner may have been divorced or widowed, and there may or may not be children from this union.

The etiquette books will tell you that it's 'terribly bad form' to refer to any previous marriage. While I agree that one shouldn't bang on about it, eulogising about former partners or, worse, making any form of comparison whatsoever between weddings or wives, I think it's insane to ignore the facts altogether. We are no longer living in the Victorian age, when divorcees wore their status like a lifelong badge of shame. No one plans to get divorced! Yes, if that first marriage was in church, the couple swore before God that they would love and cherish, etc., 'until death us do part'. And many people still believe that breaking that promise is a sin – however it came about. But most people can see that circumstances alter cases – and they make allowances.

And anyway, the day one of those people is getting married for the second time is *not* the day for self-righteous guests to get sniffy. Apart from anything else, such a blatant triumph of hope over experience should be roundly celebrated. A divorce or bereavement is a traumatic and life-changing experience for anyone. And a first marriage was an important rite of passage, however badly things turned out or however briefly the union may have lasted. If there were children, they will presumably attend the second wedding. And children of the bride or groom are not easily ignored.

Anyway, half the guests will have brought up the issue of the first wedding anyway – usually when they're bumping into long-lost relatives and trying to remember where they last saw each other. Oh yes! It was at Jane's *last* wedding. At which point they get a bit embarrassed and tend to let those words hang in the air.

So, to get back to the point, I believe some passing reference may be made to a first marriage. It may make the guests feel more comfortable, if they know there are no secrets or taboo topics. You don't have to mention it, but if you do, be matter-of-fact and don't linger on the subject.

WHAT IF ONE OF THE KEY CAST IS ILL OR DEAD – OR HAS RECENTLY DIED?

This was the case at a wedding I recently attended. The situation was acknowledged and it was a highly emotional moment. But weddings are inherently happy occasions (on the whole), so a moment after we'd all had a lump in our throats and a tear in our eye, the speechmaker recovered with a more positive thought. And the whole speech was much the better for his honesty in mentioning a difficult subject on what is supposed to be 'the happiest day of your life'.

In the same way as divorce, illness and bereavement shouldn't be dwelt on, but should be acknowledged if the victim is an important friend or family member. If the bride's mother is a widow, the toast to the bride and groom is often made by a senior male relative (such as an uncle) or by an old family friend, who has known the bride for years. Of course, there's nothing to stop the bride's mother from stepping in and taking on the role that her late husband would have played.

If a close relative has died very recently, the family may want to pay tribute to them in some way. This can best be done before the main speeches and is most easily done by an old family friend. Close family members may want to pay tribute themselves, rather than hand the task over to a friend: if this is the case at your wedding, sit down and discuss it with them in detail. The time for long eulogies and emotion was at the funeral. Close family may take on the job with equanimity, but the highly charged atmosphere of a wedding can easily lead to too many tears.

However, you should respect their wishes and discuss the situation with consideration.

DON'T end on a downer. Start positively, mention the sad bit, and then move on to end on a high note.

WHAT IF THE BRIDE OR GROOM HAS A CHILD BY A PREVIOUS RELATIONSHIP?

We touched on this in the question about previous marriages.
Of course, there need not have been an earlier marriage for there to have been a child, but the principles remain the same. The child, in 99 per cent of cases, will be present at the wedding – and, in the majority of cases, she or he will have a special role to play: as an usher, bridesmaid or page-boy. This reflects the important status of the child and may help them to accept the wedding more happily. However, a child can be the happiest bridesmaid in the land, but if Daddy doesn't mention her in his speech, she'll swiftly transform into the unhappiest. In addition, while most of the guests will be aware of the situation, there may well be some who do not.

For both these reasons, and more, it's best to mention the child in a positive and welcoming way. We saw above how many of the speeches are meant to welcome newcomers into each other's family; the child of a couple who are no longer together should be granted the courtesy of even more welcoming into what really will be their new family.

WHAT IF THE PARENTS OF THE BRIDE OR GROOM ARE DIVORCED?

Again, this was the case at one of the weddings I attended last year. Neither the bride's nor the groom's parents were still together. And while the various relationships between them had been highly strained at times over the years, they all handled it beautifully. And the bride, who had been particularly concerned, was able to enjoy her day in exactly the right way.

If the bride's parents are divorced and a stepfather played an important role in her upbringing, a wedding can be a difficult time. Assuming that both men are to be at the wedding, many brides recoil in horror at the thought of having to choose who will 'give them away' and make a speech. One way round this would be for the bride's mother to make the speech. If she doesn't feel comfortable with this, you might want to skip the speechy bit and the mother could simply propose the toast to the bride and bridegroom.

RESEARCHING YOUR SPEECH

If you've been asked to make a speech at a wedding, the chances are that you know the bride and groom well. However, this is not always the case – you could be standing in for someone else, or for other reasons you might know one half of the couple and not the other.

Whether you think you know them well or not, it's always worth doing a bit of research. You might uncover funny or tender stories that you had never heard before.

ASK FRIENDS AND FAMILY

Make a point of calling those close to the couple and asking for their special memories. Most people will be chuffed to have been asked to help, particularly if they're not making a speech themselves. Don't expect them to have a supply of anecdotes that they can trot out like a list. You'll probably need to chat to them to draw out the best stories.

A good method is to get friends and family together over a bottle of wine. Forgotten anecdotes will be remembered and they, in turn, will prompt other stories. Take a dictaphone or tape recorder, so that you don't have to sit there frantically scribbling notes. If you're the best man (or best woman) and the groom (or bride) has a very close circle of friends, it's a nice touch to mention the other members of the gang. The same goes for aunties, uncles, cousins or grandparents.

OTHER PEOPLE

It might take a bit more work, but if you can track down old teachers or schoolfriends, former colleagues and ex-bosses, you can open the floodgates for even more stories.

FAMILY ARCHIVE

Plunder old photo albums, letters, press cuttings and school books. Childhood essays about 'what I did in the summer holidays', 'what I want to be when I grow up' or 'what I would do if I was prime minister' can often prove to be rich pickings. Take the book along to the wedding and read it out verbatim. Friends and relatives may love the chance to look at the rest of the book, later on in the evening.

Borrow photos and have copies made, to show at the wedding. Refer to old press cuttings – usually for sporting or school achievements; these can be hilarious in the light of the way the subject's life has panned out since.

ANCIENT HISTORY

Get hold of a newspaper printed the day the subject was born and read out a story that has some relevance. You could enlarge a photocopy and display it while you speak.

Original back issues of most of the main national and regional newspapers (subject to availability) can be bought from Historic Newspapers. They stock papers going back to the 1800s, although some of the more popular dates may have sold out. Contact them on 01988 402221.

Or you could discover the events that happened on the day she or he was born, and tie them in to the subject's life. Someone with a shared birthday might also be amusing. You can do the same thing with the date of the wedding: someone famous might have been married on the same day, or a great war might have been declared! Think around the events for relevant jokes.

WEB TIP *The History Channel's website includes a search facility for important events that took place on any date of the year. Check it out at **www.historychannel.com***

TODAY'S NEWS

Take a look through the newspapers and see if you can adapt any current stories to your speech. If you have access to a scanner and PC, you could even make authentic-looking changes to the piece.

You might want to put copies of any photographs, cuttings and other documents into a special book, which you could present to the couple as a further memento of the big day.

STAR-CROSS'D LOVERS

Look up the couple's star signs and see if they are supposed to be well matched. Reading out the characteristics of the signs can also lead to laughs, whether through spooky accuracy or, more realistically, amusing mismatches. Adapt, add bits or even make them up if it makes them funnier.

You could also read a prediction for that star sign from the day's newspapers – if they're not funny, relevant or irrelevant enough, make them up. 'A quiet day for Librans [or whatever]' should raise a chuckle. You could even try numerology (where birth-dates and names have numerical meanings) or find out which of the Chinese animal signs the subject was born under.

A ROSE BY ANY OTHER NAME

Grab a name dictionary and look up the meanings of the couple's names. You might come up with something funny or relevant. Surnames can also be researched – and these might be particularly appropriate if the bride is to take the groom's name.

I looked up the names of some couples I know and came up with the following:

> A 'victory' together with a 'handsome at birth'.
>
> A pair whose first names are both actually Scottish surnames – neither of whom have anything to do with Scotland. And his surname means 'descendant of a sea warrior'.
>
> A 'fit to be loved' teamed up with a 'champion'.
>
> One who is 'just', together with one who is 'snub-nosed' (he actually has got quite a pointy nose).
>
> A girl who is 'lovable' together with a man who 'takes by the heel', i.e. a supplanter.

So a fair amount of ammunition for jokes, as well as opportunity to say something heartfelt, there.

JOKES

Obviously, telling jokes is a good way to enliven your speech. But there's nothing worse than a clumsy link to a joke that has nothing to do with the proceedings. Keep it topical or relevant.

SUGGESTED INTRODUCTIONS

I don't know the details of your wedding or the people concerned and it's vitally important to make your speech personal. If you've familiarised yourself with the particular jobs assigned to your role, and you've done your research, most of the work has already been done.

But that's no help when you're sitting staring at a blank sheet of paper, with an equally blank mind. Looking at this book's main section on openings (in chapter 3) should give you some hints and tips about how to make an attention-grabbing opening. If you're *still* stumped, here are a few suggestions to get you started:

FATHER OF THE BRIDE

'Ladies and gentlemen, attending my daughter's wedding today has taken me on a mental journey back – how many years?! – to my own wedding ...'

'Today is Janet and John's big day – and they've dropped a big hint that it will be an even better day if I keep my speech short, so you can all get to the bar. But it's not every day a father gives his daughter away, so I will ask for just a few minutes of your time ...'

'I had thought I might be nervous about standing up here and speaking to you all, but it's been such a wonderful day, and I'm so proud of Janet, that the nerves have just disappeared.'

'Every father looks forward with a mixture of pride and trepidation to the day when he is called upon to give his daughter away in marriage. Having been through it today I certainly feel very proud. And the only trepidation is about how I'm going to pay for this lot!'

'What a day! It's been such a pleasure to give my daughter away. My only regret is that I didn't do it years ago ...'

WHEN THE MOTHER OF THE BRIDE IS DEAD 'The bride's father traditionally speaks both for himself and on behalf of the bride's mother. Sadly, my wife is no longer with us but, if she was, I know she would be as happy and proud as I am to see Janet and John getting married today.'

WHEN THE BRIDE HAS BEEN MARRIED BEFORE 'When Janet and John came to see us to tell us they were getting married, I was delighted. As you know, Janet has been married before. I'm glad that experience hasn't put her off a second try. But, Janet, if you ever think of trying for a third time, don't come to me for help!'

WHEN BOTH HAVE BEEN MARRIED BEFORE 'Ladies and gentlemen, all marriages are special. But second ones are doubly so, because it is a time for renewed hope.'

GROOM

'Ladies and gentlemen, my wife and I would like to start by saying thank you, James, for those kind words and good wishes.'

'My wife and I would like to say thank you to you all for coming to help us celebrate our wedding today. It's been a fantastic day, thanks to my wonderful wife and to the power of Imodium, without which I wouldn't be here today.'

'Today really has been the happiest day of my life. I've had quite a good life up to now and so that's quite an achievement. The only events that have come close for me were when Chelsea won the FA Cup and when I won the junior boys' egg and spoon race.'

'When I first saw my wife, I wasted no time in going over to chat her up. But that was mainly because my mate said he was going to if I didn't. Well, I'm glad I beat him to it because that evening was the beginning of a wonderful love story.'

WHEN THEY HAVE LIVED TOGETHER FOR A LONG TIME 'A few people have asked me why we're bothering to get married after all these years. The answer is that I wanted to stand up in public and let the world know how much Janet means to me. We've been happy together for a long time, but we felt it was time to move our relationship on and make a public commitment.'

'I know Janet and I have spent a while getting round to our wedding day. It's not that we weren't sure about each other. We were just giving James a chance to save up!'

WHEN HE HAS BEEN MARRIED BEFORE 'There's a first time for everything – and sometimes a second.'

WHEN THERE ARE CHILDREN INVOLVED 'This is a very big day for Janet and myself, but it's also a big day for Janet's children, Rod, Jane and Freddie. And my first thank you is to them, for welcoming me into their family. I know that they mean the world to Janet and I know I'm very lucky to be a part of their lives.'

BEST MAN

'First of all, on behalf of the bridesmaids, I'd like to thank John for his kind words. It's traditional for the best man to compliment the bridesmaids and, on this occasion, that's certainly an easy task – don't they look lovely?'

'I'd like to share with you today some very special words I overheard while the wedding photographs were being taken. I'm sorry I don't know the names of the guests concerned, but I thought I should pass on what they said. One of the ladies confided in the other that she hadn't seen her husband for 20 years: "He went out to buy a cabbage and never came back." The other looked shocked and said: "What on earth did you do?" "Oh," said the first, "I just opened a tin of peas."'

'I'm sure you've all heard stories about people getting cold feet before a wedding – and I've got to tell you, up until this moment I wasn't sure I was actually going to make it.'

'Unaccustomed as I am to pubic spanking … er, I mean …'

'I knew early on in their relationship that John was truly in love – and not just because he started missing nights out with the lads and buying better clothes. No, I could tell by the way he looked at Janet, and I had no trouble recognising that she was the one for him.'

'It's not often that us blokes get to talk about love. But I'm delighted that I've had the opportunity to do so today. And if there are any single women among the guests, who feel touched by my sensitivity, I'll be at the bar later.'

BRIDE

'Most of you know me well. And most of you will therefore not be surprised that we've decided to break with tradition and allow the blushing bride to say a few words.'

'Surely you didn't think I was going to sit there and let John speak for me … I never have in the past!'

'Some of you might think it's a bit forward for a bride to get up and make a speech. Well, wait till I tell you how I proposed …'

'I couldn't resist this opportunity to embarrass my new husband in public. And probably not for the last time.'

WHEN SHE HAS BEEN MARRIED BEFORE 'Most of you know that this is the second time I've been a bride. I thought the first time was for life but that didn't work out. Still, the nature of mistakes is that we learn from them and I know that my marriage to John is going to be very different and I'm confident that this is my last time in the white dress.'

WHEN THERE ARE CHILDREN INVOLVED See groom (p.154).

SON STANDING IN FOR FATHER OF THE BRIDE

'"Our father, who art in heaven …" Well, mine is, and that's why I'm standing in for him today …'

SOMEONE ELSE STANDING IN FOR FATHER OF THE BRIDE

'When Mary asked me to stand in and make the speech usually performed by the father of the bride, I was very touched. I have spent a long time thinking about what my dear brother/friend would have liked to say on this occasion and one thing I do know is that he would have been very proud.'

'When I was small, my brother James was always getting me into trouble – and now look at the mess he's got me into! I'm sure he's looking down and laughing at my awkward attempts at speech-making.'

'Many of you will not know me, so I'd like to begin by introducing myself.'

STAND-IN FOR FATHER OF THE BRIDE/BEST MAN WHO'S ILL

'I know I'm probably not the person most of you expected to be speaking at this point, but Jim is unfortunately too ill to make it today. I spoke to him this morning though and he's promised me that he'll be scrutinising the video to see if I was an adequate stand-in. Jim asked me to send his apologies and best wishes to Janet and John, and I'm sure you all join me in wishing him a speedy recovery and hoping that he can soon get right back on his hang-glider!'

MOTHER OF THE BRIDE

'If my husband was still alive, I know he'd say, "Mary, you never could keep quiet!" But I think I'm entitled to say a few words today of all days. Janet was very close to her father and they are so alike in so many ways. But today is a happy occasion and so we're going to look to the future and not dwell on the past.'

WHEN SOMEONE CLOSE TO THE COUPLE HAS DIED RECENTLY

'For many of us, there is a little sadness mixed in with today's joy. And that's because of the recent loss of Jim. Those of us who knew him find it hard to believe that he's not among us today and we would like to pay tribute to him and say thank you for his life.

'But today is Janet and John's wedding day and I know Jim wouldn't want us to dwell on sad thoughts.'

IF THE STAND-IN IS THERE FOR A HAPPIER REASON

'Many of you will be surprised to see me standing here today in Steve's place. And believe me, 24 hours ago I thought I was going to be sitting around and knocking back the champagne with the rest of you.

'But John called me and told me something that Steve's girlfriends could have told me years ago – that he was unable to perform on the big occasion.'

As for finding jokes, the field is enormous. Rent out comedy videos and films, look up gags on the Net, note down funnies in papers and mags. There are plenty of wedding-joke books around, too. Ask people for their favourite joke. But remember, very often, your own raw original material will be much funnier than any stuff that's borrowed.

TOASTS

Most of the wedding speeches traditionally include a toast, and the English custom is usually to keep it simple and announce, 'To the bride and groom!' or 'To the bridesmaids'.

But you can make the occasion very special by choosing a longer toast. You may even ask someone else to propose it – particularly useful if you have other close friends or family who would not otherwise have a role to play.

Here are a few suggestions:

- May your home always be too small to hold all of your friends;

  May you both live as long as you want and never want as long as you live;

  May your troubles be less and your blessings be more,
  And nothing but happiness come through your door.

- May your love always last and your happiness always be assured.

- May the happiest day of your past be the saddest day of your future;

  May you love each other more than yesterday but less than tomorrow;

May the love you share for ever remain as beautiful as the
bride looks today;

May your wishes always come true and may you always get
more than you wish for;

May your hands be forever joined in friendship and your
hearts forever joined in love;

May you live as long as you want to and want to as long as
you live;

May your love be modern enough to survive the times and old-
fashioned enough to last for ever;

May you live long, laugh often, and love much;

May the love you feel today be present always, for ever and a day.

- It is said when a child finds true love the parents find true joy.

- May the most you ever wish for be the least you receive.

- They say you get married for better or worse.
  May your lives together be far better than worse.

WEB TIP *Find more toasts at*
***www.weddings.about.com/style/weddings/**. If you really get a kick
out of this – and public speaking in general – why not check out
Toastmasters International at **www.toastmasters.org.uk**.*

READINGS

Another way of involving close friends and family in your wedding is
to ask them to perform a reading, whether you're getting married in
church or in a civil ceremony.

If you've been asked to do a reading, I'm sure you've taken the
invitation as a huge compliment, but you're probably still very nervous
about the prospect – especially if you are going to have to read from the

Bible. And in church too! Poems also fill many people with terror, as they wrestle with the short lines and unfamiliar punctuation.

Well, fear not, my friend. Help is at hand. Read on …

It's a great honour to be asked to read at someone's wedding – but it can be scary too.

CHOOSING A READING

Sometimes kind couples will simply give you a book, tell you which page you're reading and send you off to practise.

However, others will ask you to choose – either because they can't be bothered, or because you appear to have – or claim to have – some kind of literary expertise.

IN CHURCH If the wedding is taking place in church, the vicar will normally be able to supply a selection of suitable biblical passages.

Read them through, and really consider which one is most appropriate for the couple who are getting married (not which one is the shortest, or has the least big words).

I have provided the references for some of the most popular biblical passages below, but once you've chosen, just run it past the vicar or priest for approval – it is their church, after all.

Many vicars will also allow you to read a secular text, but here things might get a bit more tricky. Your average priest or vicar is likely to give the thumbs up to the old classics – Shakespeare, Wordsworth; that kind of thing. But they may be suspicious of anything they're unfamiliar with or suspect of being too modern and trendy.

However, some vicars might be much more open-minded or open to persuasion. They may even welcome new sources into their churches.

A CIVIL CEREMONY Don't imagine that just because you're *not* in a church that anything goes. Far from it.

The first and most important thing to remember is that civil ceremonies

– whether in a State-licensed venue or in a Register Office – do not allow readings with any religious content at all. It's obvious that this means no Bible readings, prayers or hymns, but it also applies to other 'spiritual' poems, such as the ever-popular 'Desiderata' ('Go placidly amid the noise and haste').

Just like the readings in the vicar's church, you must clear any reading with the registrar, or whoever is conducting the ceremony.

The vicar and registrar are only one part of the equation though. You also need to choose something that's appropriate for the couple themselves.

Humanist weddings, or other alternative ceremonies, allow total freedom and may be worth considering if you're set on pieces that the church/Registrar won't approve of.

If you're choosing a non-religious reading, where on earth do you start?

If you're choosing for your own wedding, the following suggestions might help. If you're choosing the reading for a friend, you might want to go through it with them:

Do you have a favourite poet/author/book that might be appropriate?

Look in books of quotations under sections such as 'love' and 'marriage'. Note any particular quotations or authors that you find appealing and look into them more carefully.

There are several books of love poetry or suggested readings. Invest in one or see if your library can get it for you.

The British Humanist Association publishes a guide to non-religious wedding ceremonies, 'Sharing the Future', which includes a section on readings.

WEB TIP *Contact them via **www.humanism.org.uk**, or call 020 7430 0908.*

READINGS

Some suggested readings (I have left it to you to look them up):

Matthew 19:3–6	Ecclesiastes 4:9–12
John 15:9-13 'Song of Songs' 2:13–14, 16; 8:6–7	Matthew 19:5–6
Colossians 3:12–15	Mark 10:6–9
Genesis 2:18–24	John 2:1–11
Proverbs 5:15–19; 18:22	I Corinthians 7

RELIGIOUS READINGS If you're not very familiar with the Bible, it might seem daunting to have to choose a reading for your wedding. But the Bible really isn't difficult to read – you just need to take time.

Some families have traditional readings, which are used at all family weddings. Even if yours doesn't, you might want to ask your parents what was read at their wedding. Or if you've been asked to give a reading, you might want to choose one that was read at *your* own wedding, or at your parents' wedding. Although you won't mention that in church, you might want to explain to the couple, or the other guests, the reason behind your choice.

You also need to decide which version of the Bible you want to use. There is only one Bible, but there are a number of different versions, or translations. Your priest or vicar may have strong feelings about which you use, or may be happy for you to have the one you prefer. It's another thing that you should discuss with them in advance.

The King James's Bible is the old one, dating back to the 17th century. While some welcome it for its familarity and rich old-fashioned language, others find it out of date and difficult to understand.

There are several more modern versions – from the Revised Standard Version (RSV), which updates the traditional translations, to those like the New English Bible (NEB) or the Good News Bible, which try to be ultra-modern, replacing all the words that are no longer in common use.

Roman Catholics usually use the Jerusalem Bible, but that too is available in a newer version.

Compare these versions of I Corinthians 13:4–7 (which I chose for my own wedding, incidentally) – the first from the King James and the second from the NEB.

'Charity suffereth long, and is kind; charity envieth not; charity vaunteth not itself, is not puffed up, doth not behave itself unseemly, seeketh not her own, is not easily provoked, thinketh no evil; rejoiceth not in iniquity, but rejoiceth in the truth; beareth all things, believeth all things, hopeth all things, endureth all things.'

'Love is patient; love is kind and envies no one. Love is never boastful, nor conceited, nor rude; never selfish, nor quick to take offence. Love keeps no score of wrongs; does not gloat over other men's sins, but delights in the truth. There is nothing love cannot face; there is no limit to its faith, its hope, and its endurance.'

The Bible is divided into the Old and New Testaments and then further into a series of Books. Each Book divides into chapters, which divide further into verses. Quotations are identified first by the name of the book. After the name of the book comes the chapter number. Finally, there are the verse numbers.

Several of the books have commonly abbreviated titles. If you're not sure what you're looking for, there should be a table at the beginning of your Bible, listing all the abbreviations. It will also tell you the order of the books, so you can find them faster.

NON-RELIGIOUS READINGS Love poems are the most popular choice but poetry is such a personal thing that it's hard to narrow this down to a few suggestions. If you don't have a favourite poem or poet, you might like to start by looking at some of the following:

The Passionate Shepherd to his Love – Christopher Marlowe

> *Come live with me and be my Love,*
> *And we will all the pleasures prove*

My Love is Like a Red, Red Rose – Robert Burns

> *My love is like a red, red rose*
> *That's newly sprung in June*

A Dedication to My Wife – T S Eliot

> *To whom I owe the leaping delight*
> *That quickens my senses in our wakingtime*
> *And the rhythm that governs the repose of our sleepingtime,*
> *The breathing in unison*

If Thou Must Love Me – Elizabeth Barrett Browning

> *If thou must love me, let it be for naught*
> *Except for love's sake only*

The Bargain – Sir Philip Sidney

> *My true love hath my heart, and I have his*

WEB TIP *There are dozens of suggestions for readings on the internet. You might like to try:*

www.speeches.com
Weddings.about.com/style/weddings
www.lovepoetry.com
www.weddingguide.co.uk

CHECKLIST

Checklist for choosing a reading:

Has the reading been approved by the vicar/priest/registrar? ❏

Is it suitable? ❏

Is it about marriage, rather than just falling in love, or lust? ❏

Does the piece make sense as a piece of writing,
   without needing any further explanation? ❏

Does it fit in with the prayers, other readings and hymns? ❏

Are you sure it won't offend anyone? ❏

Is it the right length – not too short and not too long? ❏

Does the reader feel comfortable with it? ❏

SUMMARY

Rules are there to be broken – but you can only break the rules if you know what they are in the first place. You now know why traditions exist and when it's OK to change them. You should also be more inspired about choosing an appropriate reading. Let's recap:

Work out who should speak and what they should say

Stick to tradition or adapt it to your special needs – but make sure everyone's clear about their role.

Step-families, bereavement and other tricky matters

Be sensible and sensitive and no one will get hurt.

Research

Use the insider tips on research specific to wedding speeches.

Suggested intros

Getting started is often the hardest bit. Use these suggestions as a way to get going ... then it's up to you.

Toasts

Think about this charming, but neglected tradition

Readings

Offer the right passage to the right people at the right ceremony. These suggestions should give you some inspiration and help you find your way round the Bible.

10

SPEAKING TO
THE MEDIA

- **FEAR OF THE PRESS**

- **PRESS RELEASES**

- **APPROACHING THE MEDIA**

- **EXCLUSIVES – KISS & TELLS**

- **HOW TO HANDLE THAT PHONE CALL**

- **SIMPLE DOS & DON'TS**

- **MAKING THE MOST OF YOUR MEDIA TIME**

- **DEALING WITH DIFFICULT QUESTIONS**

- **EMERGENCIES & INCIDENTS**

It's ironic, but the press gets a very bad press. There are several reasons why you might find yourself at the sharp end of a journalist's pencil; or the fluffy end of a radio mike; or the wide end of a TV camera.

If you're running a campaign, you might want to use the media to publicise your cause. You might want to get some editorial coverage to help boost your business. You might witness a major accident (God forbid) or be involved in a dramatic rescue. You might find that the

spotty oik you used to date in the fifth form has now become the latest rock god. You might even get off with someone famous and decide to pose half-naked and sell your kiss and tell to the News of the World.

Whether your motives are altruistic or purely for financial gain, it's probably only a matter of time before you get your Andy Warhol 15 minutes of fame. Much of this section deals with issues you might not traditionally regard as public speaking – but in fact, speaking to the media is likely to reach a bigger audience than any conference centre or village hall. Also, you'll find lots of tips on writing press releases and other ways of attracting the media's attention.

Of course, this doesn't necessarily involve speaking, but unless you know how to get onto the news agenda, you'll never get the chance.

FEAR OF THE PRESS

You can hardly open a magazine now, or turn on the television, without some bleeding-heart celebrity complaining about press intrusion. The tragic death of Princess Diana also served to further blacken the name of the British newspaper industry. Much of the criticism has been well deserved and the crisis has made editors think twice about issues of intrusion and harassment.

However, a drawback of the negative coverage has been that ordinary people are often terrified of the press, fearing that their names will be dragged through the dirt; that they will be misquoted and misunderstood; or that they will be ridiculed. I must emphasise that this is not the case.

In the first place, you're not a celebrity. It's highly unlikely that anyone is going to go through your bins or try to trip you up into talking about something you would rather have kept quiet. Journalists are in the business of selling newspapers, it's true. And celebrity scoops certainly have a big part to play in selling newspapers. But readers also love good luck stories, amusing anecdotes, tales of the triumph of ordinary people, and they adore the idea of people pulling together for a common cause.

Real LIFE
Look at the petrol crisis of summer 2000 – the press had a field day with the idea of people power. Ordinary truckers and farmers found themselves leading a national campaign that affected almost every area of British life and dominated the front pages for days on end. Those ordinary truckers and farmers had the chance to put their views across when they were interviewed by journalists. And the journalists were happy to reflect the nation's views and give voice to the protesters.

Look too at the campaigns to find organ transplants for children. Here we have ordinary parents who found themselves in the extraordinary situation of having to fight for their child's life. By going to the media with their plea, the search for a suitable donor instantly becomes national or world-wide. Countless lives have been saved, thanks to such campaigns.

There are literally thousands and thousands of such examples – the local press in particular is constantly running various campaigns on behalf of local people.

Real LIFE
When I was a cub reporter on a local newspaper, I launched a number of campaigns on issues affecting the town where I worked. But one of the stories I'm proudest of only affected a single family. A local woman had travelled to America on holiday but while there she had suffered a sudden and serious heart attack. Luckily, she had medical insurance and was able to secure the best hospital treatment. But she was so ill that doctors advised her husband to call their daughters to warn them that their mother was

probably going to die any day. Amazingly, she pu+lled through and was able to fly home again in a matter of weeks. But on returning to the UK, she faced horrendous bills from all sides. Her husband had returned the hire car a day late and had been charged a hefty penalty fee. A credit card that had been used to make all those pricey transatlantic phone calls was demanding immediate payment because the charges were sky-high. Her husband had had to stay somewhere near the hospital. This sick woman was at her wits' end when she turned up in our newspaper office, begging for any help we could lend. I must admit, I was sceptical – we were only a tiny local paper, with none of the sway held by the nationals. But by the end of the day, I had halved the bills. The credit card company waived some of the charges and agreed to take the rest of the payment in affordable monthly sums. The car hire company scrapped the penalty fee. We ran the story as the front page splash and various local organisations rushed to help. Not only were the financial headaches solved, but the woman in question was inundated with offers of help in other ways.

If one story, in one small provincial newspaper, can do all that in one day, imagine what you can achieve for your campaign if you harness the power of the press.

OK, JOURNALISTS ARE OBVIOUSLY THE MOST WONDERFUL PEOPLE ON THE PLANET – WHAT NOW? Well, having allayed your worst fears, I would temper my advice with a few stern words of caution. You can get what you want from the press if you've got something to say, you find the right people to say it to and you play it straight.

Let's go through the process and we'll find the most important dos and don'ts along the way.

The first thing you need to do is to think about whether anyone really cares about what you want to say. You need to present your story in the most newsworthy way, by thinking like an editor.

CHECKLIST

Run through the following checklist and see if you can say yes to any of the questions:

	yes	no
Is the subject already recognised as an issue?	❏	❏
Is there anyone famous involved?	❏	❏
Is there a famous organisation involved?	❏	❏
Is the issue fashionable, topical or current?	❏	❏
Is the subject an event or problem that's happening right now?	❏	❏
Will the subject have a significant impact?	❏	❏
Will the impact be felt directly by people? Or groups of people?	❏	❏
Will the impact be felt locally? Or globally?	❏	❏
Is there a real power-struggle involved? Does it involve individuals fighting against a major organisation?	❏	❏
Do you simply have a good story to tell?	❏	❏
Does the story involve children? Or animals? Or old people? Or sick people? Or anyone else who might grab the public imagination?	❏	❏

	yes	no
Does the story have an emotional impact on those who hear it?	❏	❏
Does the story or issue have a visual side? Are there photo opportunities? Might there be an opportunity to film something dramatic?	❏	❏
Does the story fit in to a theme that always interests people, e.g. the triumph of love over circumstances; a dramatic rescue; a community who pulled together where others might have fallen apart; a local boy who saw an opportunity and pursued it to impressive ends; racism; sexism, etc.?	❏	❏
Is there anything funny about it?	❏	❏
Is there anything innovative about it?	❏	❏
Is there anything really big about it?	❏	❏
Is it a 'first' in any way?	❏	❏
Is there anything wacky about it?	❏	❏
Does it touch on issues that might be relevant to a large number of people? If they heard your story could it help them improve their life/health/understanding/consumer rights?	❏	❏
Have you organised an event that's open to the public?	❏	❏

	yes	no
Have you won an award, been appointed to an important organisation or otherwise achieved recognition for what you do?	❏	❏
Have you published a book or CD? Have you mounted an exhibition?	❏	❏
Have you provided some kind of important service to your community?	❏	❏
Are you standing for some kind of public office or important role?	❏	❏
Are you involved in a major investigation, inquiry or court case?	❏	❏
Are you offering a totally new product or service?	❏	❏
Are you looking for volunteers?	❏	❏
Are you offering training or apprenticeships?	❏	❏
Have you won the lottery? Or a lot of money/big prize in another competition?	❏	❏
Are you about to appear on television?	❏	❏
Are you offering franchises of your business?	❏	❏
Have you opened a new branch of your business? Or moved your headquarters somewhere else?	❏	❏

	yes	no
Have you received an impressive qualification? Has a member of your staff?	❏	❏
Are you throwing your office/factory open to visitors for a day?	❏	❏
Are you having a general meeting?	❏	❏
Has your company sponsored a major event?	❏	❏

If you can say 'yes' to any of those questions, you've probably got a story. The more positive answers, the better the story.

If you didn't shout 'yes' many times, that list itself should help you think of ways you could add news value to your campaign.

But there are lots of things you can do to boost the story's newsworthiness. Journalists talk about a story being 'sexy', or saying it's 'got legs', by which they mean it's a good, exciting story.

If you only answered 'yes' to the rather dull questions – 'Are you offering training?', 'Are you standing for office?' or some of the other questions towards the bottom of the list – you might need to make your story a bit more sexy.

If you are staging an event, or you run an attraction, or the like, don't forget to offer the journalist a free press ticket, or two if you can afford it. It'll be worth it in the long run.

MAKING IT SEXIER

Here are a few ideas:

1   Do a survey – especially in the 'silly season' of August, when news runs dry and journalists are desperate to fill the pages.

2   Get someone to turn it into a report – another goodie for
    August. Persuade a charity or educational organisation to lend
    their support to your report.

3   Hold a vote or election of some kind.

4   Announce an appointment.

5   Make it topical: look for an angle that chimes with something
    else that's happening in the news.

6   Hire a PR (this will cost money but might be worth considering).

7   Approach a publication or programme about mounting a joint
    event or joining in with their existing ones.

8   Approach a publication or programme about the possibility of
    them sponsoring your event. You'll get money AND publicity!

9   Tie it in with an anniversary.

10 Issue a set of guidelines, or a handy guide or a set of facts.

11 Wait for a relevant time of year and tie the campaign to it:
    parents will be more receptive about campaigns to teach
    children to swim during the summer; they'll be more
    sympathetic to the plight of the homeless during the winter.

12 Wait for a relevant date and tie the campaign to it: fertility and
    egg donation at Easter, perhaps; or a campaign for a maternity
    ward at Christmas.

13 Get someone famous involved.

14 Do something controversial.

15 Stage an event.

16 Get lots of people involved and announce their names.
    Take the journalists on a trip or outing – it must be something
    they'll really want to go on, though, and they must be sure
    they'll get a story out of it.

17 Create a competition or set of awards.

18 Form a delegation to approach the government, council or other relevant body.

19 Stage a sit-in, a blockade or other form of protest.

20 Stage a concert.

21 Organise a march.

22 Call for a boycott.

23 Write a letter to someone newsworthy or publish a letter from someone newsworthy or about something newsworthy.

24 Create a 'day' – like Red Nose Day, Jeans for Genes day – there are hundreds of these!

25 If you don't want to invite the media to an event, for any reason – or if they can't come – why not videotape the event yourself. If the event ends up in the headlines, they might use your footage.

I mentioned the 'silly season' above. If you're not sure how truly newsworthy your story is, why not wait until August. All the traditional sources of news are on holiday and stories are woefully thin on the ground. Editors will greet your story with heartfelt joy.

WEB TIP **www.lamar.colostate.edu/~hallahan/hpubty** *has lots more ideas about how to get publicity.*

You might start the ball rolling on your media campaign with a simple phone call to the right journalist, but you could – especially if you want to reach more than one publication – send out a press release.

PRESS RELEASES

I know what you're thinking. Aren't we straying off the point somewhat? This is a public speaking book. Press releases have nothing to do with public speaking. Right?

Right. But if you don't grab the attention of the journalists you're trying to reach, they won't be asking you to speak at all.

You've already decided what your story is, and you've thought of everything you can to make that story more sexy. But you still need to hone your approach.

DON'T dilute your message. If you have several angles to your story, don't confuse the media by trying to shoe-horn them all into the same press release.

DO decide what your overall message is, and stick to this for the first release.

Let's look at a fictitious example:

Real
LIFE
Seven-year-old Kerry Potts is disabled and the authorities said she couldn't go to the local school unless it had proper wheelchair access. The authority decided not to fund the alterations and told Kerry she would have to go to a school in the city centre. Her neighbour, Angela Smith, was so upset that she decided to start a fund-raising campaign.

She discussed the idea with friends and neighbours, who were very supportive. Their first idea was to do a sponsored head shave in the school hall, to help raise the money. One of them knew a local celebrity and agreed to approach him about getting involved. Another runs a local business and his staff offered to put on a barn-dance in the school gymnasium, as part of the fund-raising. At this point, Mrs Smith decided to call the local newspaper to tell them what was going on.

Let's examine how she managed the events to get maximum coverage.

Giving the press everything in one go could well get you a story – but only one story and a slightly muddled one at that.

Angela decided to break it down into several bits and do a new press release each week. She hoped this approach meant the story would be in the paper every week. The stories themselves were a little smaller but she won the support of the paper, who placed them in prominent positions on their pages.

The stories broke down roughly like this:

WEEK ONE Little Kerry is banned from village school – neighbours start fund-raising campaign.

WEEK TWO Villagers pledge to go bald to help little Kerry.

WEEK THREE Workers stage barn-dance to help little Kerry.

WEEK FOUR (having had the definite go-ahead from the celebrity) – Local star John Morton joins fight for little Kerry and wields clippers in sponsored head shave.

WEEK FIVE Morton opens garden for village party in little Kerry campaign.

Well, you get the drift. To try to put all those things into one press release would have been confusing.

PLUS a 'drip-drip' approach, with a story each week, kept Angela's campaign in people's minds for longer.

☞ **Keep your release simple and avoid hype. Remember, thousands of press releases pour into newspaper offices. Journalists don't need whizzes and bangs to make them notice yours – if you've got a good story and you tell it clearly, they'll notice. Follow our template for a good press release (see over).**

PRESS RELEASE TEMPLATE

1 DATE

2 HEADLINE
Villagers start campaign for little Kerry to attend local school.

Sums the story up in as few words as possible

3 SUBHEAD
Authorities rule that 7-year-old disabled child must travel to Donchester for education – but local people pledge to raise cash to equip the village school.

Slightly longer – expands on headline

4 INTRO
Little Marching residents have launched a fund-raising campaign, after education authorities ruled that wheelchair user Kerry Potts must attend school in Donchester city centre, twelve miles from her home.

Opens the story – keep it short

5 SECOND PARAGRAPH
The villagers decided on the action after a shock ruling that Little Marching School will not receive the government funding necessary to adapt it for wheelchair access.

Together with intro, these two paragraphs should tell the who, what, why, when, how

6 KEY QUOTE
Kerry's mother, Tanya Potts, said: 'Kerry has grown up in the village and all her friends are here. We are supporters of the local school and we don't want to send her to a much bigger school in the city centre. I'm bitterly disappointed that the authorities won't find the money to pay for the adaptations.'

Sums up the situation in the words of someone involved

7 TELL THE STORY
Mr and Mrs Potts put Kerry's name down for the local school in April, but they were told that her disability meant the building would have to be assessed for wheelchair access.

Keep it brief, but simply tell the story in chronological order

The authorities ruled that the school was not suitable, but the work necessary was assessed and applications were made for funding.

But at a meeting on Monday, the Potts heard the application had been turned down and Kerry would have to attend the nearest suitable school, Donchester City School.

8. SECOND OR MORE QUOTES

Mrs Potts added: 'Donchester City School is twelve miles from our home and it's an hour's journey, there and back. Kerry might be disabled but she shouldn't be made to feel different to the other children. She should be educated here, among her friends.'

> As you tell the story, you may want to include more quotes to illustrate it and vary the pace of the release

> Return to the main story

9. BACK TO THE STORY

The Pottses' neighbour, Mrs Angela Smith, decided to mount a campaign to raise the £5,000 needed to pay for the changes.

10. INCLUDE ALL THE DETAILS THE PUBLIC WILL NEED TO KNOW

Local people have been invited to attend a meeting at Little Marching School hall on Tuesday 19 May at 7 pm.

Mrs Smith said: 'We're asking everyone in the village to come, so that we can put our heads together and come up with some ways to raise this money for Kerry.'

> Details for people who might get involved

> Details for the press to follow up on

11. INCLUDE ALL THE DETAILS THE JOURNALISTS WILL NEED TO KNOW

Contact:

Mrs Tanya Potts – 01222 839567

Mrs Angela Smith – 01222 839574

12. NOTE TO EDITOR

Kerry suffers from spina bifida and has been unable to walk since birth.

> Optional: any background information that might not be suitable as part of the release, but would be useful

PRESS RELEASE

VILLAGERS CAMPAIGN FOR GIRL TO ATTEND LOCAL SCHOOL

Authorities rule that seven-year-old disabled child must travel to Donchester for education – but local people pledge to raise cash to equip the village school

Little Marching residents have launched a fund-raising campaign, after education authorities ruled that wheelchair user Kerry Potts must attend school in Donchester city centre, twelve miles from her home.

The villagers decided on the action after a shock ruling that Little Marching School will not receive the government funding necessary to adapt it for wheelchair access.

Kerry's mother, Tanya Potts, said: 'Kerry has grown up in the village and all her friends are here. We are supporters of the local school and we don't want to send her to a much bigger school in the city centre. I'm bitterly disappointed that the authorities won't find the money to pay for the adaptations.'

Mr and Mrs Potts put Kerry's name down for the local school in April, but they were told that her disability meant the building would have to be assessed for wheelchair access.

The authorities ruled that the school was not suitable, but the work necessary was assessed and applications were made for funding.

But at a meeting on Monday, the Pottses heard the application had been turned down and Kerry would have to attend the nearest suitable school, Donchester City School.

Mrs Potts added: 'Donchester City School is twelve miles from our home and it's an hour's journey, there and back. Kerry might be disabled but she shouldn't be made to feel different to the other children. She should be educated here, among her friends.'

The Pottses' neighbour, Mrs Angela Smith, decided to mount a campaign to raise the £5,000 needed to pay for the changes.

Local people have been invited to attend a meeting at Little Marching School hall on Tuesday 19 May at 7 pm.

Mrs Smith said: 'We're asking everyone in the village to come, so that we can put our heads together and come up with some ways to raise this money for Kerry.'

Ends

Contact:

> Mrs Tanya Potts – 01222 839567
>
> Mrs Angela Smith – 01222 839574

Note to editors: Kerry suffers from spina bifida and has been unable to walk since birth.

ILLUSTRATION 18   A finished press release should look something like this – but fit it on one page!

When writing or speaking about dates for important events, don't just say '19 May', say 'Tuesday 19 May' – it will help people to remember it.

DON'T go into a long-winded history of everything you've ever done. Try to edit it down to a few words: Clothing manufacturer N Brown and Sons, which specialises in dancewear …

DON'T write more than a single page of A4, if you can possibly help it.

DON'T try to sell your product. Keep that approach for your clients. When talking to journalists, simply provide information about it.

DON'T use long words or jargon. Newspapers don't so why should you?

DON'T try to flog them a story that's way out of date. If it happened months ago, sorry, you've missed the boat and you'll have to come up with something new.

DON'T exaggerate or hype.

DO print your release on a computer, or at least a very good typewriter. Borrow one if necessary – but NEVER hand-write releases. No one will take you seriously.

DO keep the release brief but include all the necessary background information. If you're writing about a complicated issue, the journalists will be grateful for the explanation.

DO offer to give them more information, if necessary. You might want to simplify the issue – let the editor decide exactly which areas they want to explore further.

DO explain what your company does, if you're writing about a business issue.

DO include additional information on a separate sheet if you feel you need to say more. Draw up a company biog on to a separate sheet of A4.

> **JARGONBUSTER!**
> Embargo: a request for a publication to wait until a certain date before publishing the story.

DO check, check and double check your spelling.

DO avoid clichés.

DO get someone else to read the release before you send it out.

Don't be too blatantly promotional – too false. Editors are happy to carry news, but they don't like being over-manipulated by someone trying to get a slice of the action. Make your story news, real news.

CHECKLIST FOR NEW RELEASES

Have you included:

date that you're sending the release? ❏

embargo date – if appropriate? ❏

contact name and phone number (during office hours)? ❏

headline? ❏

subhead? ❏

intro? ❏

key quote? ❏

story? ❏

all relevant dates in full (including day of the week)? ❏

all relevant times? ❏

all relevant addresses (with details of how to get there, if necessary)? ❏

full names (spelt correctly)? ❏

any background information? ❏

APPROACHING THE MEDIA

Firstly, you need to appreciate that you might get very little coverage, or even none at all. Don't be disheartened. Even the act of sending the release has made that one journalist aware of you.

But you don't want to be constantly sending releases to the wrong people. Not only is it a waste of your time and money, but any journalist finding an irrelevant release on their cluttered desk will become irritated and will throw it away. At best, they'll forget about it. At worst, they'll remember your name and mentally give you a black mark.

But there are ways to make your releases more effective:

DO get the right target.

DO log on and have a good look round if you're targeting a website.

DO phone up and ask for the name and job title of the person you need to send it to if you're satisfied that they cover your kind of story. Most magazines carry names, job titles, direct lines and even email addresses for their key staff. Look it up. If you've hit the right target, they'll be delighted to hear from you.

DON'T grab some listing for 'magazines' and send out releases willy nilly.

DON'T just send your press release off to the BBC. Read your target publication and listen to or watch the programme.

GET THE NAME RIGHT

When you get that person's name do double check the spelling and job title. I know I've got an unusual name but when I was a journalist, I was so sick of people spelling my name wrong that I often chucked away releases with barely a glance if they'd got it wrong.

Never, ever, abbreviate anyone's name without asking them. It's not friendly, it's rude. If their listing says Charles, they're Charles to you. Not Charlie, not Chas, not Chuck. Charles.

GET THE TIMING RIGHT

Glossy magazines usually have long lead times – between two and four months. And special editions, such as a Christmas issue, might be planned out even earlier than that. So contacting them in April to say you've heard they're covering your subject in May isn't much good.

But if your product is going to be a secret until the last minute, trust the journalist. Most will be more than happy to sign embargos – meaning they can't breathe a word until a certain date – if it means they're going to get the scoop.

DON'T irritate them by refusing to tell them. How will they know how much space to plan for it unless they know the facts?

GET UP TO DATE

DON'T think that because someone gave you the name of the news editor in 1973, they're still there.

DO check out that staffing column I mentioned above.

GET ON THE RIGHT SIDE OF YOUR MEDIA CONTACT

Many media guides tell you to follow up your press release with a call.

BE VERY CAREFUL WITH THIS. I used to be driven up the wall with irritating PRs – total strangers with whom I'd never done business before – phoning me up on a news day and asking me how I was. Then they plagued me by asking me if I'd received their fax. If you mailed it – they've got it. OK?

If you hear nothing and you're anxious, you can call a few days later. But be direct and to the point. Make it clear you're not hassling them.

WHAT ABOUT EMAILS?

Some journalists like to receive press releases by email – others don't. The best thing to do is to call and ask. If you do email your releases, remember:

Don't send huge attachments that will take the journalist ages to download.

Don't hound the journalist. If they don't reply to your email, take the hint and leave them alone.

Do make it clear that you can send pictures, products or other attachments, and ask the journalist to mail you back if they'd like to receive them.

Do be careful about 'netiquette'!

Do write the address of your website (the URL) if you have one. Most word-processing systems will turn this URL into a link, so the recipient can click on it and be connected directly to your website.

> **JARGONBUSTER!**
> Netiquette: from 'internet' and 'etiquette'. The correct form of behaviour to use while working on the internet.

WEB TIP *For more information about netiquette, including a quiz to test your expertise, visit **www.albion.com/netiquette**.*

EXCLUSIVES – KISS & TELLS

If your story is particularly hot, you might want to offer it to a publication as an exclusive. Or a newspaper or magazine might take the initiative and ask you not to speak to anyone else about it.

You need to think carefully about exclusives – a newspaper might promise the earth, but exclusives can end up tripping you up. If you're out to make money, you'll need to sign exclusivity deals – no paper will pay you for your story unless they're the only one carrying the tale.

> **JARGONBUSTER!**
> Exclusive: strictly speaking, a story that is only told to one publication.

But if you're talking to the press for another reason – to publicise your business, for example – exclusives can be counter-productive. If rival newspapers feel they've missed out on a great story, they might be miffed enough to run a counter-story, attacking you or your business. At the very least, they'll be much more receptive to anyone else approaching them with a less than flattering angle.

Kiss and tell stories are almost always told on an exclusive basis. The teller (and indeed kisser) can often command a high price for their story – if it concerns the right celebrity. Anyone who's constantly in the newspapers is likely to be a lucrative target – but usually only if they're married. A romp with a young, free and single celebrity might earn you a few column inches, but it's rarely going to make you rich.

DO think deeply about your motives for telling your story about a celebrity, why you should tell it, and about how it would make you look in the eyes of the world.

You can also offer exclusives by genre – you might promise that you won't speak to any other national newspaper except the *Sun*, but you might also promise to tell your story to *Marie Claire* and no other monthly women's magazine. However, this is dodgy territory and if you're going to stretch the boundaries of exclusivity, you need to make sure everyone concerned is very clear about the deal.

Publicist James Herring is well versed in helping ordinary people who suddenly find themselves in the media spotlight. He handled all the publicity for the first series of Channel 4's Big Brother. *He warns potential kiss and tellers:*

'Be extremely cautious! I think you should always think long and hard before hanging your dirty washing in public for money.

'By selling your story for money, you are inviting people into your personal life and it's hard to reclaim it.

'Bear in mind the long-term consequences; you might have £15,000 in your bank

account, but you're fair game for any media which might want to find out the other side of the story.

'If you hire a publicist to help you make money from your story, they'll be working on a commission. They'll push their fee up by asking you to talk more about a certain area – particularly if your story is a kiss and tell. They might persuade you to pose for some provocative photographs which could embarrass you further down the line.

'There's a big difference between a PR agent who's there to say how using the media will benefit you over a period of time, and somebody who's there to make a quick buck.'

If publications are really badgering you for an exclusive – or you have lots to say or show – you might be able to offer different exclusives to each. You might give one an exclusive picture, while the other gets an exclusive interview. But be careful with this – you're playing with fire.

Not every story has to be an exclusive but don't send a story to one newspaper and then expect another to run the same story a week or a month later. If they know it's appeared elsewhere previously, they'll tell you where to go. If they don't know and they run the story themselves, and then they find out, they'll never speak to you again.

IT'S NOT NEWS – BUT IS IT STILL WORTH READING?

Your story might, of course, not be 'hard' enough to make the news pages – it simply might not be news. But that doesn't mean you're dead in the water. You might still be able to get your story in print. It might be suitable to be one of the following, and you should look through your chosen publication – there might be other categories.

FEATURE General longer article. In newspapers, features are usually carried after the news pages.

REGULAR Look through your target publication and see if your story might fit into one of their regular features; they might run a 'How to ...' or 'Ask the expert' section.

PROFILE Special interview with interesting person – you! Trade papers are particularly fond of profiles. Sometimes they might also do company profiles, about a firm rather than an individual.

OP-ED PIECES/COLUMNS Mid-length articles that are very personal and opinionated.

LETTERS TO THE EDITOR

HOW TO HANDLE THAT PHONE CALL

Phew, we're back on the speaking bit now. You've thought about your story, written your press release and sent it to just the right person. They were delighted to hear from you and they want to interview you.

OR, you've decided that a press release isn't appropriate and it's better to call them.

OR, they've heard about *you* and want to chat.

FINDING YOUR CENTRAL MESSAGE

Before you open your mouth to speak to anyone, make sure you know what you want to say.

Think about your story and imagine you only have 20 seconds to make your point. What would you say?

If you're struggling, why not have a look at the section in chapter 1 which deals with finding your Objective and End Result.

DO sit down and write a list of your key points. Then be ruthless. Keep crossing off the points until you find your Objective and End Result.

DO keep them at the forefront of your mind throughout all your dealings with the media.

DO remind yourself of your Objective and End Result if you falter in your interview, and you'll be back on track.

IF YOU'RE CALLING THEM OUT OF THE BLUE

The first and most important thing is to make sure you've got the timing right – if you haven't read the section 'Get the timing right' on page 180, have a scan through it first. When phoning, timing is even more important. The time of your call can make all the difference between a friendly chat and a curt exchange.

Daily newspapers often have much shorter deadlines – although even they plan features and supplements way ahead of time. But shorter deadlines mean more intense deadlines. Ring reception and ask what is a good time to call a journalist.

Most national newspapers have their main news meeting at around 11 am. If you have a piece of news for the following day's paper, call the journalist before 11 am, so they can put your story on the main news list.

After that, the best time to call is between about 12 noon and 2.30 pm. Later, news journalists tend to come under pressure from deadlines and won't be so free to talk. Also, the later you leave it, the harder it is to squeeze stories in to the following day's paper.

Features writers are generally more flexible – call any time from around 10 am.

WHATEVER YOU DO, DON'T PHONE WITH NON-URGENT NEWS AROUND 11 am.

DON'T try to engage them in a friendly chat unless they start it.

DON'T fix meetings if you could have told them over the phone or in an email.

DO suggest lunch or a drink and then leave it up to them if you're keen to set up a relationship.

DO remember that most journalists are being pulled in 1,001 directions.

Get prepared – even if you've written a press release, have that in front of you. If you've decided not to write one, jot down what you want to say – nerves can often make you stammer, stutter and wander off the subject.

WHAT IF THEY CALL YOU?

James Herring suggests: *'If you're planning to phone a journalist, or you are expecting a call from the press, sit down first and write down exactly what you want to get across.*

'But if a journalist calls you, never feel you have to give an immediate response. It's fine to say you'll call back. You can ask them to give you all their questions over the phone, and say you'll call back with your response. The fact that you did will never appear in print and is a perfectly reasonable practice.'

In 99.99 per cent of cases, if a journalist calls you, it will be about something perfectly innocent. However, they might well be up against a deadline and putting pressure on you to answer their questions immediately. If you can, all well and good, but if you feel your personal or business reputation is at stake, you have a right to ask for a few minutes to consider your answer.

Ask the journalist to give you all the questions they're planning to ask, note them down, then ask them what the deadline is. Collect your thoughts – maybe make a few notes – and call back as soon as you can.

Keep your answers clear and to the point – if they don't ask you about a point you consider important, don't forget to bring it up yourself, and explain why it's so vital. If you are being interviewed for a news story, a journalist will normally take about 10 or 15 minutes to chat to you over the phone.

If a longer feature is planned, the journalist may want to meet you face to face. If they do conduct the interview over the phone, you might be talking for around 45 minutes, although it really depends on the publication and the subject-matter.

HELP!

I've got something to hide and I don't want to talk to any journalists.

If you possibly can, it's always better to give journalists something, rather than nothing. Saying 'no comment' comes across badly. The public view the words suspiciously and wonder what you've got to hide.

If the reporter really has hit a raw nerve, or they are questioning you about something that really must remain secret, the best thing to do is to prepare a statement. You already know that you don't have to answer questions immediately. Take the journalist's number, find out their deadline and prepare a statement. Keep it brief and unambiguous.

If the subject is legally sensitive, you might want to consult a lawyer before speaking.

'I regret that, for legal reasons, I am unable to comment on the rumours …'

'I'm sorry, but it's company policy not to comment on speculation about financial matters.'

These are both reasonable responses. Look in any newspaper and you'll see real-life examples.

If you can't talk about an issue yet, but will be able to later, offer to let the journalist know when you can discuss it.

DON'T agree to call back and then never do so.

DON'T simply make yourself unavailable.

DO ask someone else to call back and read your statement to the journalist. Even if you give a statement, a journalist will still try to wheedle more out of you. If you don't think you'll be able to remain

strong in the face of such questioning, by all means ask someone else to act as your spokesperson.

And, whatever else you do, DON'T LIE!

Never, ever, ever lie to the media.

James Herring says: *'Never lie to the media. You cannot lie to the media without it bouncing back to get you sooner or later. If you get found out – and you will – you'll lose everyone's respect, including the respect of any media who might have considered you a trustworthy source in the future. You'll have blown your opportunity.'*

SIMPLE DOS & DONT'S

Do tell the truth.

Do make sure the journalist or interviewer knows how to spell and pronounce your name.

Do make sure the journalist or interviewer knows your job title and company, or your position within the campaign – whatever background information is appropriate.

Do prepare for any interview by thinking about what questions are likely to be asked.

Do mug up on facts and figures – have them written down if you think you might forget.

Do try to chat to the interviewer or journalist beforehand, to make sure they're au fait with the subject.

Don't try to tell them anything off the record – this is very dangerous and different people sometimes have different interpretations of what 'off the record' means.

Don't ask to see the copy before it is published or broadcast. Most journalists will be highly offended by this. If they want you to see it – or any part of it – to check matters of fact, they'll ask you.

Don't let your emotions get the better of you – especially anger and especially if it's directed at the journalist. If your story is sad and you become upset, that's different, but take a deep breath and try to pull yourself together – you're there because you have something to say – don't waste your opportunity. Cry all you like after the interview.

Don't criticise those who disagree with you. Name-calling just comes across as childish and will take the focus away from the issues.

Do retain good manners and good humour throughout, however rattled you might be.

MAKING THE MOST OF YOUR MEDIA TIME

- Think before you speak – as with any form of public speaking, your adrenalin will be rushing about. A pause may seem like an age to you, but is likely to come across as thoughtfulness to the audience or the reporter.

- Keep it short – if you can make it catchy, so much the better. All journalists love a sound bite.

> **JARGONBUSTER!**
> Sound bite: a short extract of recorded (now also reported) speech which is particularly catchy and quotable. It tends to sum up a situation or feeling in just a few words.

- If you have something technical, medical or otherwise complicated to explain, think about how you can do this in simple language, but without being patronising.

- Avoid jargon, obscure references or acronyms.

- Try not to get dragged into meaningless hypothetical discussions – 'what if's – just discuss the here and now.

- Talk about your area of expertise and then shut up. Don't be dragged into subjects you don't know a lot about.

- If the journalist gets something wrong when they're asking you a question, correct the mistake then answer the question.

- Answer the question you want to answer. If you're asked a mischievous question, rephrase it into something you're happy with. Don't fumble about because someone asks you the equivalent of 'When did you stop beating your wife?'.

- If they keep on at you, repeating the question, keep on repeating your answer. You may change the words, but make it clear that you're simply reinforcing your point.

- Make sure you say important names – like the name of your company or organisation.

- If you're acting as a spokesperson for your company, organisation or campaign, reporters and the public won't distinguish between your personal opinion and the opinion of the organisation you represent. Don't get drawn into giving your personal opinions.

EXAMPLES OF SOUND BITES

'Ask not what your country can do for you, rather what you can do for your country'

'She was the People's Princess'

'There were three people in that marriage'

'I have a dream'

Don't work up to your point – work backwards. Say the most important thing first and then fill in the background if you get the chance.

Don't give one-word answers – it'll look as if you have something to hide, or at the very least like you're being awkward.

Don't guess or bluff. If you don't know, say so – but say you'll try to find out.

Don't refuse to answer unless you can help it. If you can't help it, explain why you can't answer the question: there's a legal reason; there are market sensitivities; it's too early to say, etc.

SPECIAL ADVICE FOR TELEVISION AND RADIO

Although the preceding advice has concentrated on newspapers and the rest of the printed press, pretty much all of it applies equally to television and radio. If you're being interviewed for a news piece, you'll probably only be on camera for five or ten minutes. The crew may well prefer to come to you for the filming – which at least gives you a home advantage. Although the interview will be over quickly, it can take some time to set up lights and angles, etc. Make sure you allow plenty of time for the interview. Radio interviews are usually done over the phone, and often take only five or ten minutes.

> ☞ You're the expert on your topic. Be confident. Keep your tone of voice conversational.

If you are asked to go to the television or radio studios, the researcher (or whoever you speak to) should be able to give you an idea of how long you'll be there. But don't schedule a vital meeting immediately afterwards – these things invariably over-run.

As well as finding out how long it should take, find out everything you can about the programme concerned.

Then ask yourself:

- Do I understand exactly what's expected of me?
- Can I speak knowledgeably on this subject?

Rehearse your answers, rope in friends, family or colleagues as sounding boards, and tape yourself.

CHECKLIST

Ask yourself the following questions:

Firstly, and rather obviously, which programme is
   inviting me to speak? If you're not familiar with
   the programme, ask for tapes. ❏

Is it live or pre-recorded? ❏

How long will the interview take? ❏

Where will the recording take place? If you're unfamiliar
   with the location, ask if they'll send a car for you –
   or plan your route carefully and allow plenty of time. ❏

What time do I need to be there? ❏

When will the programme be broadcast, and on
   which channel or station? ❏

Who will be interviewing me? ❏

Will I meet the interviewer beforehand? ❏

Are there other people being interviewed? Who are they?
   If you don't know the other panellists, or
   interviewees, ask for a biog, or more information. ❏

Am I being pitted against the other interviewee
   as presenting two opposing arguments? ❏

- If you're appearing on the radio, a simple tape recorder will do.

- If you're going on television, try to borrow or hire a video
  camera.

- Play the tape back and look at it with a critical eye. If you have a problem with your voice, see the section on 'Your voice' in chapter 6.

- If you have odd physical mannerisms, look up the relevant sections in chapter 6.

DON'T read from a prepared statement. Assume you're being taped from the moment you get there until the moment you leave.

DON'T ramble on but give them enough material to use.

DO practise answering questions in 20 seconds or less. They'll probably use 20-second chunks anyway, so practise squeezing your message into these chunks.

DO practice what you want to say.

DO correct any mistakes politely and try not to be fazed by interruptions. Ask to be allowed to finish and give a proper answer to the question.

DON'T argue with the reporter. Correct mistakes but keep a sense of perspective. Often, the reporter will have been instructed to try to wind you up. Don't fall for it!

DON'T waffle. When you've answered a question, shut up. It's hugely tempting to blather on to avoid silence, but don't!

DON'T answer a question with a question. If you're asked, 'What do you think about educating disabled children alongside the able-bodied?', don't say, 'What do you mean by disabled?' Either you'll sound aggressive or evasive.

DO take a deep breath and start your answer again if you're not being interviewed live and you make a mistake. It will seem weird but they will be able to edit out the first attempt. Don't ruin this by apologising at length. (I bet the interviewer fluffs at least one question and he's supposed to be the professional!)

DON'T worry if they ask you to run through your answer two, three or even more times. It happens all the time and they won't lose patience. Honestly! It might not even be your fault – there might be a problem with the equipment. Be grateful that you'll have several opportunities to practise making your point.

DO simply stop and say 'I'm sorry, I haven't answered that very well – let me try again' if you make a mistake when you're being interviewed live. They've invited you there to put across your point of view, so they'll be pleased if you do so clearly and concisely.

I worked in television for several years and I've been to many recordings and shoots. Even the most professional, experienced and admired presenters make mistakes – all the time. And even if you're an avid fan of *It'll Be Alright On The Night*, you'd still be shocked if you could see how many takes are needed to get something right. After a while, presenters stop worrying and just concentrate on getting it right. Take a leaf out of their book and make mistakes like a pro!

SPECIAL TV TIPS

Get there early but expect to start late and finish late. TV is *always* late. But they'll scream blue murder if *you're* late. Check the following for help on what to wear.

Dress smartly from head to toe, just in case they film a long shot of you. But remember that the camera will probably only focus on your head and shoulders – don't wear anything fussy, revealing (unless you're doing it on purpose) or bulky. Stick to simple lines. Wear something that's comfortable.

Avoid very short skirts – you might be seated for the interview. At best, it could be unflattering (squashed-up cellulite never looks good). At worst you could 'do a Sharon Stone', if you know what I mean. Also avoid bright colours – they might clash with the set and jump out at the viewer – and never wear busy patterns, or contrasty stripes and small checks – the camera won't be able to cope and you'll look like a bizarre kind of kaleidoscope. Don't wear high contrasts like black and white, for the same reason.

Plain colours in flattering, soft shades are best. Black can make you look like you're in mourning – viewers switching on halfway through might think a member of the royal family has died, or something. Avoid too much jewellery – noises that in real life sound like tinkles and clinks will be amplified into clunking great crashes that will drown out your words of wisdom.

Remember Tony Blair at the 2000 Labour Party conference: TV lights are hot stuff and they make you sweat. Wear deodorant, choose a lightweight suit and if you have a real tendency to perspire, wear a plain white T-shirt under your shirt. It will soak up a lot of yukky sweat.

Empty your pockets – odd bulges will only look worse on television – and if you're wearing a tie, straighten it. If you're wearing trousers, make sure your socks are long enough so you're not showing a flash of leg. Make sure your shirt is tucked in. Turn off your mobile or pager – or leave it in another room.

WHAT ABOUT HAIR AND MAKEUP?

Make sure your hair is clean, and style it so it's off your face. Overlong fringes or weird wispy bits will throw funny shadows and the viewers will think you're ready for Hallowe'en.

Just wear your normal makeup – if you need more, they'll organise that. If you're a man, they'll powder you if you're looking shiny, so don't worry.

HELP! MY BODY HAS TURNED AGAINST ME!

VOICE See the section on 'Your voice' in chapter 6.

The sound man will ask you to speak so that he can get his 'levels'.

Now is the time to use your normal voice at its normal level. And sit in the position you're going to sit in during the interview.

It doesn't really matter what you say to set your
level – no one cares. Most people say their name
and where they're from. Some say a few lines of a
nursery rhyme or poem.

During the interview, try to sit more or less still,
without looking as if you're practising for musical
statues. The levels have been set, so there's no need
to lean into the mike. If your voice is wavering
about because of nerves, try some of the relaxation
and breathing exercises in this book.

> **JARGONBUSTER!**
> Levels: sound equipment
> has gauges that show
> the amount of sound
> being picked up.
> The sound man can
> set each microphone
> to the right level,
> so that you'll be heard
> properly, without
> deafening anyone.

HANDS If you're sitting at a desk, put your hands on top of it. If you
don't have a desk but you're sitting down, fold your hands in your lap
– hiding your hands will at best make you look shifty; at worst like
you're fiddling with yourself.

If you're standing up, don't cross your arms. Hands in pockets can
look casual – maybe too casual, depending on the circumstances. If you
feel really uncomfortable, try holding a book, or file, or something
relevant. If you still feel uncomfortable, ask if you can do the interview
sitting down.

DON'T be afraid to gesticulate. But,

**DON'T wave your fist, point or make any rude signs. It comes across
terribly badly on television.**

LEGS Sit up straight. Don't swivel about. If you cross your legs, it will
make your thighs look fat. And if you uncross them on camera, you'll
look like that Kenny Everett character who waved 'her' legs around like
a windmill. Or like Sharon Stone in *Fatal Attraction*. This might be
a good idea if you're launching a career as a topless model but isn't so
wise for the rest of us.

**DO either cross your legs at the ankles or keep your feet together,
sliding one slightly ahead of the other. A good trick is to swivel your
knees to one side – it's the most flattering way to sit.**

DO lean forward very slightly in your chair. Slouching back will make you look uninterested or afraid.

DO try sitting in front of a mirror in your chosen outfit – find the best way to sit and make sure your slip isn't going to show.

DON'T leap to your feet as soon as you've finished speaking. We've all seen that done and it's excruciating. Just sit still, exactly where you are and look poised.

DON'T face squarely on to the camera if you do have to stand. If you swivel your body round slightly, you will look slimmer – and don't forget, the camera adds about 10 pounds, so most of us need all the help we can get!

Here's how to do it:

- Stand with your right foot in front of the other.

- Imagine your feet are the hands of a clock – but six inches or so apart.

- Point your right foot to 12 o'clock.

- Point your left foot to 10 o'clock.

- Put slightly more weight on your right foot (you can switch this around to the other side, if you feel more comfortable).

This stance is very solid, so you'll look slim *and* you won't fall over. Bonus!

TORSO Don't sway or rock, and keep your shoulders back.

HEAD Hold it high and don't wave it about. Nod if you agree, by all means.

EYES Look at the journalist – pay attention at all times, because if the camera picks up your wandering gaze, it will make you look shifty. Unless you're looking up at the sky, which will make you look like you're pleading with God. Or you're looking at the ground, which will make you look like you're either asleep or praying. And never try to look into the camera. It will make you look like a newsreader. Or Uri Geller.

DON'T gaze around the studio (however fascinating it might be and however many people are running around).

DON'T avoid eye contact with the journalist.

DO wear your glasses if you need to. The lighting man will fix it so there's not too much glare from the lenses. But you won't be able to wear photochromic lenses because they'll just go dark as soon as the lights go on and you'll look like an ageing Hollywood star or a boxer the morning after the fight.

ENTIRE BODY If you feel like you've lost control of your entire body, it's probably stress. As opposed to St Vitus's Dance or some kind of fit. Be aware of how you behave during stress – you might need to ask someone else. If you're aware that you normally tap your foot, fiddle with your hair or grimace, you'll be less likely to do it.

DEALING WITH DIFFICULT QUESTIONS

As I've already said, the overwhelming majority of journalists are honest and accurate.

But there are a few bad apples – if your subject has anything to do with politics, you might find yourself on the opposite side to the journalist, for example. Although they are supposed to be unbiased, some can't and others simply won't be. There are also times when even good journalists might feel the need to give you a hard time. Let's go through some of the tricky bits.

LOADED QUESTIONS

The journalist builds his case by making a number of statements and then comes in with the killer: the loaded question.

'The local education authorities have suffered a major cutback in funding this year. Most schools don't have enough books or computer equipment. Why should we spend so much money adapting one village school for one child?'

WHAT SHOULD I SAY? Start by either rejecting or accepting the statements and then link to your Objective.

'In fact, local authorities have been given additional grants for computer equipment, which frees cash for other areas of spending this year. However, we accept that they are not prepared to spend the money on these adaptations. But we think there's an important issue at the heart of this – and that's the right of physically disabled children to be part of mainstream education. And that's why we've launched the fund-raising campaign – so that Kerry, and other children like her, can go to the school of their choice.'

HOBSON'S CHOICE

The reporter asks you to choose between two extremes, neither of which is desirable.

'Would you prefer the licence fee to be spent on obscure arts programmes that fall into the public service remit or should the BBC devote the cash to popular shows that win big audiences?'

WHAT SHOULD I SAY? Don't feel you have to plump for one or the other. Say you reject both arguments and return to your Objective.

'Neither of those options is acceptable on its own. As part of the BBC's public service remit, it has to serve all kinds of audiences and we feel we distribute the licence fee effectively. Just because a programme has a smaller audience, it doesn't mean we shouldn't serve that audience. We just need to be as sensible as we've always been.'

HYPOTHETICALS

The reporter creates a hypothetical situation and follows up with a question.

'Imagine a big multinational company has offered to donate £10,000 to your environment group, but you know they are one of the biggest polluters in the area?'

WHAT SHOULD I SAY? Don't get pulled into the hypothetical – you could end up tying yourself in knots. Revert to your Objective if possible.

'Nothing like that has ever happened. You seem to be asking about where we get our funds from. Our members pay an annual subscription and help us by staging fund-raising events. These moneys and any other donations are clearly shown in our accounts, which can be viewed by anyone at our website – *Environment.com*.'

THE DOG WITH A BONE

The reporter won't give it up and keeps coming back to you with the same question.

'But what if they really offered you a lot of money? Wouldn't it be immoral to refuse?'

WHAT SHOULD I SAY? Don't fall into the trap of giving them what they want, either to make them happy or to shut them up. Rephrase your answer if you want, but remember your Objective.

'I can't really comment on situations that don't exist. We are entirely open about our funding and always strive to work towards our aim of protecting the environment. That's our main concern – and at the moment we're particularly concerned about the amount of pollution in the sea and the filth washing up on British beaches.'

COMMENT ON A COMMENT ON A COMMENT

Stories can sometimes spin out of control because no one has bothered to find out the true facts, which are now buried under a mountain of hype, misquotes and misinformation.

'What do you think about Fred Benson's accusation that you are out of touch and inefficient?'

WHAT SHOULD I SAY? If you didn't directly hear someone make a particular comment, don't be drawn into commenting on it yourself. The comments may have been taken out of context. Try to go back to your Objective.

'Fred has certainly never said anything like that to me! I've worked with Fred for years and if he has any criticisms I'm sure he wouldn't hold back in coming and saying them straight to me!' Then link back to your Objective.

UNITED WE STAND!

A journalist might try to cause trouble by exposing (or creating) a split within your organisation.

'Don't you think £2 million is a hell of a lot to have spent on the brand-new office building?'

WHAT SHOULD I SAY? If you're not the expert on a particular area, say so. If asked about something that falls into a colleague's remit, refer the journalist back to the right person.

'I only control my own budget – you'd have to speak to Malcolm Williams about the new office! I do know that Malcolm has substantially increased my own budget this year and I'm delighted that it's meant I can invest in 200 extra hours of programming, including a fantastic adaptation of *Wuthering Heights*, which starts next Sunday at 8 pm.'

THAT'S JUST PLAIN WRONG!

The reporter asks you a question based on totally incorrect information, or information you perceive as wrong.

'When are schools going to get the funding they deserve?'

WHAT SHOULD I SAY? Correct them straight away, or the audience might accept the information or inference. Go back to your Objective.

'I'm convinced that schools already receive a good level of funding.

The budget went up 15 per cent above inflation this year and we've been able to equip 15 more schools with brand-new computer equipment.'

THE TWISTER

The reporter twists your words to turn them back on you.

'You mean our children have been struggling with poor equipment until now?'

WHAT SHOULD I SAY? Restate your comment, or expand on it, so there's no misunderstanding.

'Let me make myself clear: school equipment in our area is already well above the national average. But the extra money has meant we've achieved our target of having five pupils to each computer. The national average is eight pupils per computer.'

DON'T PUT WORDS IN MY MOUTH!

Don't repeat negative words. Journalists sometimes ask aggressive and negative questions.

'Many people have complained that the standard of teaching today is appalling. What do you say to them?'

WHAT SHOULD I SAY? Well, what you *shouldn't* say is, *'I don't think the standard of teaching is appalling.'* They could edit out the question and it will sound as if you brought it up. Always turn it round and emphasise the positive.

'You'll see from the last set of exam results that pupils are getting higher grades than ever before.'

ONE THING AFTER ANOTHER

The reporter asks you a whole lot of questions, all at once.

WHAT SHOULD I SAY? Just answer the one you want to answer – the one that will link most easily to your Objective.

☞ No matter how hot your story, always remember, the press is doing you a favour, not the other way round. Don't call them saying: 'I'd like to place a story with you' or 'I'd like some editorial'.

INTERRUPTING

The journalist fires another question while you're only halfway through answering the previous one.

What should I say? Don't forget the rule that you should always be polite. Just ask that you be allowed to finish answering the last question first.

DEAD AIR

You finish your answer but the reporter says nothing and there's a big, fat embarrassing silence.

WHAT SHOULD I SAY? Nothing at all. They're controlling the interview so it's their problem. If you really feel uncomfortable, why not say: 'Does that answer your question?'

THE KNOCK

The reporter comes to your house or your office and either knocks on your door or ambushes you just outside.

WHAT SHOULD I SAY? We've all seen this on the television – on *Watchdog* and *Roger Cook*, etc. What do you think of the people who run away? You think they're scoundrels with something to hide, right? And what about the people who answer pleasantly, or appear later in the studio? You might think they've done something wrong, but you don't think they're crooks. They'll probably try to put it right.

If you get ambushed, resist the temptation to run away. It doesn't matter how busy or surprised you are, turn and face the journalist.

Use the tips for when a journalist phones you out of the blue – ask them what they want, what questions they need to ask and when they need to hear from you. Tell them when you'll be able to get back to them – AND DO IT.

If you really can't discuss the matter, call the journalist and tell them you are going to issue a statement (see above for tips on making a statement). You can either read this on camera or to the mike, or you can simply send it to the journalist. For reporters from newspapers or magazines it's obviously fine to send a written statement. For broadcast media, it's better to appear on camera, or, for radio, read the statement to the reporter. Be firm about supplementary questions and say, 'I'm sorry, I've given you my statement. I really can't say any more about it at this stage, for the reasons I've already mentioned. I'll be happy to talk to you further when this becomes public.'

If you can grant an interview and you're confident about handling it then and there, why not invite the journalist in? You will look much more professional if you are interviewed at your desk, on home territory, than if you give an interview in the car park, with your hair being blown about by the wind and with your hands full of papers, briefcase and mobile phone. By inviting the reporter in, you are also giving a subliminal message that you have nothing to hide.

They have tried to surprise you, but you can take control of the situation.

It's not uncommon for reporters to ambush a news source outside their office or home. Respond as if the reporter had called you on the phone. You might ask what the story is about and when they need the information. Tell the reporter when you or someone else will be able to get back to them. You are not obligated to consent to the ambush interview if you are unprepared or the time is inconvenient.

HMM, THAT'S A TOUGHIE!

The journalist asks you a very difficult question – it's not that you don't know the answer, it's finding the right way to say it.

WHAT SHOULD I SAY? Simply pause for thought. As we have discovered before, pauses seem worse to you than to anyone listening. If you're being interviewed for a newspaper, the reporter can't *write* a pause. And they're unlikely even to mention that you paused.

And if you are doing a recorded broadcast interview, pauses are usually edited out.

Even if it is live, you'll simply look thoughtful. Which you are. The chances are, the audience will recognise that it's a difficult subject and they'll respect you for giving it due thought.

EMERGENCIES, ACCIDENTS & INCIDENTS

It may be that your company is somehow involved in an accident – a gas explosion in the office, for example. I know these are horrible thoughts but you might be involved in an accident – or you might witness a crime or a crash.

You might be a member of the services, called to a major incident and it suddenly falls to you to speak to the waiting press.

Whatever the emergency, it's a difficult situation. Emotions may be running high – if people are injured, survivors and relatives will be angry and looking for someone to blame. The media will be on even tighter deadlines than usual and the niceties might go straight out of the window.

Keep a cool head, remember a few golden rules and you'll get through.

SHOULDN'T I BE DOING SOMETHING MORE USEFUL?

In an emergency, you might feel that you'd be better off elsewhere – and you might also think the media would be better off elsewhere – anywhere except here, making matters worse! You might rather be in the thick of things, carrying on helping people. You might rather be with your colleagues, finding out what the hell went wrong. You might rather be at the hospital, finding out if your own friends or family are all right.

But if you're there in an official capacity (not just as a witness), you really are doing something useful if you're making the necessary statement to the press.

Remember that relatives might be worried and they're going to get their information from the media. If they don't hear what's going on, they too might come to the scene and hamper the rescue or clean-up.

Give the media clear, concise, regular messages to keep them off your back and give everyone the information to which they have a right.

If the emergency services are involved, special systems will swing into action and phone lines will be manned by spokespeople. But journalists will always prefer to speak to someone at the scene than to a trained spokesperson in a cosy warm office.

They will grab witnesses, bystanders, survivors – anyone. And sometimes rumour and conjecture can dramatically exaggerate the scale of the problem. Keep things under control by giving calm, factual briefings whenever you have new information.

PEOPLE ARE NUMBER ONE

Whatever has happened, remember that people should be your number one concern. Mention victims or survivors first and decline to comment about other matters, such as money.

If someone has been injured, her mother won't thank you for talking about how much it's going to cost you to sort out the damage.

BE REALISTIC

Just as you shouldn't allow an accident to be hyped out of control by rumours and speculation, don't try to play down a tragedy.

DON'T SPECULATE

As soon as there's an accident of any kind, reporters will want to know if anyone was hurt and how badly. The second thing they'll want to know is how it happened.

DON'T get drawn into speculation. Simply say that you are investigating as a matter of urgency and you will let them know as soon as there are any conclusions.

The public enquiries for the rail disasters of the last few years have made their reports months and even years after the tragedies. In the aftermath of accidents – such as the Concorde crash in Paris – the newspapers are full of possible causes. But if *you* jump the gun and start speculating, you may look foolish or cause more panic.

DON'T BLAME INDIVIDUALS OR GROUPS

This is an extension of the previous point. Don't attempt to lay blame with anyone personally. Don't discuss previous incidents or problems. If these are relevant, they will emerge in the fullness of time. If they're not, you risk a serious libel action.

> **JARGONBUSTER!**
> Biog: what the rest of us might call a CV. Your real CV condensed into a few sentences – a useful reference for journalists.

If someone in your company or organisation has been arrested, do not discuss their previous behaviour record. Such information could prejudice a fair trial and you'll find yourself in the dock, too.

DO say: 'I have a story you might be interested in' or 'I'm going to send you my biog. I just wanted to let you know that if you're doing any stories about x, I might be able to help, or comment.'

WEB TIP   *My favourite place for links to sites packed with media tips is www.newsbureau.com.*

SUMMARY

If you don't get much coverage, don't be disheartened. Think about why your story or interview wasn't used, or was cut to almost nothing.

If you really, hand on heart, think you've done everything right, remember there might have been another reason.

It might have been a busy news day; the next time might be a slow day. The subject-matter might have been unfashionable; it might come back into the spotlight (or you could make it more current). The news editor who was on duty that day might not have liked it, but their colleague might love it and will run your next story. You might have happened upon one of the editor's pet hates. The journalist might have filed a badly written story because they had a headache – they'll get better. The sub-editor might have been having a bad day.

But don't be put off.

James Herring says: *'Ultimately, journalists are in the business of finding news and entertaining their readership. You shouldn't be scared of approaching them with your story.*

'This is especially true if you want to talk to them about your business, or a charity venture. Most journalists will be very glad to hear from you.

'Usually someone, somewhere will want to know your story – even if it's a straightforward "local boy done good" piece for your local paper.

'And once you've got it in print, it's much easier to get in print again.

'Don't be scared of the media – use it. It's there for you.'

11

PROBLEMS AND
TROUBLESHOOTING

- LIBEL & SLANDER
- HECKLING
- NERVES
- PROBLEMS WITH THE VENUE
- WHEN MACHINERY LETS YOU DOWN

This is the chapter to read if you've got problems. Well, with public speaking anyway. It's a general rule of life that if something can go wrong, it will. Don't be disheartened. There is seldom a problem that can't be sorted out with a little thought and enough determination.

Many of the problems you might encounter have been covered in previous chapters, but it does no harm to recap and stress that you can overcome them!

LIBEL & SLANDER

The law on libel and slander – collectively known as 'defamation' – is so complicated that this book can only give you a rough guide to the main pitfalls. If you're anxious to say something and you're concerned it could be defamatory, make an appointment to see your nearest friendly libel lawyer.

WHAT DOES 'DEFAMATION' MEAN?

The lawyer-speak definition of defamation is that the law recognises that every woman/man has the right to have the estimation in which he stands in the opinion of others unaffected by false and defamatory statements and imputations.

Stripped down to the bare minimum, it covers anything said or written about a person that makes you think less of him/her.

A defamatory statement is one which does one of the following to the person it's about:

1 exposes them to hatred, ridicule or contempt

2 causes them to be shunned or avoided

3 lowers them in the estimation of right-thinking members of society generally

4 disparages them in their business, trade, office or profession

If it's written down (or permanent, such as a picture), it's libel. If it's spoken it's slander. The only exceptions are that defamatory statements made on television, radio or in a play count as libel.

The trouble with the definition of libel is that no one has been able to think up a form of words that explains it all properly, covering all eventualities. One of the main problems relates to that phrase in point 3: 'right-thinking members of society generally'. When a lawyer is deciding whether something is defamatory, they try to think what this imaginary person might possibly think. And with changing times comes a changing 'right-thinking' person. What was defamatory 20 years ago might not be so now. So you can see how these things are open to different interpretations.

As I said before, this is a hugely complicated legal issue – far too complicated to go into here. Just beware that even repeating something that's already been said on television or written in a newspaper could find you in extremely hot water.

If you want to know more about slander, and defamation laws in general, try McNae's Essential Law for Journalists, published by Butterworths, for a concise no-nonsense explanation.

HECKLING

See chapter 7, page 114, 'Dealing with difficult people'.

NERVES

See chapter 6, page 89, Nerves.

PROBLEMS WITH THE VENUE

See chapter 5, page 78, 'Coping with the venue'.

WHEN MACHINERY LETS YOU DOWN

See chapter 4, page 48, 'Words are not enough'.

12
CONCLUSION

Well, good luck with it. I hope this book has helped boost your speaking confidence – and given you a few new ideas and tips to help.

If you only bought it in the hope of making your point more clearly in meetings, I hope your horizons are now somewhat wider.

Remember – there's nothing to it!

At the very beginning of the book, I gave you a tip and told you to remember it, even if you forgot everything else:

Who? What? Why? When? Where? How?

Well, I'm actually going to ask you to remember one more tip, as well. It's my best public speaking tip, boiled right down to its simplest form. It's just:

STAND UP, SPEAK UP and SHUT UP.

USEFUL QUOTATIONS

ABILITY

FORBES, Malcolm S. (1919–1990)
Ability will never catch up with the demand for it.

NAPOLEON I (1769–1821)
Men take only their needs into consideration, never their abilities.

LA ROCHEFOUCAULD (1613–1680)
There is great ability in knowing how to conceal one's ability.

SHAW, George Bernard (1856–1950)
Martyrdom is the only way a man can become famous without ability.

WILDE, Oscar (1854–1900)
I think that God, in creating man, somewhat overestimated his ability.

ACCIDENTS

BENCHLEY, Robert (1889–1945)
My only solution for the problem of habitual accidents is for everybody to stay in bed all day. Even then, there is always the chance that you will fall out.
[*Chips off the Old Bentley*]

WILKES, John (1727–1797)
The chapter of accidents is the longest chapter in the book.
[Attr.]

ACTION

ARISTOTLE (384–322 BC)
Our actions determine our dispositions.
[*Nicomachean Ethics*]

BERGSON, Henri Louis (1859–1941)
Think like a man of action, act like a man of thought.

BLAKE, William (1757–1827)
He who desires but acts not, breeds pestilence.

CARNEGIE, Andrew (1835–1919)
As I grow older, I pay less attention to what men say. I just watch what they do.

DE GAULLE, Charles (1890–1970)
Deliberation is the work of many men. Action, of one alone.
[*War Memoirs*]

HUXLEY, T.H. (1825–1895)
The great end of life is not knowledge but action.
[*Science and Culture* (1877)]

SHAW, George Bernard (1856–1950)
Activity is the only road to knowledge.
[*Man and Superman* (1903)]

ADVERSITY

HAZLITT, William (1778–1830)
Prosperity is a great teacher; adversity a greater.

HORACE (65–8 BC)
Adversity has the effect of eliciting talents, which in prosperous circumstances would have lain dormant.

ADVICE

ADAMS, Douglas (1952–2001)
Don't panic.
[*The Hitch Hiker's Guide to the Galaxy* (1979)]

BURTON, Robert (1577–1640)
Who cannot give good counsel? 'tis cheap, it costs them nothing.
[*Anatomy of Melancholy* (1621)]

COSBY, Bill (1937–)
A word to the wise ain't necessary – it's the stupid ones who need the advice.

HORACE (65–8 BC)
A good scare is worth more than good advice.

LA ROCHEFOUCAULD (1613–1680)
One gives nothing so generously as advice.
[*Maximes* (1678)]

STEINBECK, John (1902–1968)
No one wants advice – only corroboration.
[Attr.]

WILDE, Oscar (1854–1900)
The only thing to do with good advice is to pass it on. It is never of any use to oneself.

AGE

ALLEN, Woody (1935–)
I recently turned sixty. Practically a third of my life is over.
[*The Observer Review*, 1996]

BENNY, Jack (1894–1974)
Age is strictly a case of mind over matter. If you don't mind, it doesn't matter.
[*New York Times*, February 1974]

CHEVALIER, Maurice (1888–1972)
I prefer old age to the alternative.
[Attr.]

DAY, Doris (1924–)
The really frightening thing about middle age is the knowledge that you'll grow out of it.
[A. E. Hotchner *Doris Day: Her Own Story* (1976)]

HOPE, Bob (1903–2003)
I don't generally feel anything until noon, then it's time for my nap.
[*International Herald Tribune*, 1990]

MARX, Groucho (1895–1977)
Age is not a particularly interesting subject. Anyone can get old. All you have to do is live long enough.
[*Groucho and Me* (1959)]

ORWELL, George (1903–1950)
At 50, everyone has the face he deserves.
[*Notebook*, 1949]

REAGAN, Ronald (1911–)
I am delighted to be with you. In fact, at my age, I am delighted to be anywhere.
[Speech at the Oxford Union, 1992]

SANTAYANA, George (1863–1952)
The young man who has not wept is a savage, and the old man who will not laugh is a fool.
[*Dialogues in Limbo* (1925)]

SEXTON, Anne (1928–1974)
In a dream you are never eighty.
['Old' (1962)]

TUCKER, Sophie (1884–1966)
[Asked, when 80, the secret of longevity] Keep breathing.
[Attr.]

WORDSWORTH, William (1770–1850)
The wiser mind
Mourns less for what age takes away
Than what it leaves behind.
['The Fountain' (1800)]

ALCOHOL

BECON, Thomas (1512–1567)
For when the wine is in, the wit is out.
[*Catechism* (1560)]

BEHAN, Brendan (1923–1964)
I only take a drink on two occasions – when I'm thirsty and when I'm not.
[In McCnn, *The Wit of Brendan Behan*]

BELLOC, Hilaire (1870–1953)
Strong Brother in God and last Companion: Wine.
[*Short Talks with the Dead and Others* (1926)]

BENCHLEY, Robert (1889–1945)
[Reply when asked if he realised that drinking was a slow death]
So who's in a hurry?
[Attr.]

BURNS, Robert (1759–1796)
Freedom and whisky gang thegither,
Tak aff your dram!
['The Author's Earnest Cry and Prayer' (1786)]

BURTON, Sir Richard (1925–1984)
I have to think hard to name an interesting man who does not drink.

CONNOLLY, Billy (1942–)
A well-balanced person has a drink in each hand.
[*Gullible's Travels*]

COOPER, Derek (1925–)
[Highland saying]
One whisky is all right; two is too much; three is too few.
[*A Taste of Scotch* (1989)]

COPE, Wendy (1945–)
All you need is love, love
or, failing that, alcohol.
[Variation on a Lennon and McCartney song]

FIELDS, W.C. (1880–1946)
I cook with wine, sometimes I even add it to the food.
[Attr.]

FLOYD, Keith (1943–)
All my life I have been a very thirsty person.
[*The Sunday Times*, February 2001]

JOHNSON, Samuel (1709–1784)
Claret is the liquor for boys; port for men; but he who aspires to be a hero must drink brandy.
[In Boswell, *The Life of Samuel Johnson* (1791)]

MENCKEN, H.L. (1880–1956)
I've made it a rule never to drink by daylight and never to refuse a drink after dark.
[*New York Post*,1945]

NASH, Ogden (1902–1971)
Candy
Is dandy
But liquor
Is quicker.
['Reflections on Ice-Breaking' (1931)]

THOMAS, Dylan (1914–1953)
An alcoholic is someone you don't like who drinks as much as you do.
[Attr.]

AMBITION

DENHAM, Sir John (1615–1669)
Ambition is like love, impatient both of delays and rivals.

KENEALLY, Thomas (1935–)
It's only when you abandon your ambitions that they become possible.
[*Australian*, 1983]

LEARY, Timothy (1920–1996)
Women who seek to be equal with men lack ambition.

ANGER

DILLER, Phyllis (1917–1974)
Never go to bed mad. Stay up and fight.
[*Phyllis Diller's Housekeeping Hints*]

HALIFAX, Lord (1633–1695)
Anger is never without an Argument, but seldom with a good one.
[*Thoughts and Reflections* (1750)]

HAZLITT, William (1778–1830)
Spleen can subsist on any kind of food.
['On Wit and Humour' (1819)]

TWAIN, Mark (1835–1910)
When angry count four; when very angry swear.
[*Pudd'nhead Wilson's Calendar* (1894)]

APPEARANCE

BROWN, James (1933–)
Hair is the first thing. And teeth the second. Hair and teeth. A man got those two things he's got it all.
[*The Godfather of Soul* (1986)]

DANIELS, R. G. (1916–1993)
The most delightful advantage of being bald – one can hear snowflakes.
[*The Observer*, 1976]

DICKENS, Charles (1812–1870)
He might have brought an action against his countenance for libel, and won heavy damages.
[*Oliver Twist* (1838)]

LAUGHTON, Charles (1899–1962)
I have a face like the behind of an elephant.

WILDE, Oscar (1854–1900)
It is only shallow people who do not judge by appearances.
[*The Picture of Dorian Gray* (1891)]

WINDSOR, Duchess of (Wallis Simpson) (1896–1986)
One can never be too thin or too rich.
[Attr.]

ART

BACON, Francis (1909–1993)
The job of the artist is always to deepen the mystery.
[*Sunday Telegraph*,1964]

BEAVERBROOK, Lord (1879–1964)
Buy old masters. They fetch a better price than old mistresses.

DEBUSSY, Claude (1862–1918)
Art is the most beautiful of all lies.
[*Monsieur Croche, antidilettante*]

HIRST, Damien (1965–)
[On winning the Turner Prize]
It's amazing what you can do with an E in A-level art, twisted imagination and a chainsaw.
[*The Observer*, 1995]

INGRES, J.A.D. (1780–1867)
Drawing is the true test of art.
[*Pensées d'Ingres* (1922)]

LANDSEER, Sir Edwin Henry (1802–1873)
If people only knew as much about painting as I do, they would never buy my pictures.
[In Campbell Lennie, *Landseer the Victorian Paragon*]

MUSSET, Alfred de (1810–1857)
Great artists have no homeland.
[*Lorenzaccio* (1834)]

SARGENT, John Singer (1856–1925)
Every time I paint a portrait I lose a friend.
[In Bentley and Esar, *Treasury of Humorous Quotations* (1951)]

WILDE, Oscar (1854–1900)
All art is quite useless.
[*The Picture of Dorian Gray* (1891)]

BACHELORS

ALEICHEM, Sholom (1859–1916)
A bachelor is a man who comes to work each morning from a different direction.

MENCKEN, H.L. (1880–1956)
Bachelors know more about women than married men do. If they didn't, they'd be married too.

WILDE, Oscar (1854–1900)
Nowadays, all the married men live like bachelors, and all the bachelors like married men.
[*The Picture of Dorian Gray* (1891)]

BEAUTY

BACON, Francis (1561–1626)
There is no excellent beauty, that hath not some strangeness in the proportion.
[*Essays* (1625)]

BURCHILL, Julie (1960–)
It has been said that a pretty face is a passport. But it's not, it's a visa, and it runs out fast.
[*Mail on Sunday* 1988]

CERNUDA, Luis (1902–1963)
Everything beautiful has its moment and then passes away.

CONFUCIUS (c.550–c.478 BC)
Everything has its beauty but not everyone sees it.
[*Analects*]

GAINSBOURG, Serge (1928–1991)
Ugliness is, in a way, superior to beauty because it lasts.
[*The Scotsman*, 1998]

JOHNSON, Samuel (1709–1784)
What ills from beauty spring.
[*The Vanity of Human Wishes* (1749)]

LOREN, Sophia (1934–)
Nothing makes a woman more beautiful than the belief she is beautiful.

SAKI (1870–1916)
I always say beauty is only sin deep.
['Reginald's Choir Treat' (1904)]

SOCRATES (469–399 BC)
Beauty is a short-lived tyranny.

BELIEF

COWARD, Sir Noël (1899–1973)
Life without faith is an arid business.
[*Blithe Spirit* (1941)]

MENCKEN, H.L. (1880–1956)
Faith may be defined briefly as an illogical belief in the occurrence of the improbable.
[*Prejudices* (1927)]

ORWELL, George (1903–1950)
Doublethink means the power of holding two contradictory beliefs in one's mind simultaneously, and accepting both of them.
[*Nineteen Eighty-Four* (1949)]

STORR, Dr Anthony (1920–)
One man's faith is another man's delusion.
[*Feet of Clay* (1996)]

TURGENEV, Ivan (1818–1883)
The courage to believe in nothing.
[*Fathers and Sons* (1862)]

VALÉRY, Paul (1871–1945)
What has always been believed by everyone, everywhere, will most likely turn out to be false.
[*Moralities*, 1932]

BREVITY

FONTAINE, Jean de la (1621–1695)
But the shortest works are always the best.
[*Fables*, 'Les lapins']

HORACE (65–8 BC)
I labour to be brief, and I become obscure.
[*Ars Poetica*, line 25]

PARKER, Dorothy (1893–1967)
Brevity is the soul of lingerie.
[Caption written for *Vogue* (1916)]

BUSINESS

AUSTEN, Jane (1775–1817)
Business, you know, may bring money, but friendship hardly ever does.
[*Emma* (1816)]

BALZAC, Honoré de (1799–1850)
Generous people make bad shopkeepers.
[*Illusions perdues* (1843)]

BARNUM, Phineas T. (1810–1891)
Every crowd has a silver lining.
[Attr.]

FORD, Henry (1863–1947)
A business that makes nothing but money is a poor kind of business.
[Interview]

FRANKLIN, Benjamin (1706–1790)
No nation was ever ruined by trade.
[*Essays*]

GETTY, John Paul (1892–1976)
The meek shall inherit the earth, but not the mineral rights.
[Robert Lenzner *The Great Getty* (1985)]

ONASSIS, Aristotle (1906–1975)
The secret of business is to know something that nobody else knows.
[*The Economist*, 1991]

PUZO, Mario (1920–)
He's a businessman. I'll make him an offer he can't refuse.
[*The Godfather* (1969)]

YOUNG, Andrew (1932–)
Nothing is illegal if one hundred businessmen decide to do it.
[Attr.]

CHANGE

HERACLITUS (c.540–c.480 BC)
You cannot step twice into the same river.
[In Plato, *Cratylus*]

THOREAU, Henry David (1817–1862)
Things do not change; we change.
[*Walden* (1854)]

CHARACTER

GOETHE (1749–1832)
Talent is formed in quiet retreat,
Character in the headlong rush of life.
[*Torquato Tasso* (1790)]

KARR, Alphonse (1808–1890)
Every man has three characters: that which he exhibits, that which he has, and that which he thinks he has.
[Attr.]

SIMPSON, O. J. (1947–)
The only thing that endures is character. Fame and wealth – all that is illusion. All that endures is character.
[*The Guardian*, 1995]

WILSON, Woodrow (1856–1924)
Character is a by-product; it is produced in the great manufacture of daily duty.
[Speech, 1915]

CHILDREN

FROST, David (1939–)
Having one child makes you a parent; having two you are a referee.
[*The Independent*, 1989]

KNOX, Ronald (1888–1957)
[Definition of a baby]
A loud noise at one end and no sense of responsibility at the other.
[Attr.]

LARKIN, Philip (1922–1985)
As a child, I thought I hated everybody, but when I grew up I realized it was just children I didn't like.

COMEDY

GRIFFITHS, Trevor (1935–)
Comedy is medicine.
[*The Comedians* (1979)]

PRIESTLEY, J.B. (1894–1984)
Comedy, we may say, is society
protecting itself – with a smile.
[*George Meredith* (1926)]

COMMON SENSE

DESCARTES, René (1596–1650)
Common sense is the best distributed
thing in the world, for we all think we
possess a good share of it.
[*Discours de la Méthode* (1637)]

EINSTEIN, Albert (1879–1955)
Common sense is the collection of
prejudices acquired by age eighteen.
[Attr.]

EMERSON, Ralph Waldo (1803–1882)
Nothing astonishes men so much as
common-sense and plain dealing.
['Art' (1841)]

CONVERSATION

BAGEHOT, Walter (1826–1877)
The habit of common and continuous
speech is a symptom of mental
deficiency.
[*Literary Studies* (1879)]

BOSWELL, James (1740–1795)
Johnson: Well, we had a good talk.
Boswell: Yes, Sir; you tossed and gored
several persons.
[*The Life of Samuel Johnson* (1791)]

**TALLEYRAND, Charles-Maurice de
(1754–1838)**
Speech was given to man to disguise
his thoughts.
[Attr.]

TANNEN, Deborah (1945–)
Each person's life is lived as a series of
conversations.
[*The Observer*, 1992]

COURAGE

**IBÁRRURI, Dolores ('La Pasionaria')
(1895–1989)**
It is better to die on your feet than to
live on your knees.
[Speech, Paris, 1936]

USTINOV, Sir Peter (1921–)
Courage is often lack of insight,
whereas cowardice in many cases is
based on good information.
[Attr.]

COWARDICE

SHAW, George Bernard (1856–1950)
As an old soldier I admit the
cowardice: it's as universal as sea
sickness, and matters just as little.
[*Man and Superman* (1903)]

VOLTAIRE (1694–1778)
Marriage is the only adventure open
to the cowardly.
[Attr.]

DANGER

BURKE, Edmund (1729–1797)
Dangers by being despised grow
great.
[Speech on the Petition of the
Unitarians, 1792]

CORNEILLE, Pierre (1606–1684)
When we conquer without danger our
triumph is without glory.
[*Le Cid* (1637)]

EMERSON, Ralph Waldo (1803–1882)
In skating over thin ice, our safety is in
our speed.
['Prudence' (1841)]

DEATH

BOWRA, Sir Maurice (1898–1971)
Any amusing deaths lately?
[Attr.]

BUTLER, Samuel (1835–1902)
When you have told anyone you have
left him a legacy the only decent thing
to do is to die at once.
[In Festing Jones, *Samuel Butler:
A Memoir*]

FONTAINE, Jean de la (1621–1695)
Death does not take the wise man by
surprise, he is always prepared to leave.
['La Mort et le mourant']

HENDRIX, Jimi (1942–1970)
Once you're dead, you're made for life.
[Attr.]

LARKIN, Philip (1922–1985)
The anaesthetic from which none
come round.
['Aubade' (1988)]

MAETERLINCK, Maurice (1862–1949)
The living are just the dead on
holiday.
[Attr.]

MOLIÈRE (1622–1673)
One dies only once, and then for such a long time!
[Le Dépit Amoureux (1656)]

SCHOPENHAUER, Arthur (1788–1860)
After your death you will be what you were before your birth.
[Parerga and Paralipomena (1851)]

TWAIN, Mark (1835–1910)
The report of my death was an exaggeration.
[Cable, 1897]

YOUNG, Edward (1683–1765)
Life is the desert, life the solitude;
Death joins us to the great majority.
[The Revenge (1721)]

DEBT

FOX, Henry Stephen (1791–1846)
[Remark after an illness]
I am so changed that my oldest creditors would hardly know me.
[Quoted by Byron in a letter to John Murray, 1817]

FRANKLIN, Benjamin (1706–1790)
Creditors have better memories than debtors.
[Poor Richard's Almanac (1758)]

MUMFORD, Ethel (1878–1940)
In the midst of life we are in debt.
[Altogether New Cynic's Calendar (1907)]

WILDE, Oscar (1854–1900)
It is only by not paying one's bills that one can hope to live in the memory of the commercial classes.
[The Chameleon, 1894]

WODEHOUSE, P.G. (1881–1975)
I don't owe a penny to a single soul – not counting tradesmen, of course.
['Jeeves and the Hard-Boiled Egg' (1919)]

DESTINY

AESCHYLUS (525–456 BC)
Things are where things are, and, as fate has willed,
So shall they be fulfilled.
[Agamemnon, trans. Browning]

BACON, Francis (1561–1626)
If a man look sharply, and attentively, he shall see Fortune: for though she be blind, yet she is not invisible.
[Essays (1625)]

BOWEN, Elizabeth (1899–1973)
Fate is not an eagle, it creeps like a rat.
[The House in Paris (1935)]

CHURCHILL, Sir Winston (1874–1965)
I felt as if I were walking with destiny, and that all my past life had been but a preparation for this hour and this trial.
[The Gathering Storm]

CLAUDIUS CAECUS, Appius (4th–3rd century BC)
Each man is the architect of his own destiny.
[In Sallust, Ad Caesarem]

CRISP, Quentin (1908–1999)
Believe in fate, but lean forward where fate can see you.
[Attr.]

DELILLE, Abbé Jacques (1738–1813)
Relations are made by fate, friends by choice.
[Malheur et pitié (1803)]

FORD, John (c.1586–1639)
Tempt not the stars, young man, thou canst not play
With the severity of fate.
[The Broken Heart (1633)]

GAY, John (1685–1732)
'Tis a gross error, held in schools,
That Fortune always favours fools.
[Fables (1738)]

HARE, Maurice Evan (1886–1967)
There once was a man who said,
'Damn!
It is borne in upon me I am
An engine that moves
In predestinate grooves,
I'm not even a bus, I'm a tram.'
['Limerick', 1905]

HORACE (65–8 BC)
Do not ask – it is forbidden to know – what end the gods have in store for me or for you.
[Odes]

JONSON, Ben (1572–1637)
Blind Fortune still
Bestows her gifts on such as cannot use them.
[Every Man out of His Humour (1599)]

LOOS, Anita (1893–1981)
Fate keeps on happening.
　　[Gentlemen Prefer Blondes (1925)]

SCHOPENHAUER, Arthur (1788–1860)
Fate shuffles the cards and we play.
　　['Aphorisms for Wisdom' (1851)]

SHAKESPEARE, William (1564–1616)
Men at some time are masters of their fates:
The fault, dear Brutus, is not in our stars,
But in ourselves, that we are underlings.
　　[Julius Caesar, I.ii]

SINGER, Isaac Bashevis (1904–1991)
We have to believe in free will. We've got no choice.
　　[The Times, 1982]

TERENCE (c.190–159 BC)
Fortune favours the brave.
　　[Phormio]

DUTY

ANONYMOUS
Straight is the line of Duty
Curved is the line of Beauty
Follow the first and thou shallt see
The second ever following thee.

BIERCE, Ambrose (1842–c.1914)
Duty: That which sternly impels us in the direction of profit, along the line of desire.
　　[The Enlarged Devil's Dictionary (1967)]

HOOPER, Ellen Sturgis (1816–1841)
I slept, and dreamed that life was Beauty;
I woke, and found that life was Duty.
　　['Beauty and Duty' (1840)]

IBSEN, Henrik (1828–1906)
What's a man's first duty? The answer's brief: To be himself.
　　[Peer Gynt (1867)]

LEE, Robert E. (1807–1870)
Duty then is the sublimest word in our language. Do your duty in all things. You cannot do more. You should never wish to do less.
　　[Inscription in the Hall of Fame]

NELSON, Lord (1758–1805)
[Nelson's last signal at the Battle of Trafalgar, 1805]

England expects every man to do his duty.
　　[In Southey, The Life of Nelson (1860)]

SHAW, George Bernard (1856–1950)
When a stupid man is doing something he is ashamed of, he always declares that it is his duty.
　　[Caesar and Cleopatra (1901)]

STEVENSON, Robert Louis (1850–1894)
There is no duty we so much underrate as the duty of being happy.
　　[Virginibus Puerisque (1881)]

TENNYSON, Alfred, Lord (1809–1892)
O hard, when love and duty clash!
　　[The Princess (1847)]

WILDE, Oscar (1854–1900)
Duty is what one expects of others, it is not what one does oneself.
　　[A Woman of No Importance (1893)]

EDUCATION

ADDISON, Joseph (1672–1719)
What sculpture is to a block of marble, education is to a human soul.

ARISTOTLE (384–322 BC)
The roots of education are bitter, but the fruit is sweet.
　　[In Diogenes Laertius, Lives of Philosophers]

BACON, Francis (1561–1626)
Reading maketh a full man; conference a ready man; and writing an exact man.
　　[Essays (1625)]

BANKHEAD, Tallulah (1903–1968)
I read Shakespeare and the Bible and I can shoot dice. That's what I call a liberal education.
　　[Attr.]

BIERCE, Ambrose (1842–c.1914)
Education: That which discloses to the wise and disguises from the foolish their lack of understanding.
　　[The Cynic's Word Book (1906)]

BROUGHAM, Lord Henry (1778–1868)
Education makes a people easy to lead, but difficult to drive; easy to govern, but impossible to enslave.
　　[Attr.]

BUCHAN, John (1875–1940)
To live for a time close to great minds is the best kind of education.
[*Memory Hold the Door*]

BUSH, George W. (1946–)
[On returning to Yale to accept an honorary degree]
To those of you who received honors, awards and distinctions, I say well done. And to the C students, I say you, too, can be president of the United States.
[*The Sunday Times*, May 2001]

CHESTERTON, G.K. (1874–1936)
Education is simply the soul of a society as it passes from one generation to another.
[*The Observer*, 1924]

COWARD, Sir Noël (1899–1973)
I've over-educated myself in all the things I shouldn't have known at all.
[*Mild Oats* (1931)]

DICKENS, Charles (1812–1870)
Now, what I want is, Facts. Teach these boys and girls nothing but Facts. Facts alone are wanted in life. Plant nothing else, and root out everything else ... Stick to Facts, sir!
[*Hard Times* (1854)]

DIOGENES (THE CYNIC) (c.400–325 BC)
Education is something that tempers the young and consoles the old, gives wealth to the poor and adorns the rich.
[In Diogenes Laertius, *Lives of Eminent Philosophers*]

EMERSON, Ralph Waldo (1803–1882)
I pay the schoolmaster, but 'tis the schoolboys that educate my son.
[*Journals*]

FRANZEN, Jonathan (1959–)
One pretty good definition of college is that it's a place where people are made to read difficult books.

HUXLEY, Aldous (1894–1963)
The solemn foolery of scholarship for scholarship's sake.
[*The Perennial Philosophy* (1945)]

JOHNSON, Samuel (1709–1784)
All intellectual improvement arises from leisure.
[In Boswell, *The Life of Samuel Johnson* (1791)]

KANT, Immanuel (1724–1804)
Man is the only creature which must be educated.
[*On Pedagogy* (1803)]

KRAUS, Karl (1874–1936)
Education is what most people receive, many pass on and few actually have.
[*Pro domo et mundo* (1912)]

ROUSSEAU, Jean-Jacques (1712–1778)
One is only curious in proportion to one's level of education.
[*Émile ou De l'éducation* (1762)]

SKINNER, B.F. (1904–1990)
Education is what survives when what has been learned has been forgotten.
[*New Scientist*, 1964]

USTINOV, Sir Peter (1921–)
People at the top of the tree are those without qualifications to detain them at the bottom.
[Attr.]

WILDE, Oscar (1854–1900)
Education is an admirable thing, but it is well to remember from time to time that nothing that is worth knowing can be taught.
['The Critic as Artist' (1891)]

ZAPPA, Frank (1940–1993)
If you want to get laid, go to college. If you want an education, go to the library.

ENVY

BEERBOHM, Sir Max (1872–1956)
The dullard's envy of brilliant men is always assuaged by the suspicion that they will come to a bad end.
[*Zuleika Dobson* (1911)]

CHURCHILL, Charles (1731–1764)
Who wit with jealous eye surveys,
And sickens at another's praise.
[*The Ghost* (1763)]

FIELDING, Henry (1707–1754)
Some folks rail against other folks because other folks have what some folks would be glad of.
[*Joseph Andrews* (1742)]

GAY, John (1685–1732)
Fools may our scorn, not envy raise,
For envy is a kind of praise.
[*Fables* (1727)]

MOORE, Brian (1921–1999)
How many works of the imagination have been goaded into life by envy of an untalented contemporary's success.
[*An Answer from Limbo* (1994)]

SHAKESPEARE, William (1564–1616)
[Of Cassius]
Such men as he be never at heart's ease
Whiles they behold a greater than themselves,
And therefore are they very dangerous.
[*Julius Caesar*, I.ii]

EXPERIENCE

ALI, Muhammad (1942–)
The man who views the world at fifty the same as he did at twenty has wasted thirty years of his life.
[Playboy Magazine, November 1975]

ANONYMOUS
Experience is the comb that nature gives us when we are bald.

ANTRIM, Minna (1861–1950)
Experience is a good teacher, but she sends in terrific bills.
[*Naked Truth and Veiled Allusions* (1902)]

BAX, Arnold (1883–1953)
You should make a point of trying every experience once, excepting incest and folk-dancing.
[*Farewell My Youth* (1943)]

BOWEN, Elizabeth (1899–1973)
Experience isn't interesting till it begins to repeat itself – in fact, till it does that, it hardly is experience.
[*The Death of the Heart* (1938)]

DISRAELI, Benjamin (1804–1881)
Experience is the child of Thought, and Thought is the child of Action. We cannot learn men from books.
[*Vivian Grey* (1826)]

EMERSON, Ralph Waldo (1803–1882)
The years teach much which the days never know.
['Experience' (1844)]

FADIMAN, Clifton (1904–1999)
Experience teaches you that the man who looks you straight in the eye, particularly if he adds a firm handshake, is hiding something.
[*Enter, Conversing*]

FROUDE, James Anthony (1818–1894)
Experience teaches slowly, and at the cost of mistakes.
[*Short Studies on Great Subjects* (1877)]

HOLMES, Oliver Wendell (1809–1894)
A moment's insight is sometimes worth a life's experience.
[*The Professor at the Breakfast-Table* (1860)]

HUXLEY, Aldous (1894–1963)
Experience is not what happens to a man. It is what a man does with what happens to him.
[Attr.]

MACCAIG, Norman (1910–1996)
Experience teaches that it doesn't.
[*A World of Difference* (1983)]

POMFRET, John (1667–1702)
We live and learn, but not the wiser grow.
['Reason' (1700)]

SHAW, George Bernard (1856–1950)
Men are wise in proportion, not to their experience, but to their capacity for experience.

WILDE, Oscar (1854–1900)
Experience is the name every one gives to their mistakes.
[*Lady Windermere's Fan* (1892)]

FACTS

HUXLEY, Aldous (1894–1963)
Facts do not cease to exist because they are ignored.
[*Proper Studies* (1927)]

JAMES, Henry (1843–1916)
The fatal futility of Fact.
[*Prefaces* (1897)]

FAILURE

CIANO, Count Galeazzo (1903–1944)
As always, victory finds a hundred fathers, but defeat is an orphan.
[*Diary*, 1942]

HARE, Augustus (1792–1834)
Half the failures in life arise from pulling in one's horse as he is leaping.
[*Guesses at Truth* (1827)]

HELLER, Joseph (1923–1999)
He was a self-made man who owed
his lack of success to nobody.
[*Catch-22* (1961)]

KEATS, John (1795–1821)
I would sooner fail than not be among
the greatest.
[Letter to James Hessey, 1818]

NEWMAN, Paul (1925–)
Show me a good loser and I'll show
you a loser.
[*The Observer*, 1982]

SHAKESPEARE, William (1564–1616)
Macbeth: If we should fail?
Lady Macbeth: We fail!
But screw your courage to the sticking
place,
And we'll not fail.
[*Macbeth*, I.vii]

WILDE, Oscar (1854–1900)
We women adore failures. They lean
on us.
[*A Woman of No Importance* (1893)]

FAME

BERNERS, Lord (1883–1950)
[Of T.E. Lawrence]
He's always backing into the limelight.
[Attr.]

BOORSTIN, Daniel J. (1914–)
The celebrity is a person who is
known for his well-knownness.
[*The Image* (1962)]

BYRON, Lord (1788–1824)
[Remark on the instantaneous success
of Childe Harold]
I awoke one morning and found
myself famous.
[In Moore, *Letters and Journals of
Lord Byron* (1830)]

**CALDERÓN DE LA BARCA, Pedro
(1600–1681)**
Fame, like water, bears up the lighter
things, and lets the weighty sink.
[Attr.]

CATO THE ELDER (234–149 BC)
I would much rather have men ask
why I have no statue than why I have
one.
[In Plutarch, *Lives*]

CURTIS, Tony (1925–)
It is like having a kind of Alzheimer's
disease where everyone knows you
and you don't know anyone.
[*The Sunday Times*, April 2001]

GRAINGER, James (c.1721–1766)
What is fame? an empty bubble;
Gold? a transient, shining trouble.
['Solitude' (1755)]

GREENE, Graham (1904–1991)
Fame is a powerful aphrodisiac.
[*Radio Times*, 1964]

HUGO, Victor (1802–1885)
Fame? It's glory in small change.
[*Ruy Blas* (1838)]

HUXLEY, Aldous (1894–1963)
I'm afraid of losing my obscurity.
Genuineness only thrives in the dark.
Like celery.
[*Those Barren Leaves* (1925)]

MONTAIGNE, Michel de (1533–1592)
Fame and tranquillity cannot dwell
under the same roof.
[*Essais* (1580)]

PECK, Gregory (1916–2003)
[On the fact that no-one in a crowded
restaurant recognized him]
If you have to tell them who you are,
you aren't anybody.
[In S. Harris, *Pieces of Eight*]

TACITUS (AD c.56–c.120)
The desire for fame is the last thing to
be put aside, even by the wise.
[*Histories*]

WARHOL, Andy (c.1926–1987)
In the future everyone will be world
famous for fifteen minutes.
[Catalogue for an exhibition, 1968]

WILDE, Oscar (1854–1900)
There is only one thing in the world
worse than being talked about, and
that is not being talked about.
[*The Picture of Dorian Gray* (1891)]

FAMILIES

BEERBOHM, Sir Max (1872–1956)
They were a tense and peculiar family,
the Oedipuses, weren't they?
[Attr.]

DICKENS, Charles (1812–1870)
Accidents will occur in the best-
regulated families.
[David Copperfield (1850)]

ELIZABETH II (1926–)
Like all the best families, we have our
share of eccentricities, of impetuous
and wayward youngsters and of
family disagreements.
[Daily Mail, October 1989]

HAZLITT, William (1778–1830)
A person may be indebted for a nose
or an eye, for a graceful carriage or a
voluble discourse, to a great-aunt or
uncle, whose existence he has
scarcely heard of.
[London Magazine, 1821]

HOPE, Anthony (1863–1933)
Good families are generally worse
than any others.
[The Prisoner of Zenda (1894)]

LEACH, Sir Edmund (1910–1989)
Far from being the basis of the good
society, the family, with its narrow
privacy and tawdry secrets, is the
source of all our discontents.
[BBC Reith Lecture, 1967]

LINCOLN, Abraham (1809–1865)
I don't know who my grandfather was;
I am much more concerned to know
what his grandson will be.
[In Gross, Lincoln's Own Stories]

MARX, Groucho (1895–1977)
You're a disgrace to our family name
of Wagstaff, if such a thing is possible.
[Horse Feathers, film, 1932]

MITCHELL, Julian (1935–)
The sink is the great symbol of the
bloodiness of family life. All life is bad,
but family life is worse.
[As Far as You Can Go (1963)]

**THACKERAY, William Makepeace
(1811–1863)**
If a man's character is to be abused,
say what you will, there's nobody like
a relation to do the business.
[Vanity Fair (1848)]

TOLSTOY, Leo (1828–1910)
All happy families resemble one
another, but every unhappy family is
unhappy in its own way.
[Anna Karenina (1877)]

WODEHOUSE, P.G. (1881–1975)
It is no use telling me that there are
bad aunts and good aunts. At the core
they are all alike. Sooner or later, out
pops the cloven hoof.
[The Code of the Woosters (1938)]

FASHION

BAILEY, David (1938–)
I never cared for fashion much,
amusing little seams and witty little
pleats: it was the girls I liked.
[The Independent, November 1990]

BEATON, Cecil (1904–1980)
[On the miniskirt]
Never in the history of fashion has so
little material been raised so high to
reveal so much that needs to be
covered so badly.

CASSINI, Oleg (1913–)
Fashion anticipates, and elegance is a
state of mind.
[In My Own Fashion (1987)]

RADNER, Gilda (1946–1989)
I base most of my fashion taste on
what doesn't itch.
[It's Always Something (1989)]

FEAR

ALLEN, Woody (1935–)
I'm really a timid person – I was
beaten up by Quakers.
[Sleeper, film, 1973]

CERVANTES, Miguel de (1547–1616)
Fear has many eyes and can see
things which are underground.
[Don Quixote I (1605)]

CHURCHILL, Sir Winston (1874–1965)
When I look back on all these worries I
remember the story of the old man
who said on his deathbed that he had
had a lot of trouble in his life, most of
which had never happened.
[Their Finest Hour]

CURIE, Marie (1867–1934)
Nothing in life is to be feared, it is
only to be understood. Now is the
time to understand more, so that we
may fear less.
[Attr.]

FOCH, Ferdinand (1851–1929)
None but a coward dares to boast that he has never known fear.
[Attr.]

PLATO (c.429–347 BC)
Nothing in the affairs of men is worthy of great anxiety.
[Republic]

ROOSEVELT, Franklin Delano (1882–1945)
The only thing we have to fear is fear itself.
[First Inaugural Address, 1933]

SHAW, George Bernard (1856–1950)
There is only one universal passion: fear.
[The Man of Destiny (1898)]

STEPHENS, James (1882–1950)
Curiosity will conquer fear even more than bravery will.
[The Crock of Gold (1912)]

VOLTAIRE (1694–1778)
Fear follows crime, and is its punishment.
[Sémiramis (1748)]

FLATTERY

BIERCE, Ambrose (1842–c.1914)
Flatter: To impress another with a sense of one's own merit.
[The Enlarged Devil's Dictionary (1961)]

FONTAINE, Jean de la (1621–1695)
My dear Monsieur, know that every flatterer lives at the expense of the one who listens to him.
['Le corbeau et le renard']

HALIFAX, Lord (1633–1695)
It is flattering some Men to endure them.
['Of Company' (1750)]

SHAW, George Bernard (1856–1950)
What really flatters a man is that you think him worth flattering.
[John Bull's Other Island (1907)]

FOOD

ALLEN, Woody (1935–)
I will not eat oysters. I want my food dead. Not sick. Not wounded. Dead.

BAREHAM, Lindsey (1948–)
Good mashed potato is one of the great luxuries of life and I don't blame Elvis for eating it every night for the last year of his life.
[In Praise of the Potato (1989)]

BRAND, Jo (1957–)
Anything is good if it's made of chocolate.

BRILLAT-SAVARIN, Anthelme (1755–1826)
Tell me what you eat and I will tell you what you are.
[Physiologie du Goût (1825)]

CERVANTES, Miguel de (1547–1616)
Hunger is the best sauce in the world.
[Don Quixote (1615)]

DE VRIES, Peter (1910–1993)
Gluttony is an emotional escape, a sign something is eating us.
[Comfort me with Apples (1956)]

FADIMAN, Clifton (1904–1999)
Cheese – milk's leap toward immortality.
[Any Number Can Play (1957)]

FRANKLIN, Benjamin (1706–1790)
To lengthen thy life, lessen thy meals.
[Poor Richard's Almanac (1733)]

FULLER, Thomas (1608–1661)
He was a very valiant man who first ventured on eating of oysters.
[The History of the Worthies of England (1662)]

GARFIELD, James A. (1831–1881)
Man cannot live by bread alone; he must have peanut butter.
[Inaugural address, 4 March 1881]

HERBERT, George (1593–1633)
A cheerful look makes a dish a feast.
[Jacula Prudentum (1640)]

JOHNSON, Samuel (1709–1784)
I look upon it, that he who does not mind his belly will hardly mind anything else.
[In Boswell, The Life of Samuel Johnson (1791)]

LEBOWITZ, Fran (1946–)
Food is an important part of a balanced diet.
[Metropolitan Life (1978)]

MOLIÈRE (1622–1673)
One should eat to live, not live to eat.
[*L'Avare* (1669)]

MONROE, Marilyn (1926–1962)
[On having matzo balls for supper at Arthur Miller's parents]
Isn't there another part of the matzo you can eat?
[Attr.]

PETER, Laurence J. (1919–1990)
The noblest of all dogs is the hot-dog; it feeds the hand that bites it.
[*Quotations for Our Time* (1977)]

ROUSSEAU, Émile (1929–)
Great eaters of meat are in general more cruel and ferocious than other men. The English are known for their cruelty.
[Attr.]

SECOMBE, Sir Harry (1921–2001)
My advice if you insist on slimming: Eat as much as you like – just don't swallow it.
[*Daily Herald*, 1962]

SHAKESPEARE, William (1564–1616)
Methinks sometimes I have no more wit than a Christian or an ordinary man has; but I am a great eater of beef, and I believe that does harm to my wit.
[*Twelfth Night*, I.iii]

SHAW, George Bernard (1856–1950)
There is no love sincerer than the love of food.
[*Man and Superman* (1903)]

SWIFT, Jonathan (1667–1745)
If a lump of soot falls into the soup and you cannot conveniently get it out, stir it well in and it will give the soup a French taste.

VOLTAIRE (1694–1778)
[On learning that coffee was considered a slow poison]
I think it must be so, for I have been drinking it for sixty-five years and I am not dead yet.
[Attr.]

WEBSTER, John (c.1580–c.1625)
I saw him even now going the way of all flesh, that is to say towards the kitchen.
[*Westward Hoe* (1607)]

WODEHOUSE, P.G. (1881–1975)
The lunches of fifty-seven years had caused his chest to slip down to the mezzanine floor.
[*The Heart of a Goof* (1926)]

FOOLISHNESS

BARNUM, Phineas T. (1810–1891)
There's a sucker born every minute.
[Attr.]

BLAKE, William (1757–1827)
If the fool would persist in his folly he would become wise.
['Proverbs of Hell' (1793)]

COWPER, William (1731–1800)
A fool must now and then be right, by chance.
['Conversation' (1782)]

FIELDING, Henry (1707–1754)
One fool at least in every married couple.
[*Amelia* (1751)]

FRANKLIN, Benjamin (1706–1790)
Experience keeps a dear school, but fools will learn in no other.
[*Poor Richard's Almanac* (1743)]

IBSEN, Henrik (1828–1906)
Fools are in a terrible, overwhelming majority, all the wide world over.
[*An Enemy of the People* (1882)]

POPE, Alexander (1688–1744)
For Fools rush in where Angels fear to tread.
[*An Essay on Criticism* (1711)]

ROWLAND, Helen (1875–1950)
The follies which a man regrets most in his life are those which he didn't commit when he had the opportunity.
[*A Guide to Men* (1922)]

SCHILLER, Johann Christoph Friedrich (1759–1805)
Gods themselves struggle in vain with stupidity.
[*The Maid of Orleans* (1801)]

STEVENSON, Robert Louis (1850–1894)
For God's sake give me the young man who has brains enough to make a fool of himself!
[*Virginibus Puerisque* (1881)]

SWIFT, Jonathan (1667–1745)
Hated by fools, and fools to hate,
Be that my motto and my fate.
['To Mr Delany' (1718)]

THOREAU, Henry David (1817–1862)
Any fool can make a rule and every
fool will mind it.
[Attr.]

TUSSER, Thomas (c.1524–1580)
A fool and his money be soon at
debate.
[*Five Hundred Points of Good
Husbandry* (1557)]

YOUNG, Edward (1683–1765)
Be wise with speed;
A fool at forty is a fool indeed.
[*Love of Fame, the Universal Passion*
(1728)]

FORGIVENESS

FROST, Robert (1874–1963)
Forgive, O Lord, my little jokes on
Thee
And I'll forgive Thy great big one on
me.
['Cluster of Faith' (1962)]

HEINE, Heinrich (1797–1856)
We should forgive our enemies, but
only after they have been hanged first.

KENNEDY, Robert F. (1925–1968)
Always forgive your enemies – but
never forget their names.
[Attr.]

FREEDOM

ADDISON, Joseph (1672–1719)
A day, an hour of virtuous liberty
Is worth a whole eternity in bondage.
[*Cato* (1713)]

COLERIDGE, Hartley (1796–1849)
But what is Freedom? Rightly
understood,
A universal licence to be good.
['Liberty' (1833)]

CONNOLLY, James (1868–1916)
Apostles of Freedom are ever idolised
when dead, but crucified when alive.
[*Workers Republic*, 1898]

DIDEROT, Denis (1713–1784)
Men will never be free until the last
king is strangled with the entrails of
the last priest.
[*Dithyrambe sur la Fête des Rois*]

HAZLITT, William (1778–1830)
The love of liberty is the love of
others; the love of power is the love of
ourselves.
[*Political Essays* (1819)]

HENRY, Patrick (1736–1799)
Give me liberty, or give me death!
[Speech, 1775]

KAFKA, Franz (1883–1924)
It's often better to be in chains than to
be free.
[*The Trial* (1925)]

KING, Martin Luther (1929–1968)
Free at last, free at last, thank God
Almighty, we are free at last!
[Speech, 1963]

LINCOLN, Abraham (1809–1865)
Those who deny freedom to others,
deserve it not for themselves.
[Speech, 1856]

ROUSSEAU, Jean-Jacques (1712–1778)
Man was born free, and everywhere
he is in chains.
[*Du Contrat Social* (1762)]

SARTRE, Jean-Paul (1905–1980)
Man is condemned to be free.
[*Existentialism and Humanism*]

SHAW, George Bernard (1856–1950)
Liberty means responsibility. That is
why most men dread it.
[*Man and Superman* (1903)]

WASHINGTON, George (1732–1799)
Liberty, when it begins to take root, is
a plant of rapid growth.
[Letter, 1788]

WILSON, Woodrow (1856–1924)
The history of liberty is a history of
resistance.
[Speech, 1912]

FRIENDSHIP

BACON, Francis (1561–1626)
It is the worst solitude, to have no true
friendships.
[*The Advancement of Learning* (1605)]

BIERCE, Ambrose (1842–c.1914)
Antipathy: The sentiment inspired by one's friend's friend.
[*The Enlarged Devil's Dictionary* (1961)]

BYRON, Lord (1788–1824)
Friendship is Love without his wings.
['L'amitié est l'amour sans ailes' (1806)]

COLTON, Charles Caleb (c.1780–1832)
Friendship often ends in love; but love in friendship – never.
[*Lacon* (1820)]

JOHNSON, Samuel (1709–1784)
If a man does not make new acquaintance as he advances through life, he will soon find himself left alone. A man, Sir, should keep his friendship in constant repair.
[In Boswell, *The Life of Samuel Johnson* (1791)]

KINGSMILL, Hugh (1889–1949)
Friends are God's apology for relations.
[In Ingrams, *God's Apology* (1977)]

LA ROCHEFOUCAULD (1613–1680)
In the misfortunes of our closest friends, we always find something which is not displeasing to us.
[*Maximes* (1665)]

SHAKESPEARE, William (1564–1616)
Friendship is constant in all other things Save in the office and affairs of love.
[*Much Ado About Nothing*, II.i]

VIDAL, Gore (1925–)
Whenever a friend succeeds, a little something in me dies.
[*The Sunday Times Magazine*, 1973]

WAUGH, Evelyn (1903–1966)
We cherish our friends not for their ability to amuse us, but for our ability to amuse them.
[Attr.]

THE FUTURE

ACHESON, Dean (1893–1971)
Always remember that the future comes one day at a time.
[*Sketches From Life*]

BERRA, Yogi (1925–)
The future ain't what it used to be.
[Attr.]

BIERCE, Ambrose (1842–c.1914)
Future: That period of time in which our affairs prosper, our friends are true and our happiness is assured.
[*The Cynic's Word Book* (1906)]

CONFUCIUS (c.550–c.478 BC)
Study the past, if you would divine the future.
[*Analects*]

CRISP, Quentin (1908–1999)
I still lived in the future – a habit which is the death of happiness.
[*The Naked Civil Servant* (1968)]

EINSTEIN, Albert (1879–1955)
I never think of the future. It comes soon enough.
[Interview, 1930]

JOHNSON, Samuel (1709–1784)
The future is purchased by the present.
[Attr.]

MAUGHAM, William Somerset (1874–1965)
It is bad enough to know the past; it would be intolerable to know the future.
[In R. Hughes *Foreign Devil* (1972)]

MITCHELL, Margaret (1900–1949)
After all, tomorrow is another day.
[*Gone with the Wind* (1936)]

ORWELL, George (1903–1950)
If you want a picture of the future, imagine a boot stamping on a human face – for ever.
[*Nineteen Eighty-Four* (1949)]

PROUST, Marcel (1871–1922)
What we call our future is the shadow which our past throws in front of us.
[*A l'ombre des jeunes filles en fleurs* (1918)]

QUAYLE, Dan (1947–)
The future will be better tomorrow.
[Attr.]

GENEROSITY

BARRIE, Sir J.M. (1860–1937)
Never ascribe to an opponent motives meaner than your own.
[Address, St Andrews University, 1922]

CORNEILLE, Pierre (1606–1684)
The manner of giving is worth more than the gift.
[*Le Menteur* (1643)]

GIBBS, Sir Philip (1877–1962)
It is better to give than to lend, and it costs about the same.
[Attr.]

LAUTRÉAMONT, Comte de (1846–1870)
Generosity enjoys the happiness of others, as though it were responsible for it.

TALLEYRAND, Charles-Maurice de (1754–1838)
Don't trust first impulses; they are always generous.
[Attr.]

GENIUS

ANONYMOUS
The difference between genius and stupidity is that genius has its limits.

DALI, Salvador (1904–1989)
I'm going to live forever. Geniuses don't die.
[The Observer, 1986]

DOYLE, Sir Arthur Conan (1859–1930)
Mediocrity knows nothing higher than itself, but talent instantly recognizes genius.
[The Valley of Fear (1914)]

EDISON, Thomas Alva (1847–1931)
Genius is one per cent inspiration and ninety-nine per cent perspiration.
[Life, 1932]

HAZLITT, William (1778–1830)
Rules and models destroy genius and art.
['Thoughts on Taste' (1818)]

HOPE, Anthony (1863–1933)
Unless one is a genius, it is best to aim at being intelligible.
[The Dolly Dialogues (1894)]

HOPKINS, Jane Ellice (1836–1904)
Gift, like genius, I often think, only means an infinite capacity for taking pains.
[Work amongst Working Men, 1870]

SWIFT, Jonathan (1667–1745)
When a true genius appears in the world, you may know him by this sign, that the dunces are all in confederacy against him.
[Thoughts on Various Subjects (1711)]

VIDAL, Gore (1925–)
[Of Andy Warhol]
A genius with the IQ of a moron.
[The Observer, June 1989]

WHISTLER, James McNeill (1834–1903)
[Replying to a lady inquiring whether he thought genius hereditary]
I cannot tell you that, madam. Heaven has granted me no offspring.
[In Seitz, Whistler Stories (1913)]

WILDE, Oscar (1854–1900)
[At the New York Customs]
I have nothing to declare except my genius.
[In Harris, Oscar Wilde (1918)]

GLORY

ANONYMOUS
Sic transit gloria mundi.
Thus passes the glory of the world.
[Spoken during the coronation of a new Pope]

BLAKE, William (1757–1827)
The pride of the peacock is the glory of God.
['Proverbs of Hell' (c. 1793)]

FONTAINE, Jean de la (1621–1695)
No flowery path leads to glory.
['Les deux aventuriers et le talisman']

SHAKESPEARE, William (1564–1616)
Like madness is the glory of this life.
[Timon of Athens, I.ii]

GOALS

KAFKA, Franz (1883–1924)
There is a goal but no way of reaching it; what we call the way is hesitation.
[Reflections on Sin, Sorrow, Hope and the True Way]

LONGFELLOW, Henry Wadsworth (1807–1882)
If you would hit the mark, you must aim a little above it;
Every arrow that flies feels the attraction of earth.
['Elegiac Verse' (1880)]

SANTAYANA, George (1863–1952)
Fanaticism consists in redoubling your effort when you have forgotten your aim.
[The Life of Reason (1906)]

SMITH, Logan Pearsall (1865–1946)
When people come and talk to you of
their aspirations, before they leave
you had better count your spoons.
[*Afterthoughts* (1931)]

STEVENSON, Robert Louis (1850–1894)
An aspiration is a joy forever.
[*Virginibus Puerisque* (1881)]

HAPPINESS

ADAMS, Scott (1957–)
Smile, it confuses people.
[*The Dilbert Principle*]

ARISTOTLE (384–322 BC)
One swallow does not make a
summer, neither does one fine day;
similarly one day or brief time of
happiness does not make a person
entirely happy.
[*Nicomachean Ethics*]

BENJAMIN, Walter (1892–1940)
To be happy is to be able to become
aware of oneself without fright.

BERGMAN, Ingrid (1915–1982)
Happiness is good health – and a bad
memory.
[In Simon Rose, *Classic Film Guide*
(1995)]

ELIOT, George (1819–1880)
The happiest women, like the happiest
nations, have no history.
[*The Mill on the Floss* (1860)]

EMERSON, Ralph Waldo (1803–1882)
To fill the hour, – that is happiness.
[*Essays, Second Series* (1844)]

FRANKLIN, Benjamin (1706–1790)
Be in general virtuous, and you will be
happy.
['On Early Marriages']

JEFFERSON, Thomas (1743–1826)
It is neither wealth nor splendor; but
tranquility and occupation which give
you happiness.
[Letter to Mrs. A.S. Marks]

JOHNSON, Samuel (1709–1784)
There is nothing which has yet been
contrived by man, by which so much
happiness is produced as by a good
tavern or inn.
[In Boswell, *The Life of Samuel
Johnson* (1791)]

MILL, John Stuart (1806–1873)
Ask yourself whether you are happy,
and you cease to be so.
[*Autobiography* (1873)]

ROUSSEAU, Jean-Jacques (1712–1778)
Happiness: a good bank account, a
good cook, and a good digestion.
[*Treasury of Humorous Quotations*]

SHAKESPEARE, William (1564–1616)
O, how bitter a thing it is to look into
happiness through another man's
eyes!
[*As You Like It*, V.ii]

SHAW, George Bernard (1856–1950)
A lifetime of happiness! No man alive
could bear it: it would be hell on earth.
[*Man and Superman* (1903)]

TOLSTOY, Leo (1828–1910)
If you want to be happy, be.
[Attr.]

WHATELY, Richard (1787–1863)
Happiness is no laughing matter.
[*Apophthegms* (1854)]

HEROES

**CORNUEL, Madame Anne-Marie Bigot
de (1605–1694)**
No man is a hero to his valet.
[In *Lettres de Mlle Aïssé á Madame C*
(1787)]

MORELL, Thomas (1703–1784)
See, the conquering hero comes!
Sound the trumpets, beat the drums!
[*Joshua* (1748)]

ROGERS, Will (1879–1935)
Heroing is one of the shortest-lived
professions there is.
[In Grove, *The Will Rogers Book* (1961)]

HOME

ACE, Jane (1905–1974)
Home wasn't built in a day.
[In G. Ace, *The Fine Art of Hypochondria*
(1966)]

ANONYMOUS
Be it ever so humble there's no place
like home for sending one slowly
crackers.

BEAUVOIR, Simone de (1908–1986)
The ideal of happiness has always taken material form in the house, whether cottage or castle; it stands for permanence and separation from the world.
[*The Second Sex* (1949)]

DE WOLFE, Elsie (1865–1950)
It is the personality of the mistress that the home expresses. Men are forever guests in our homes, no matter how much happiness they may find there.
[*The House in Good Taste* (1920)]

DOUGLAS, Norman (1868–1952)
Many a man who thinks to found a home discovers that he has merely opened a tavern for his friends.
[*South Wind* (1917)]

FLETCHER, John (1579–1625)
Charity and beating begins at home.
[*Wit Without Money* (c. 1614)]

FROST, Robert (1874–1963)
'Home is the place where, when you have to go there,
They have to take you in.'
'I should have called it
Something you somehow haven't to deserve.'
['The Death of the Hired Man' (1914)]

LUCE, Clare Boothe (1903–1987)
A man's home may seem to be his castle on the outside; inside, it is more often his nursery.
[Attr.]

MEYER, Agnes (1887–c.1970)
What the nation must realise is that the home, when both parents work, is non-existent. Once we have honestly faced the fact, we must act accordingly.
[*Washington Post*, 1943]

MORE, Hannah (1745–1833)
The sober comfort, all the peace which springs
From the large aggregate of little things;
On these small cares of daughter, wife, or friend,
The almost sacred joys of home depend.
['Sensibility' (1782)]

MORRIS, William (1834–1896)
If you want a golden rule that will fit everybody, this is it: Have nothing in your houses that you do not know to be useful, or believe to be beautiful.
[*Hopes and Fears for Art* (1882)]

ROWLAND, Helen (1875–1950)
'Home' is any four walls that enclose the right person.
[*Reflections of a Bachelor Girl* (1909)]

SHAW, George Bernard (1856–1950)
The great advantage of a hotel is that it's a refuge from home life.
[*You Never Can Tell* (1898)]

STOWE, Harriet Beecher (1811–1896)
Home is a place not only of strong affections, but of entire unreserve; it is life's undress rehearsal, its backroom, its dressing room, from which we go forth to more careful and guarded intercourse, leaving behind us much debris of cast-off and everyday clothing.
[*Little Foxes* (1866)]

THATCHER, Margaret (1925–)
Home is where you come to when you have nothing better to do.
[*Vanity Fair* May 1991]

HONESTY

BLAKE, William (1757–1827)
Always be ready to speak your mind, and a base man will avoid you.
[Attr.]

CARLYLE, Thomas (1795–1881)
Make yourself an honest man and then you may be sure there is one rascal less in the world.
[Attr.]

COWARD, Sir Noël (1899–1973)
It's discouraging to think how many people are shocked by honesty and how few by deceit.

CROMWELL, Oliver (1599–1658)
A few honest men are better than numbers.
[Letter to Sir William Spring, 1643]

DEFOE, Daniel (c.1661–1731)
Necessity makes an honest man a knave.
[*Serious Reflections of Robinson Crusoe* (1720)]

FITZGERALD, F. Scott (1896–1940)
I am one of the few honest people that
I have ever known.
[*The Great Gatsby* (1926)]

RICHELIEU, Cardinal (1585–1642)
If you give me six lines written by the
most honest man, I will find
something in them to hang him.
[Attr.]

WHATELY, Richard (1787–1863)
Honesty is the best policy, but he who
is governed by that maxim is not an
honest man.
[*Apophthegms* (1854)]

HONOUR

EMERSON, Ralph Waldo (1803–1882)
The louder he talked of his honor, the
faster we counted our spoons.
[*Conduct of Life* (1860)]

HARE, Augustus (1792–1834)
Purity is the feminine, Truth the
masculine, of Honour.
[*Guesses at Truth* (1827)]

MARX, Groucho (1895–1977)
Remember, men, we're fighting for
this woman's honour; which is
probably more than she ever did.
[*Duck Soup*, film, 1933]

RACINE, Jean (1639–1699)
Without money, honour is no more
than a disease.
[*Les Plaideurs* (1668)]

HOPE

BACON, Francis (1561–1626)
Hope is a good breakfast, but it is a
bad supper.
['Apophthegms']

CHESTERTON, G.K. (1874–1936)
Hope is the power of being cheerful in
circumstances which we know to be
desperate.
[*Heretics* (1905)]

FRANKLIN, Benjamin (1706–1790)
He that lives upon hope will die
fasting.
[*Poor Richard's Almanac* (1758)]

HERBERT, George (1593–1633)
He that lives in hope danceth without
music.
[*Jacula Prudentum* (1640)]

KERR, Jean (1923–)
Hope is the feeling you have that the
feeling you have isn't permanent.
[*Finishing Touches* (1973)]

OSBORNE, John (1929–1994)
[A notice in his bathroom]
Since I gave up hope I feel so much
better.
[*The Independent*, 1994]

TERENCE (c.190–159 BC)
Where there's life, there's hope.
[*Heauton Timoroumenos*]

HUMANITY AND HUMAN NATURE

AUDEN, W.H. (1907–1973)
Man is a history-making creature who
can neither repeat his past nor leave it
behind.
[*The Dyer's Hand* (1963)]

BACON, Francis (1561–1626)
There is in human nature generally
more of the fool than of the wise.
[*Essays* (1625)]

BEAUMARCHAIS (1732–1799)
Drinking when we're not thirsty and
making love all the time, madam, that
is all there is to distinguish us from
other animals.
[*Le Barbier de Seville* (1775)]

BEERBOHM, Sir Max (1872–1956)
Mankind is divisible into two great
classes: hosts and guests.
[Attr.]

BRONOWSKI, Jacob (1908–1974)
Every animal leaves traces of what it
was; man alone leaves traces of what
he created.
[*The Ascent of Man* (1973)]

BURNS, Robert (1759–1796)
Man's inhumanity to man
Makes countless thousands mourn!
['Man was made to Mourn, a Dirge'
(1784)]

BUTLER, Samuel (1835–1902)
Man is the only animal that can
remain on friendly terms with the
victims he intends to eat until he eats
them.
[*Samuel Butler's Notebooks* (1951)]

CAGE, Nicolas (1964–)
We are here to ruin ourselves and to break our hearts and love the wrong people and die.

CAMUS, Albert (1913–1960)
A single sentence will suffice for modern man: he fornicated and read the papers.
[*The Fall* (1956)]

CONFUCIUS (c.550–c.478 BC)
Men's natures are alike; it is their habits that carry them far apart.
[*Analects*]

DONLEAVY, J.P. (1926–)
I got disappointed in human nature as well and gave it up because I found it too much like my own.
[*Fairy Tales of New York* (1961)]

DONNE, John (1572–1631)
No man is an Island, entire of it self; every man is a piece of Continent, a part of the main ... any man's death diminishes me, because I am involved in Mankind;
And therefore never send to know for whom the bell tolls; it tolls for thee.
[*Devotions upon Emergent Occasions* (1624)]

FROUDE, James Anthony (1818–1894)
Wild animals never kill for sport. Man is the only one to whom the torture and death of his fellow creatures is amusing in itself.
[*Oceana, or England and her Colonies* (1886)]

GANDHI (1869–1948)
Human nature will only find itself when it finally realizes that to be human it has to cease to be beastly or brutal.
[*In Search of the Supreme*]

GOLDSMITH, Oliver (c.1728–1774)
Man wants but little here below,
Nor wants that little long.
[*The Vicar of Wakefield* (1766)]

GORKY, Maxim (1868–1936)
Man and man alone is, I believe, the creator of all things and all ideas.
[Attr.]

KEATS, John (1795–1821)
Scenery is fine – but human nature is finer.
[Letter to Benjamin Bailey, 1818]

LAING, R.D. (1927–1989)
We are all murderers and prostitutes – no matter to what culture, society, class, nation one belongs, no matter how normal, moral, or mature one takes oneself to be.

MILLIGAN, Spike (1918–2002)
I support all the causes that are trying to increase the sensitivity of the human race to the odious things that they do. We're a pretty horrendous crowd.
[Quoted in *The Herald*, February 2002]

PLAUTUS, Titus Maccius (c.254–184 BC)
Man is a wolf to man.
[*Asinaria*]

PROTAGORAS (c.485–c.410 BC)
Man is the measure of all things.
[In Plato, *Theaetetus*]

SHAW, George Bernard (1856–1950)
Man can climb to the highest summits; but he cannot dwell there long.
[*Candida* (1898)]

TWAIN, Mark (1835–1910)
Man is the Only Animal that Blushes. Or needs to.
[*Following the Equator* (1897)]

VALÉRY, Paul (1871–1945)
A man is infinitely more complicated than his thoughts.
[In Auden, *A Certain World*]

WILDE, Oscar (1854–1900)
It is absurd to divide people into good and bad. People are either charming or tedious.
[*Lady Windermere's Fan* (1892)]

HUMOUR

ADDISON, Joseph (1672–1719)
If we may believe our logicians, man is distinguished from all other creatures by the faculty of laughter.
[*The Spectator*, 1712]

ALBEE, Edward (1928–)
I have a fine sense of the ridiculous, but no sense of humour.
[*Who's Afraid of Virginia Woolf* (1962)]

BARKER, Ronnie (1929–)
The marvellous thing about a joke with a double meaning is that it can only mean one thing.
[Attr.]

BEAUMARCHAIS (1732–1799)
I make myself laugh at everything, for fear of having to cry.
[*Le Barbier de Seville* (1775)]

BRACKEN, Brendan, First Viscount (1901–1958)
It's a good deed to forget a poor joke.
[*The Observer*, 1943]

BROWN, Thomas Edward (1830–1897)
A rich man's joke is always funny.
['The Doctor' (1887)]

BUTLER, Samuel (1835–1902)
The most perfect humour and irony is generally quite unconscious.
[*Life and Habit* (1877)]

CARLYLE, Thomas (1795–1881)
No man who has once heartily and wholly laughed can be altogether irreclaimably bad.
[*Sartor Resartus* (1834)]

CHAMFORT, Nicolas (1741–1794)
The most wasted of all days is the day one did not laugh.
[*Maximes et pensées* (1796)]

CHURCHILL, Charles (1731–1764)
A joke's a very serious thing.
[*The Ghost* (1763)]

COLBY, Frank Moore (1865–1925)
Men will confess to treason, murder, arson, false teeth, or a wig. How many of them will own up to a lack of humour?
[*Essays*]

ELIOT, George (1819–1880)
A difference of taste in jokes is a great strain on the affections.
[*Daniel Deronda* (1876)]

ROGERS, Will (1879–1935)
Everything is funny as long as it is happening to someone else.
[*The Illiterate Digest* (1924)]

SHAW, George Bernard (1856–1950)
My way of joking is to tell the truth. It's the funniest joke in the world.
[*John Bull's Other Island* (1907)]

IDEALISM

FORD, Henry (1863–1947)
An idealist is a person who helps other people to be prosperous.

KING, Martin Luther (1929–1968)
I submit to you that if a man hasn't discovered something he will die for, he isn't fit to live.
[Speech in Detroit, June 23, 1963]

TARKINGTON, Booth (1869–1946)
An ideal wife is any woman who has an ideal husband.
[Attr.]

THATCHER, Margaret (1925–)
If a woman like Eva Peron with no ideals can get that far, think how far I can go with all the ideals that I have.
[*The Sunday Times*, 1980]

IDEAS

ALAIN (Emile-Auguste Chartier) (1868–1951)
Nothing is more dangerous than an idea, when you only have one idea.
[*Remarks on Religion* (1938)]

BOWEN, Elizabeth (1899–1973)
One can live in the shadow of an idea without grasping it.
[*The Heat of the Day* (1949)]

CAGE, John (1912–1992)
I don't understand why people are frightened of new ideas. I'm frightened of the old ones.

GEDDES, Patrick (1854–1932)
When an idea is dead it is embalmed in a textbook.
[In Boardman, *The Worlds of Patrick Geddes* (1978)]

HUGO, Victor (1802–1885)
One can resist the invasion of an army; but one cannot resist the invasion of ideas.
[*Histoire d'un Crime* (1852)]

MARQUIS, Don (1878–1937)
An idea isn't responsible for the people who believe in it.
[*New York Sun*]

PAXMAN, Jeremy (1950–)
The English way with ideas is not to

kill them but to let them die of neglect.
[*The Observer*, 1998]

SWIFT, Jonathan (1667–1745)
A nice man is a man of nasty ideas.
[*Thoughts on Various Subjects* (1711)]

INTELLIGENCE

ALLEN, Woody (1935–)
My brain: it's my second favourite organ.
[*Sleeper,* film, 1973]

BOGARDE, Dirk (1921–1999)
I'm not very clever, but I'm quite intelligent.
[Attr.]

DOYLE, Sir Arthur Conan (1859–1930)
I am a brain, Watson. The rest of me is a mere appendix.
[*The Case Book of Sherlock Holmes* (1927)]

LA ROCHEFOUCAULD (1613–1680)
The height of cleverness is to be able to conceal it.
[*Maximes* (1678)]

NIETZSCHE, Friedrich Wilhelm (1844–1900)
Wit is the epigram for the death of an emotion.
[*Human, All too Human* (1886)]

SCHOPENHAUER, Arthur (1788–1860)
Intellect is invisible to the man who has none.
[*Aphorismen zur Lebensweisheit*]

KINDNESS

ANONYMOUS
Be kind to unkind people – they need it the most.

CONFUCIUS (c.550–c.478 BC)
Recompense injury with justice, and recompense kindness with kindness.
[*Analects*]

GIDE, André (1869–1951)
True kindness presupposes the faculty of imagining as one's own the suffering and joy of others.
[Attr.]

SHAKESPEARE, William (1564–1616)
I must be cruel, only to be kind.
[*Hamlet*, III.iv]

WILLIAMS, Tennessee (1911–1983)
I have always depended on the kindness of strangers.
[*A Streetcar Named Desire* (1947)]

KNOWLEDGE

ADAMS, Henry (1838–1918)
They know enough who know how to learn.
[*The Education of Henry Adams* (1918)]

BACON, Francis (1561–1626)
Knowledge itself is power.
['Of Heresies' (1597)]

THE BIBLE
He that increaseth knowledge increaseth sorrow.
[*Ecclesiastes*, 1:18]

HOLMES, Oliver Wendell (1809–1894)
It is the province of knowledge to speak and it is the privilege of wisdom to listen.
[*The Poet at the Breakfast-Table* (1872)]

MACAULAY, Lord (1800–1859)
Knowledge advances by steps, and not by leaps.
['History' (1828)]

MUMFORD, Ethel (1878–1940)
Knowledge is power if you know it about the right person.
[In Cowan, *The Wit of Women*]

RUSSELL, Bertrand (1872–1970)
There is much pleasure to be gained from useless knowledge.

LANGUAGE

CHURCHILL, Sir Winston (1874–1965)
[Marginal comment on a document]
This is the sort of English up with which I will not put.
[In Gowers, *Plain Words* (1948)]

EMERSON, Ralph Waldo (1803–1882)
Language is fossil poetry.
['The Poet' (1844)]

FRANKLIN, Benjamin (1706–1790)
Write with the learned, pronounce with the vulgar.
[*Poor Richard's Almanac* (1738)]

GOETHE (1749–1832)
Whoever is not acquainted with foreign languages knows nothing of his own.
[*On Art and Antiquity* (1827)]

GOLDWYN, Samuel (1882–1974)
Let's have some new clichés.
[*The Observer*, 1948]

JOHNSON, Samuel (1709–1784)
Language is the dress of thought.
[*The Lives of the Most Eminent
English Poets* (1781)]

LIVELY, Penelope (1933–2000)
Language tethers us to the world;
without it we spin like atoms.
[*Moon Tiger* (1987)]

MILLIGAN, Spike (1918–2002)
The cliché is the handrail of the
crippled mind.
[Quoted in *The Herald*, February 2002]

PARKER, Dorothy (1893–1967)
[Of an acquaintance]
You know, she speaks eighteen
languages. And she can't say 'No' in
any of them.
[In J. Keats, *You Might As Well Live* (1970)]

SHAW, George Bernard (1856–1950)
England and America are two
countries separated by the same
language.
[*Reader's Digest*, 1942]

TOMLIN, Lily (1939–)
Man invented language in order to
satisfy his deep need to complain.
[In Pinker, *The Language Instinct* (1994)]

LEADERSHIP

ATWOOD, Margaret (1939–)
We still think of a powerful man as a
born leader and a powerful woman as
an anomaly.

CARNEGIE, Andrew (1835–1919)
No man will make a great leader who
wants to do it all himself, or to get all
the credit for doing it.

POWELL, Colin (1937–)
The day people stop bringing you
their problems is the day you have
stopped leading them.
[*My American Journey*]

LEARNING

ARISTOTLE (384–322 BC)
What we have to learn to do, we learn
by doing.
[*Nicomachean Ethics*]

ASCHAM, Roger (1515–1568)
There is no such whetstone, to
sharpen a good wit and encourage a
will to learning, as is praise.
[*The Scholemaster* (1570)]

CHESTERFIELD, Lord (1694–1773)
Wear your learning, like your watch, in
a private pocket; and do not merely
pull it out and strike it merely to show
you have one.
[Letter to his son, 1748]

CONFUCIUS (c.550–c.478 BC)
Learning without thought is labour
lost; thought without learning is
perilous.
[*Analects*]

HUXLEY, T.H. (1825–1895)
Try to learn something about
everything and everything about
something.
[Memorial stone]

POPE, Alexander (1688–1744)
A little learning is a dangerous thing;
Drink deep, or taste not the Pierian
spring:
There shallow draughts intoxicate the
brain,
And drinking largely sobers us again.
[*An Essay on Criticism* (1711)]

LIES

ANONYMOUS
An abomination unto the Lord, but a
very present help in time of trouble.
[Definition of a lie]

ARMSTRONG, Sir Robert (1927–)
[Replying to an allegation in court that a
letter he had written on behalf of the
British Government had contained a lie]
It contains a misleading impression,
not a lie. It was being economical with
the truth.
[*The Observer*, 1986]

BUTLER, Samuel (1835–1902)
Any fool can tell the truth, but it
requires a man of some sense to know
how to lie well.
[*The Note-Books of Samuel Butler* (1912)]

BYRON, Lord (1788–1824)
And, after all, what is a lie? 'Tis but
The truth in masquerade.
[*Don Juan* (1824)]

CALLAGHAN, James (1912–)
A lie can be half-way round the world
before the truth has got its boots on.
[Speech, 1976]

CORNEILLE, Pierre (1606–1684)
One needs a good memory after
telling lies.
[*Le Menteur* (1643)]

DAVIES, Robertson (1913–1995)
Better a noble lie than a miserable
truth.
[In Twigg, *Conversations with Twenty-
four Canadian Writers* (1981)]

HERVEY, Lord (1696–1743)
Whoever would lie usefully should lie
seldom.
[In Croker, *Memoirs of the Reign of
George II* (1848)]

HITLER, Adolf (1889–1945)
The broad mass of a nation ... will
more easily fall victim to a big lie than
to a small one.
[*Mein Kampf* (1925)]

IBSEN, Henrik (1828–1906)
Take the saving lie from the average
man and you take his happiness away,
too.
[*The Wild Duck* (1884)]

**NIETZSCHE, Friedrich Wilhelm
(1844–1900)**
We need lies ... in order to live.
[*Fragments* (1880–1889)]

PROUST, Marcel (1871–1922)
One of those telegrams of which M. de
Guermantes had wittily fixed the
formula: 'Cannot come, lie follows'.
[*Le Temps retrouvé* (1926)]

SAKI (1870–1916)
A little inaccuracy sometimes saves
tons of explanation.
[*The Square Egg* (1924)]

WILDE, Oscar (1854–1900)
The final revelation is that Lying, the
telling of beautiful untrue things, is the
proper aim of Art.
['The Decay of Lying' (1889)]

LIFE

ADAMS, Henry (1838–1918)
Chaos often breeds life, when order
breeds habit.
[*The Education of Henry Adams* (1918)]

ADAMS, Scott (1957–)
Accept that some days you're the
pigeon, and some days you're the
statue.
[*The Dilbert Principle*]

ADLER, Polly (1900–1953)
I am one of those people who just
can't help getting a kick out of life –
even when it's a kick in the teeth.
[*A House Is Not a Home* (1953)]

AURELIUS, Marcus (121–180)
Remember that no one loses any other
life than this which he now lives, nor
lives any other than this which he now
loses.
[*Meditations*]

BALFOUR, A.J. (1848–1930)
Nothing matters very much, and very
few things matter at all.
[Attr.]

BENNETT, Alan (1934–)
You know life ... it's rather like
opening a tin of sardines. We are all of
us looking for the key.
[*Beyond the Fringe* (1962)]

BROWNE, Sir Thomas (1605–1682)
The long habit of living indisposeth us
for dying.
[*Hydriotaphia: Urn Burial* (1658)]

BUCHAN, John (1875–1940)
It's a great life if you don't weaken.
[*Mr Standfast* (1919)]

BUTLER, Samuel (1835–1902)
Life is one long process of getting
tired.
[*The Note-Books of Samuel Butler*
(1912)]

CHAPLIN, Charlie (1889–1977)
Life is a tragedy when seen in close-
up, but a comedy in long-shot.
[*The Guardian*, 1977]

CONRAN, Shirley (1932–)
Life is too short to stuff a mushroom.
[*Superwoman* (1975)]

DAWKINS, Richard (1941–)
The essence of life is statistical
improbability on a colossal scale.
[*The Blind Watchmaker* (1986)]

EINSTEIN, Albert (1879–1955)
Only a life lived for others is a life worthwhile.
['Defining Success']

HUBBARD, Elbert (1856–1915)
Life is just one damned thing after another.
[*Philistine*, 1909]

JOHNSON, Samuel (1709–1784)
Human life is everywhere a state in which much is to be endured, and little to be enjoyed.
[*Rasselas* (1759)]

KIERKEGAARD, Søren (1813–1855)
Life can only be understood backwards; but it must be lived forwards.
[*Life*]

LARKIN, Philip (1922–1985)
Life is first boredom, then fear.

LENNON, John (1940–1980)
Life is what happens to you when you're busy making other plans.
['Beautiful Boy', song, 1980]

MARTIAL (c.AD 40–c.104)
Believe me, 'I shall live' is not the saying of a wise man. Tomorrow's life is too late: live today.
[*Epigrammata*]

PASCAL, Blaise (1623–1662)
The last act is bloody, however delightful the rest of the play may be.
[*Pensées* (1670)]

RANKIN, Ian (1960–)
People talk about life as a river, but it's not like that at all, it's a series of punctuations.

THOMAS, Dylan (1914–1953)
Oh, isn't life a terrible thing, thank God?
[*Under Milk Wood* (1954)]

WEST, Mae (1892–1980)
You only live once, but if you do it right, once is enough.

LITERATURE

BROOKNER, Anita (1938–)
Dr Weiss, at forty, knew that her life had been ruined by literature.
[*A Start in Life* (1981)]

CONNOLLY, Cyril (1903–1974)
Literature is the art of writing something that will be read twice; journalism what will be grasped at once.
[*Enemies of Promise* (1938)]

HELLER, Joseph (1923–1999)
He knew everything about literature except how to enjoy it.
[*Catch-22* (1961)]

LODGE, David (1935–)
Literature is mostly about having sex and not much about having children; life is the other way round.
[*The British Museum is Falling Down* (1965)]

TWAIN, Mark (1835–1910)
[Definition of a classic]
Something that everybody wants to have read and nobody wants to read.
['The Disappearance of Literature']

WILDER, Thornton (1897–1975)
Literature is the orchestration of platitudes.
[*Time*, 1953]

LONELINESS

BURSTYN, Ellen (1932–)
What a lovely surprise to finally discover how unlonely being alone can be.

DALAI LAMA (1935–)
Spend some time alone every day.

HUBBARD, Elbert (1856–1915)
Loneliness is to endure the presence of one who does not understand.
[Attr.]

SARTON, May (1912–)
Loneliness is the poverty of self; solitude is the richness of self.
[*Mrs Stevens Hears the Mermaids Singing* (1993)]

LOVE

ANOUILH, Jean (1910–1987)
Love is, above all else, the gift of oneself.
[*Ardèle ou la Marguerite* (1949)]

THE BIBLE
Greater love hath no man than this, that

a man lay down his life for his friends.
[*John*, 15:13]

BRICE, Fanny (1891–1951)
I never liked the men I loved, and
never loved the men I liked.
[Norman Katkov *The Fabulous Fanny*
(1952)]

**BROWNING, Elizabeth Barrett
(1806–1861)**
How do I love thee? Let me count the
ways.
[*Sonnets from the Portuguese* (1850)]

BURNS, Robert (1759–1796)
O, my luve's like a red, red, rose
That's newly sprung in June.
O, my luve's like the melodie,
That's sweetly play'd in tune.
['A Red Red Rose' (1794)]

CHER (1946–)
If grass can grow through cement,
love can find you at every time in your
life.
[*The Times*, 1998]

CHEVALIER, Maurice (1888–1972)
Many a man has fallen in love with a
girl in a light so dim he would not
have chosen a suit by it.
[Attr.]

DIDEROT, Denis (1713–1784)
They say that love takes wit away
from those who have it, and gives it to
those who have none.
[*Paradoxe sur le Comédien*]

DOUGLAS, Lord Alfred (1870–1945)
I am the Love that dare not speak its
name.
['Two Loves' (1896)]

ELLIS, Havelock (1859–1939)
Love is friendship plus sex.
[Attr.]

FLETCHER, Phineas (1582–1650)
Love is like linen often chang'd, the
sweeter.
[*Sicelides* (1614)]

LARKIN, Philip (1922–1985)
What will survive of us is love.
['An Arundel Tomb' (1964)]

LINDSAY, Norman (1879–1969)
The best love affairs are those we
never had.
[*Bohemians of the Bulletin* (1965)]

**NIETZSCHE, Friedrich Wilhelm
(1844–1900)**
There is always some madness in
love. But there is also always some
reason in madness.
[*On Reading and Writing*]

RACINE, Jean (1639–1699)
Ah, I have loved him too much not to
hate him!
[*Andromaque* (1667)]

TROLLOPE, Anthony (1815–1882)
Love is like any other luxury. You have
no right to it unless you can afford it.
[*The Way We Live Now* (1875)]

MARRIAGE

ALLEN, Woody (1935–)
It was partially my fault that we got
divorced ... I tended to place my wife
under a pedestal.
[At a nightclub in Chicago, 1964]

**ASTOR, Nancy, Viscountess
(1879–1964)**
I married beneath me – all women do.
[*Dictionary of National Biography*]

AUSTEN, Jane (1775–1817)
It is a truth universally acknowledged,
that a single man in possession of a
good fortune, must be in want of a
wife.
[*Pride and Prejudice* (1813)]

BACON, Francis (1561–1626)
Wives are young men's mistresses,
companions for middle age, and old
men's nurses.
['Of Marriage and Single Life' (1625)]

BURTON, Robert (1577–1640)
One was never married, and that's his
hell; another is, and that's his plague.
[*Anatomy of Melancholy* (1621)]

**COLERIDGE, Samuel Taylor
(1772–1834)**
The most happy marriage I can picture
or imagine to myself would be union
of a deaf man to a blind woman.
[In Allsop, *Recollections* (1836)]

FARQUHAR, George (1678–1707)
It is a maxim that man and wife
should never have it in their power to
hang one another.
[*The Beaux' Stratagem* (1707)]

FELTZ, Vanessa (1962–)
Marriage 2001-style, as I know to my cost, is entirely expendable, more easily disposable than a McDonald's wrapper.
[*The Sunday Times*, April 2001]

GABOR, Zsa-Zsa (1919–)
Husbands are like fires. They go out when unattended.
[*Newsweek*, 1960]

MARX, Groucho (1895–1977)
I was married by a judge. I should have asked for a jury.

MURRAY, Jenni (1950–)
Marriage is an insult and women should not touch it.
[Attr.]

WILDER, Thornton (1897–1975)
The best part of married life is the fights. The rest is merely so-so.
[*The Matchmaker* (1954)]

WINTERS, Shelley (1922–)
In Hollywood all marriages are happy. It's trying to live together afterwards that causes the problems.
[Attr.]

MEMORY

APOLLINAIRE, Guillaume (1880–1918)
Memories are hunting horns whose sound dies away in the wind.
['Cors de Chasse' (1913)]

ARNOLD, Matthew (1822–1888)
And we forget because we must And not because we will.
['Absence' (1852)]

CAMPBELL, Thomas (1777–1844)
To live in hearts we leave behind Is not to die.
['Hallowed Ground']

DISRAELI, Benjamin (1804–1881)
Nobody is forgotten when it is convenient to remember him.
[Attr.]

LA ROCHEFOUCAULD (1613–1680)
Everyone complains of his memory; nobody of his judgment.
[*Maximes* (1678)]

MIND

LA ROCHEFOUCAULD (1613–1680)
The mind is always fooled by the heart.
[*Maximes* (1678)]

WELCH, Raquel (1940–)
The mind can also be an erogenous zone.
[Attr.]

MODESTY

CHURCHILL, Sir Winston (1874–1965)
[Of Clement Attlee]
He is a modest man who has a good deal to be modest about.
[In *Chicago Sunday Tribune Magazine of Books*, 1954]

GILBERT, W.S. (1836–1911)
Wherever valour true is found, True modesty will there abound.
[*The Yeoman of the Guard* (1888)]

SITWELL, Dame Edith (1887–1964)
I have often wished I had time to cultivate modesty... But I am too busy thinking about myself.
[*The Observer*, April 1950]

MONEY AND WEALTH

ASTOR, John Jacob (1763–1848)
A man who has a million dollars is as well off as if he were rich.
[Attr.]

BACON, Francis (1561–1626)
And money is like muck, not good except it be spread.
['Of Seditions and Troubles' (1625)]

BALDWIN, James (1924–1987)
Money, it turned out, was exactly like sex, you thought of nothing else if you didn't have it and thought of other things if you did.
[*Nobody Knows My Name* (1961)]

BARING, Maurice (1874–1945)
If you would know what the Lord God thinks of money, you have only to look at those to whom He gives it.
[Attr.]

BEHN, Aphra (1640–1689)
Money speaks sense in a language all nations understand.
[*The Rover* (1677)]

THE BIBLE

The love of money is the root of all evil.

[*I Timothy*, 6:10]

BUTLER, Samuel (1835–1902)

It has been said that the love of money is the root of all evil. The want of money is so quite as truly.

[*Erewhon* (1872)]

DYLAN, Bob (1941–)

Money doesn't talk, it swears.

['It's Alright, Ma (I'm Only Bleeding)' (1965)]

FLYNN, Errol (1909–1959)

My difficulty is trying to reconcile my gross habits with my net income.

[Attr.]

GETTY, John Paul (1892–1976)

If you can actually count your money you are not really a rich man.

[In A. Barrow, *Gossip*]

HORACE (65–8 BC)

Make money: make it honestly if possible; if not, make it by any means.

[*Epistles*]

LAWRENCE, D.H. (1885–1930)

Money is our madness, our vast collective madness.

['Money-Madness' (1929)]

MCLUHAN, Marshall (1911–1980)

Money is a poor man's credit card.

MILLIGAN, Spike (1918–2002)

Money can't buy friends, but you can get a better class of enemy.

[*Puckoon* (1963)]

PARSONS, Tony (1953–)

There are few things in this world more reassuring than an unhappy Lottery winner.

[*The Observer*, 1998]

RIVERS, Joan (1937–)

People say that money is not the key to happiness, but I always figured if you have enough money, you can have a key made.

[*Enter Talking* (1986)]

RUNYON, Damon (1884–1946)

Always try to rub up against money, for if you rub up against money long enough, some of it may rub off on you.

[*Furthermore* (1938)]

THATCHER, Margaret (1925–)

Pennies do not come from heaven. They have to be earned here on earth.

[*The Sunday Telegraph*, 1982]

TUCKER, Sophie (1884–1966)

I've been poor and I've been rich. Rich is better.

[In Cowan, *The Wit of Women*]

TWAIN, Mark (1835–1910)

A banker is a person who lends you his umbrella when the sun is shining and wants it back the minute it rains.

[Attr.]

VOLTAIRE (1694–1778)

I advice you to go on living solely to enrage those who are paying you annuities.

WILLIAMS, Tennessee (1911–1983)

You can be young without money but you can't be old without it.

[*Cat on a Hot Tin Roof* (1955)]

MORALITY

JONG, Erica (1942–)

Your morals are like roads through the Alps. They make these hairpin turns all the time.

[*Fear of Flying* (1973)]

KRAUS, Karl (1874–1936)

Morality is the tendency to throw out the bath along with the baby.

[*Pro domo et mundo* (1912)]

MACAULAY, Lord (1800–1859)

We know of no spectacle so ridiculous as the British public in one of its periodical fits of morality.

['Moore's Life of Byron' (1843)]

SACHS, Rabbi Jonathon

Values are tapes we play in the Walkman of the mind; any tune we choose so long as it does not disturb others.

WILDE, Oscar (1854–1900)

Morality is simply the attitude we adopt towards people whom we personally dislike.

[*An Ideal Husband* (1895)]

NATURE

BRIDGES, Robert (1844–1930)
Man masters nature not by force but by understanding.

BROWNE, Sir Thomas (1605–1682)
All things are artificial, for nature is the art of God.
[*Religio Medici* (1643)]

FIELDING, Henry (1707–1754)
All Nature wears one universal grin.
[*Tom Thumb the Great* (1731)]

HAWKING, Stephen (1942–)
There are grounds for cautious optimism that we may now be near the end of the search for the ultimate laws of nature.
[*A Brief History of Time* (1988)]

HORACE (65–8 BC)
You may drive out Nature with a pitchfork, but she always comes hurrying back.
[*Epistles*]

RABELAIS, François (c.1494–c.1553)
Nature abhors a vacuum.
[*Gargantua* (1534)]

OPTIMISM

CABELL, James Branch (1879–1958)
The optimist proclaims that we live in the best of all possible worlds; and the pessimist fears this is true.
[*The Silver Stallion* (1926)]

CHURCHILL, Sir Winston (1874–1965)
A pessimist sees the difficulty in every opportunity; an optimist sees the opportunity in every difficulty.

ELLIS, Havelock (1859–1939)
The place where optimism most flourishes is the lunatic asylum.
[*The Dance of Life*]

VOLTAIRE (1694–1778)
Everything is for the best in the best of all possible worlds.
[*Candide* (1759)]

PEACE

BIERCE, Ambrose (1842–c.1914)
Peace: In international affairs, a period of cheating between two periods of fighting.
[*The Cynic's Word Book* (1906)]

TACITUS (AD c.56–c.120)
They create a desert, and call it peace.
[*Agricola*]

WILSON, Woodrow (1856–1924)
There is a price which is too great to pay for peace, and that price can be put in one word. One cannot pay the price of self-respect.
[Speech, 1916]

PESSIMISM

BENNETT, Arnold (1867–1931)
Pessimism, when you get used to it, is just as agreeable as optimism.
[*Things That Have Interested Me*]

LOWELL, Robert (1917–1977)
If we see light at the end of the tunnel, It's the light of the oncoming train.
['Since 1939' (1977)]

PETER, Laurence J. (1919–1990)
A pessimist is a man who looks both ways before crossing a one-way street.
[Attr.]

PHILOSOPHY

CICERO (106–43 BC)
But somehow there is nothing so absurd that some philosopher has not said it.
[*De Divinatione*]

PASCAL, Blaise (1623–1662)
To ridicule philosophy is truly to philosophize.
[*Pensées* (1670)]

POETRY

ASHBERY, John (1927–)
There is the view that poetry should improve your life. I think people confuse it with the Salvation Army.
[*International Herald Tribune*, October 1989]

BARROW, Isaac (1630–1677)
Poetry is a kind of ingenious nonsense.
[In Spence, *Anecdotes*]

CAGE, John (1912–1992)
I have nothing to say, I am saying it, and that is poetry.
[*Silence* (1961)]

FROST, Robert (1874–1963)
Poetry is a way of taking life by the throat.
>[In Sergeant, *Robert Frost: the Trial by Existence* (1960)]

MACAULAY, Lord (1800–1859)
As civilization advances, poetry almost necessarily declines.
>[*Collected Essays* (1843)]

VALÉRY, Paul (1871–1945)
A poem is never finished, only abandoned.
>[In Auden, *A Certain World*]

WAIN, John (1925–1994)
Poetry is to prose as dancing is to walking.
>[BBC broadcast, 1976]

POLITICS

ABBOTT, Diane (1953–)
Being an MP is the sort of job all working-class parents want for their children – clean, indoors and no heavy lifting.
>[*The Observer*, 1994]

ADAMS, Douglas (1952–2001)
Anyone who is capable of getting themselves made President should on no account be allowed to do the job.
>[*The Hitch Hiker's Guide to the Galaxy* (1979)]

ARISTOTLE (384–322 BC)
Man is by nature a political animal.
>[Politics]

BISMARCK, Prince Otto von (1815–1898)
Politics is the art of the possible.
>[Remark, 1863]

CLARK, Alan (1928–1999)
There are no true friends in politics. We are all sharks circling and waiting, for traces of blood to appear in the water.
>[*Diary*, 1990]

DE GAULLE, Charles (1890–1970)
I have come to the conclusion that politics are too serious a matter to be left to the politicians.
>[Attr.]

FIELDS, W.C. (1880–1946)
Hell, I never vote *for* anybody. I always vote *against*.
>[In Taylor, *W. C. Fields: His Follies and Fortunes* (1950)]

GALBRAITH, J.K. (1908–)
There are times in politics when you must be on the right side and lose.
>[*The Observer*, 1968]

HIGHTOWER, Jim (1933–)
Only things in the middle of the road are yellow lines and dead armadillos.
>[Attr.]

PARRIS, Matthew (1949–)
Being an MP feeds your vanity and starves your self-respect.
>[*The Times*, 1994]

SOMOZA, Anastasio (1925–1980)
You won the elections. But I won the count.
>[*The Guardian*, 1977]

VALÉRY, Paul (1871–1945)
Politics is the art of preventing people from becoming involved in affairs which concern them.
>[*As Such 2* (1943)]

VIDAL, Gore (1925–)
'Politics' is made up of two words. 'Poli,' which is Greek for 'many,' and 'tics,' which are bloodsucking insects.
>[Attr.]

POWER

AMIS, Kingsley (1922–1995)
Generally, nobody behaves decently when they have power.
>[*Radio Times*, 1992]

ANDREOTTI, Giulio (1919–2001)
Power wears down the man who doesn't have it.
>[In Biagi, *The Good and the Bad* (1989)]

KISSINGER, Henry (1923–)
Power is the ultimate aphrodisiac.
>[Attr.]

KUNDERA, Milan (1929–)
The struggle of man against power is the struggle of memory against forgetting.
>[Attr.]

MALCOLM X (1925–1965)
Power never takes a back step – only in the face of more power.
[*Malcolm X Speaks*, 1965]

MAO TSE-TUNG (1893–1976)
Every Communist must grasp the truth. Political power grows out of the barrel of a gun.
[Speech, 1938]

STEVENSON, Adlai (1900–1965)
Power corrupts, but lack of power corrupts absolutely.
[*The Observer*, 1963]

PRAISE

GAY, John (1685–1732)
Praising all alike, is praising none.
['A Letter to a Lady' (1714)]

LA ROCHEFOUCAULD (1613–1680)
Refusal of praise reveals a desire to be praised twice over.
[*Maximes* (1678)]

PRIDE

POPE, Alexander (1688–1744)
Pride, the never-failing vice of fools.
[*An Essay on Criticism* (1711)]

RENARD, Jules (1864–1910)
Be modest! It is the kind of pride least likely to offend.
[*Journal*]

PRINCIPLES

ADLER, Alfred (1870–1937)
It is easier to fight for one's principles than to live up to them.
[Attr.]

BALDWIN, Stanley (1867–1947)
I would rather be an opportunist and float than go to the bottom with my principles round my neck.
[Attr.]

LONG, Huey (1893–1935)
The time has come for all good men to rise above principle.
[Attr.]

MELBOURNE, Lord (1779–1848)
Nobody ever did anything very foolish except from some strong principle.
[Attr.]

ROOSEVELT, Franklin Delano (1882–1945)
To stand upon the ramparts and die for our principles is heroic, but to sally forth to battle and win for our principles is something more than heroic.
[Speech, 1928]

SADE, Marquis de (1740–1814)
All universal moral principles are idle fancies.
[*The 120 Days of Sodom* (1784)]

PROGRESS

BENN, Tony (1925–)
It's the same each time with progress. First they ignore you, then they say you're mad, then dangerous, then there's a pause and then you can't find anyone who disagrees with you.
[*The Observer*, October 1991]

BORGES, Jorge Luis (1899–1986)
We have stopped believing in progress. What progress that is!
[Ibarra, Borges et Borges]

ELLIS, Havelock (1859–1939)
What we call 'Progress' is the exchange of one nuisance for another nuisance.
[Impressions and Comments (1914)]

LEM, Stanislaw (1909–1966)
Is it progress if a cannibal uses knife and fork?
[*Unkempt Thoughts* (1962)]

THURBER, James (1894–1961)
Progress was all right; only it went on too long.
[Attr.]

PROMISES

SERVICE, Robert W. (1874–1958)
A promise made is a debt unpaid.
['The Cremation of Sam McGee' (1907)]

SWIFT, Jonathan (1667–1745)
Promises and pie-crusts are made to be broken, they say.
[*Polite Conversation* (1738)]

TWAIN, Mark (1835–1910)
To promise not to do a thing is the surest way in the world to make a body want to go and do that very thing.
[*The Adventures of Tom Sawyer* (1876)]

REALISM

BURGESS, Anthony (1917–1993)
Reality is what I see, not what you see.
[*The Sunday Times Magazine*, 1983]

DICK, Phillip K. (1928–1982)
Reality is that which, when you stop
believing it, doesn't go away.

ELIOT, T.S. (1888–1965)
Human kind
Cannot bear very much reality.
[*Four Quartets* (1944)]

KHRUSHCHEV, Nikita (1894–1971)
If you cannot catch a bird of paradise,
better take a wet hen.
[Attr.]

TWAIN, Mark (1835–1910)
Don't part with your illusions. When
they are gone, you may still exist, but
you have ceased to live.
[*Pudd'nhead Wilson's Calendar* (1894)]

SCIENCE

ARCHIMEDES (c.287–212 BC)
Give me a place to stand, and I will
move the Earth.
[*On levers*]

BRONOWSKI, Jacob (1908–1974)
Science has nothing to be ashamed of,
even in the ruins of Nagasaki.
[*Science and Human Values*]

CRONENBERG, David (1943–)
A virus is only doing its job.
[*Sunday Telegraph*, 1992]

FREUD, Sigmund (1856–1939)
Science is not illusion. But it would be
an illusion to suppose that we could
get anywhere else what it cannot give
us.

NEWTON, Isaac (1642–1727)
If I have seen further it is by standing
on the shoulders of giants.
[Letter to Robert Hooke, 1675–76]

POPPER, Sir Karl (1902–1994)
Science may be described as the art of
systematic oversimplification.
[*The Observer*, 1982]

ROUX, Joseph (1834–1886)
Science is for those who learn; poetry,
for those who know.
[*Meditations of a Parish Priest* (1886)]

SANTAYANA, George (1863–1952)
If all the arts aspire to the condition of
music, all the sciences aspire to the
condition of mathematics.
[*The Observer*, 1928]

WINSTON, Robert (1940–)
Science is 90% boredom.
[*The Sunday Times*, July 2001]

SECRETS

CLARK, Alan (1928–1999)
[On being asked whether he had any
embarrassing skeletons in the
cupboard]
Dear boy, I can hardly close the door.
[*The Observer*, 1998]

CONGREVE, William (1670–1729)
I know that's a secret, for it's
whispered everywhere.
[*Love for Love* (1695)]

FRANKLIN, Benjamin (1706–1790)
Three may keep a secret, if two of
them are dead.
[*Poor Richard's Almanac* (1735)]

SELF

ARNOLD, Matthew (1822–1888)
Resolve to be thyself; and know,
that he,
Who finds himself, loses his misery!
['Self-Dependence' (1852)]

BURNS, Robert (1759–1796)
O wad some Power the giftie gie us
To see oursels as ithers see us!
['To a Louse' (1786)]

MOLIÈRE (1622–1673)
We should look long and carefully at
ourselves before we consider judging
others.
[*Le Misanthrope* (1666)]

MONTAIGNE, Michel de (1533–1592)
The greatest thing in the world is to
know how to belong to oneself.
[*Essais* (1580)]

SHAKESPEARE, William (1564–1616)
This above all – to thine own self be
true,
And it must follow, as the night the day,
Thou canst not then be false to any
man.
[*Hamlet*, I.iii]

WILDE, Oscar (1854–1900)
Other people are quite dreadful. The only possible society is oneself.
[*An Ideal Husband* (1895)]

SEX

BURCHILL, Julie (1960–)
Sex, on the whole, was meant to be short, nasty and brutish. If what you want is cuddling, you should buy a puppy.
[*Sex and Sensibility* (1992)]

CAMPBELL, Mrs Patrick (1865–1940)
I don't mind where people make love, so long as they don't do it in the street and frighten the horses.
[Attr.]

CHANDLER, Raymond (1888–1959)
She gave me a smile I could feel in my hip pocket.
[*Farewell, My Lovely* (1940)]

CHESTERFIELD, Lord (1694–1773)
The pleasure is momentary, the position ridiculous, and the expense damnable.
[Attr.]

EKLAND, Britt (1942–)
I say I don't sleep with married men, but what I mean is that I don't sleep with happily married men.
[Attr.]

EPHRON, Nora (1941–)
Women need a reason to have sex. Men need a place.
[*When Harry Met Sally*, film, 1989]

GREER, Germaine (1939–)
No sex is better than bad sex.
[Attr.]

LEIFER, Carol (1956–)
Making love to a woman is like buying real estate: location, location, location.

NASH, Ogden (1902–1971)
Home is heaven and orgies are vile
But you need an orgy, once in a while.
['Home, Sweet Home' (1935)]

NEWBOLD, H.L. (1890–1971)
Sex is between the ears as well as between the legs.
[*Mega-Nutrients for Your Nerves*]

WELDON, Fay (1931–)
Reading about sex in yesterday's novels is like watching people smoke in old films.
[*The Guardian*, December 1989]

SILENCE

BACON, Francis (1561–1626)
Silence is the virtue of fools.
[*Of the Dignity and Advancement of Learning* (1623)]

LINCOLN, Abraham (1809–1865)
Better to remain silent and be thought a fool than to speak out and remove all doubt.
[Attr.]

MANDELSTAM, Nadezhda (1899–1980)
If nothing else is left, one must scream. Silence is the real crime against humanity.
[*Hope Against Hope* (1970)]

TUPPER, Martin (1810–1889)
Well-timed silence hath more eloquence than speech.
[*Proverbial Philosophy* (1838)]

SPORT AND GAMES

ALI, Muhammad (1942–)
Float like a butterfly, sting like a bee.
[Catchphrase]

BENNETT, Alan (1934–)
If you think squash is a competitive activity, try flower arrangement.
[*Talking Heads* (1988)]

DEMPSEY, Jack (1895–1983)
Kill the other guy before he kills you.
[Motto]

FORD, Henry (1863–1947)
Exercise is bunk. If you are healthy, you don't need it: if you are sick, you shouldn't take it.
[Attr.]

GRACE, W.G. (1848–1915)
[Refusing to leave the crease after being bowled first ball in front of a large crowd]
They came to see me bat not to see you bowl.
[Attr.]

JERROLD, Douglas William (1803–1857)
The only athletic sport I ever mastered was backgammon.
[In W. Jerrold, *Douglas Jerrold* (1914)]

LOUIS, Joe (1914–1981)
[Referring to the speed of an opponent, Billy Conn]
He can run, but he can't hide.
[Attr.]

NAVRATILOVA, Martina (1956–)
The moment of victory is much too short to live for that and nothing else.
[*The Guardian*, June 1989]

PALMER, Arnold (1929–)
The more I practise the luckier I get.
[Attr.]

PAXMAN, Jeremy (1950–)
Internationally, football has become a substitute for war.
[*The Sunday Times*, June 2000]

PELÉ (1940–)
Football? It's the beautiful game.
[Attr.]

SHANKLY, Bill (1914–1981)
Some people think football is a matter of life and death. I don't like that attitude. I can assure them it is much more serious than that.
[Remark on BBC TV, 1981]

TWAIN, Mark (1835–1910)
Golf is a good walk spoiled.
[Attr.]

WILDE, Oscar (1854–1900)
The English country gentleman galloping after a fox – the unspeakable in full pursuit of the uneatable.
[*A Woman of No Importance* (1893)]

SUCCESS

ADAMS, Joey (b. 1911)
Rockefeller once explained the secret of success. 'Get up early, work late – and strike oil.'

BROWNING, Robert (1812–1889)
A minute's success pays the failure of years.
['Apollo and the Fates' (1887)]

RUSSELL, Rosalind (1911–1976)
Success is a public affair. Failure is a private funeral.
[*Life Is a Banquet* (1977)]

VIDAL, Gore (1925–)
It is not enough to succeed. Others must fail.
[In Irvine, *Antipanegyric for Tom Driberg* (1976)]

TALENT

DEGAS, Edgar (1834–1917)
Everybody has talent at twenty-five. The difficult thing is to have it at fifty.
[In Gammell, *The Shop-Talk of Edgar Degas* (1961)]

TASTE

BENNETT, Arnold (1867–1931)
Good taste is better than bad taste, but bad taste is better than no taste.
[*The Observer*, 1930]

REYNOLDS, Sir Joshua (1723–1792)
Taste does not come by chance: it is a long and laborious task to acquire it.
[In Northcote, *Life of Sir Joshua Reynolds* (1818)]

VALÉRY, Paul (1871–1945)
Taste is created from a thousand distastes.
[*Unsaid Things*]

TEMPTATION

ANONYMOUS
The trouble with resisting temptation is it may never come your way again.

BECKFORD, William (1760–1844)
I am not over-fond of resisting temptation.
[*Vathek* (1787)]

WILDE, Oscar (1854–1900)
I couldn't help it. I can resist everything except temptation.
[*Lady Windermere's Fan* (1892)]

THOUGHT

BIERCE, Ambrose (1842–c.1914)
Brain: An apparatus with which we think that we think.
[*The Cynic's Word Book* (1906)]

CONFUCIUS (c.550–c.478 BC)
Learning without thought is labour lost; thought without learning is perilous.
[*Analects*]

JAMES, William (1842–1910)
A great many people think they are thinking when they are merely rearranging their prejudices.
[Attr.]

NEWTON, Isaac (1642–1727)
If I have done the public any service, it is due to patient thought.
[Letter to Dr Bentley, 1713]

REITH, Lord (1889–1971)
You can't think rationally on an empty stomach, and a whole lot of people can't do it on a full one either.
[Attr.]

RUSSELL, Bertrand (1872–1970)
Many people would sooner die than think. In fact they do.
[In Flew, *Thinking about Thinking* (1975)]

SHAKESPEARE, William (1564–1616)
There is nothing either good or bad, but thinking makes it so.
[*Hamlet*, II.ii]

TIME

BOUCICAULT, Dion (1822–1890)
Men talk of killing time, while time quietly kills them.
[*London Assurance* (1841)]

COWARD, Sir Noël (1899–1973)
Time is the reef upon which all our frail mystic ships are wrecked.
[*Blithe Spirit* (1941)]

EMERSON, Ralph Waldo (1803–1882)
A day is a miniature eternity.
[*Journals*]

MARX, Groucho (1895–1977)
Time wounds all heels.
[Attr.]

ROGERS, Will (1879–1935)
Half our life is spent trying to find something to do with the time we have rushed through life trying to save.
[*New York Times*, 1930]

SARTRE, Jean-Paul (1905–1980)
Three o'clock is always too late or too early for anything you want to do. An odd moment in the afternoon.
[*La Nausée*]

SHAKESPEARE, William (1564–1616)
I wasted time, and now doth time waste me.
[*Richard II*, V.v]

YOUNG, Edward (1683–1765)
Procrastination is the Thief of Time.
[*Night-Thoughts on Life, Death and Immortality* (1742–1746)]

TRAVEL

CLARKSON, Jeremy
To argue that a car is simply a means of conveyance is like arguing that Blenheim Palace is simply a house.
[*The Sunday Times*, 1999]

DREW, Elizabeth (1887–1965)
Too often travel, instead of broadening the mind, merely lengthens the conversation.
[*The Literature of Gossip* (1964)]

ELIOT, T.S. (1888–1965)
The first condition of understanding a foreign country is to smell it.
[Attr.]

GEORGE VI (1895–1952)
Abroad is bloody.
[In Auden, *A Certain World* (1970)]

MACAULAY, Dame Rose (1881–1958)
The great and recurrent question about abroad is, is it worth getting there?
[Attr.]

MOORE, George (1852–1933)
A man travels the world over in search of what he needs and returns home to find it.
[*The Brook Kerith* (1916)]

SCOTT, Captain Robert (1868–1912)
[Of the South Pole]
Great God! this is an awful place.
[*Journal*, 1912]

STERNE, Laurence (1713–1768)
A man should know something of his own country too, before he goes abroad.
[*Tristram Shandy* (1767)]

VIZINCZEY, Stephen (1933–)
I was told I am a true cosmopolitan. I
am unhappy everywhere.
[*The Guardian*, 1968]

TRUST

ANONYMOUS
Trust in Allah, but tie your camel.
[Old Muslim Proverb]

JEFFERSON, Thomas (1743–1826)
When a man assumes a public trust,
he should consider himself as public
property.
[Remark, 1807]

SALISBURY, Harrison
Never trust a chief of state in
sunglasses.
[*Times Literary Supplement*,
28 February 2003]

WILLIAMS, Tennessee (1911–1983)
We have to distrust each other. It's our
only defence against betrayal.
[*Camino Real* (1953)]

TRUTH

AGAR, Herbert Sebastian (1897–1980)
The truth which makes men free is for
the most part the truth which men
prefer not to hear.
[*A Time for Greatness* (1942)]

ARNOLD, Matthew (1822–1888)
Truth sits upon the lips of dying men.
['Sohrab and Rustum' (1853)]

BALDWIN, Stanley (1867–1947)
A platitude is simply a truth repeated
until people get tired of hearing it.
[Attr.]

BATAILLE, Georges (1897–1962)
I believe that truth has only one face:
that of a violent contradiction.
[*The Deadman*]

BLAKE, William (1757–1827)
A truth thats told with bad intent
Beats all the Lies you can invent.
['Auguries of Innocence' (c. 1803)]

BRAQUE, Georges (1882–1963)
Truth exists; only lies are invented.
[*Day and Night, Notebooks* (1952)]

DOYLE, Sir Arthur Conan (1859–1930)
It is an old maxim of mine that when
you have excluded the impossible,
whatever remains, however
improbable, must be the truth.
['The Beryl Coronet' (1892)]

DRYDEN, John (1631–1700)
I never saw any good that came of
telling truth.
[*Amphitryon* (1690)]

SHAW, George Bernard (1856–1950)
All great truths begin as blasphemies.
[*Annajanska* (1919)]

WILDE, Oscar (1854–1900)
If one tells the truth, one is sure,
sooner or later, to be found out.
[*The Chameleon*, 1894]

WRIGHT, Frank Lloyd (1869–1959)
The truth is more important than the
facts.
[In Simcox, *Treasury of Quotations*]

TYRANNY

BROWNING, Robert (1812–1889)
Oppression makes the wise man mad.
[*Luria* (1846)]

BURKE, Edmund (1729–1797)
Bad laws are the worst sort of tyranny.
[*Speech at Bristol* (1780)]

MILL, John Stuart (1806–1873)
Whatever crushes individuality is
despotism, by whatever name it may
be called.
[*On Liberty* (1859)]

PITT, William (1708–1778)
Where law ends, there tyranny begins.
[Speech, 1770]

VANITY

COWLEY, Hannah (1743–1809)
Vanity, like murder, will out.
[*The Belle's Stratagem* (1780)]

**STEVENSON, Robert Louis
(1850–1894)**
Vanity dies hard; in some obstinate
cases it outlives the man.
[*Prince Otto*]

VICTORY

KENNEDY, John F. (1917–1963)
Victory has a thousand fathers but
defeat is an orphan.
[Attr.]

MACARTHUR, Douglas (1880–1964)
In war there is no substitute for
victory.
[Speech to Congress, 1951]

VIRTUE

BACON, Francis (1561–1626)
Virtue is like a rich stone, best plain
set.
['Of Beauty' (1625)]

BRECHT, Bertolt (1898–1956)
Whenever there are such great virtues,
it's proof that something's fishy.
[Mother Courage and her Children (1941)]

BROWNE, Sir Thomas (1605–1682)
There is no road or ready way to
virtue.
[Religio Medici (1643)]

COLETTE (1873–1954)
My virtue's still far too small, I don't
trot it out and about yet.
[Claudine at School (1900)]

GOLDSMITH, Oliver (c.1728–1774)
The virtue which requires to be ever
guarded, is scarce worth the sentinel.
[The Vicar of Wakefield (1766)]

MILTON, John (1608–1674)
Most men admire
Vertue, who follow not her lore.
[Paradise Regained (1671)]

SKINNER, Cornelia Otis (1901–1979)
Woman's virtue is man's greatest
invention.

WASHINGTON, George (1732–1799)
Few men have virtue to withstand the
highest bidder.
[Moral Maxims]

WAR

BELLOC, Hilaire (1870–1953)
Whatever happens, we have got
The Maxim Gun, and they have not.
[Modern Traveller (1898)]

THE BIBLE
All they that take the sword shall
perish with the sword.
[Matthew, 26:52]

BIERCE, Ambrose (1842–c.1914)
War is God's way of teaching
Americans geography.

BORGES, Jorge Luis (1899–1986)
[On the Falklands War of 1982]
The Falklands thing was a fight
between two bald men over a comb.
[Time, 1983]

CLAUSEWITZ, Karl von (1780–1831)
War is nothing but a continuation of
politics by other means.
[On War (1834)]

ERASMUS (c.1466–1536)
War is sweet to those who do not
fight.
[Adagia (1500)]

HOOVER, Herbert Clark (1874–1964)
Older men declare war. But it is youth
that must fight and die.
[Speech, 1944]

JOHNSON, Hiram (1866–1945)
The first casualty when war comes is
truth.
[Speech, US Senate, 1917]

MACDONALD, Ramsay (1866–1937)
We hear war called murder. It is not: it
is suicide.
[The Observer, 1930]

RUSSELL, Bertrand (1872–1970)
War does not determine who is right –
only who is left.

SANDBURG, Carl (1878–1967)
Sometime they'll give a war and
nobody will come.
[The People, Yes (1936)]

TROTSKY, Leon (1879–1940)
You may not be interested in war, but
war is interested in you.

WILDE, Oscar (1854–1900)
As long as war is regarded as wicked
it will always have its fascination.
When it is looked upon as vulgar, it
will cease to be popular.
[The Critic as Artist (1890)]

WIT

**MAUGHAM, William Somerset
(1874–1965)**
Impropriety is the soul of wit.
[The Moon and Sixpence (1919)]

SKELTON, Robin (1925–)
Anything said off the cuff has usually
been written on it first.
[Attr.]

STERNE, Laurence (1713–1768)
An ounce of a man's own wit is worth
a ton of other people's.
[*Tristram Shandy* (1759–1767)]

WORK

BENCHLEY, Robert (1889–1945)
I do most of my work sitting down;
that's where I shine.
[Attr.]

BUTLER, Samuel (1835–1902)
Every man's work, whether it be
literature or music or pictures or
architecture or anything else, is always
a portrait of himself.
[*The Way of All Flesh* (1903)]

COWARD, Sir Noël (1899–1973)
Work is much more fun than fun.
[*The Observer*, 1963]

CURIE, Marie (1867–1934)
One never notices what has been
done; one can only see what remains
to be done ...
[Letter to her brother, 1894]

KATZENBERG, Jeffrey (1951–)
If you don't show up for work on
Saturday, don't bother coming in on
Sunday.
[Attr.]

PARKINSON, C. Northcote (1909–1993)
Work expands so as to fill the time
available for its completion.
[Parkinson's Law (1958)]

PETER, Laurence J. (1919–1990)
In a hierarchy every employee tends to
rise to his level of incompetence.
[*The Peter Principle – Why Things
Always Go Wrong* (1969)]

REAGAN, Ronald (1911–)
They say hard work never hurt
anybody, but I figure why take the
chance.
[Attr.]

ROUSSEAU, Jean-Jacques (1712–1778)
It is too difficult to think nobly when
one thinks only of earning a living.

STANTON, Elizabeth Cady (1815–1902)
Woman has been the great unpaid
laborer of the world.
[In Anthony and Gage, *History of
Woman Suffrage* (1881)]

VOLTAIRE (1694–1778)
Work keeps away those three great
evils: boredom, vice, and poverty.
[*Candide* (1759)]

WILDE, Oscar (1854–1900)
Work is the curse of the drinking
classes.
[In Pearson, *Life of Oscar Wilde* (1946)]

THE WORLD

DIDEROT, Denis (1713–1784)
What a fine comedy this world would
be if one did not play a part in it!
[Letters to Sophie Volland]

FIRBANK, Ronald (1886–1926)
The world is disgracefully managed,
one hardly knows to whom to
complain.
[*Vainglory* (1915)]

HEMINGWAY, Ernest (1898–1961)
The world is a fine place and worth
the fighting for.
[*For Whom the Bell Tolls* (1940)]

MARQUIS, Don (1878–1937)
Ours is a world where people don't
know what they want and are willing
to go through hell to get it.
[In *Treasury of Humorous Quotations*]

WALPOLE, Horace (1717–1797)
This world is a comedy to those that
think, and a tragedy to those that feel.
[Letter to Anne, Countess of Upper
Ossory, 1776]

YOUTH

ASQUITH, Herbert (1852–1928)
Youth would be an ideal state if it
came a little later in life.
[*The Observer*, 1923]

DISRAELI, Benjamin (1804–1881)
Youth is a blunder; Manhood a
struggle; Old Age a regret.
[*Coningsby* (1844)]

**MAUGHAM, William Somerset
(1874–1965)**
It is an illusion that youth is happy, an
illusion of those who have lost it.

SHAW, George Bernard (1856–1950)
Youth, which is forgiven everything,
forgives itself nothing: age, which
forgives itself everything, is forgiven
nothing.
[*Man and Superman* (1903)]

It's all that the young can do for the
old, to shock them and keep them up
to date.
[*Fanny's First Play* (1911)]

WILDE, Oscar (1854–1900)
The old-fashioned respect for the
young is fast dying out.
[*The Importance of Being Earnest* (1895)]

WILSON, Woodrow (1856–1924)
Generally young men are regarded as
radicals. This is a popular
misconception. The most conservative
persons I ever met are college
undergraduates.
[Speech, 1905]